Gentleman George?

Gentleman George?

The Contradictory Life of George Duffield

George Duffield
with Michael Tanner

This book is dedicated to the memory of Jack Waugh,
the man to whom I owe everything

Published in 2002 by Highdown
An imprint of Raceform Ltd
Compton, Newbury, Berkshire, RG20 6NL
Raceform Ltd is a wholly owned subsidiary of MGN Ltd

A catalogue record for this book is available from the British Library.

ISBN 1-904317-03-0

Designed by Sam Pentin
Printed by Mackays of Chatham

Photographic acknowledgments for cover:
Front: David Parry/Raceform;
Back top: Sporting Life
Back bottom: Toby Melville/Press Association

CONTENTS

FOREWORD

In the great passage of British history, no event more graphically illustrated the moment when the 'stiff upper lip culture', that had won the Nation an Empire, had finally given way to the 'wobbly lower lip culture', that had lost the Nation the Empire, than the public reaction inspired by the death of Diana, Princess of Wales.

Although George Duffield's lengthy career as a Flat-race jockey has both spanned and adapted to these two phases in the development of the British psyche, his own nature has remained firmly locked into the tough-as-teak, never complain and never explain variety rather than the happy-clappy, touchy-feely and trained counselling era that is more popular today.

Born and raised in what was then a thriving Northern mining community (sadly soon to be recalled only in charming but sentimental films such as *Brassed Off*), he was apprenticed as a jockey for seven years in the Dickensian conditions that prevailed everywhere at that period. He served not less than five years of his time before being entrusted with even one ride in public.

Despite this tardy start, his career in the saddle as an apprentice jockey eventually began a slow but steady climb, only to plummet again once out of his time. Finally there followed the long grind back that enabled his career to reach its zenith at an age when most sportsmen are physically unrecognisable from the athlete of their prime and are to be seen in public only propping up bars and regaling an increasingly bored and diminishing audience with details of their increasingly distant past triumphs.

George may have different views himself, but I have always believed that the defining moment of his career probably arrived immediately he became a fully fledged jockey.

His Guv'nor, Mr John Oxley, was enduring a dreadful season. It is my view that the most common disease known to the racehorse is probably 'trainer error'. Fortunately, it is seldom reported and Mr Oxley, in common with all racehorse trainers (and I include particularly myself), followed the time-honoured system of apportioning blame for the failure of his team on the racecourse as follows: pedigree, the ground, the distance, the course, the jockey, the handicapper, the health of the stable, the horse's determination and last of all, of course, the trainer's methods!

As a result, the new stable jockey, Duffield, had to go.

All of us need jolting out of our complacency at times and the young George was now compelled by circumstances to gaze over the precipice of his career and at the waves pounding the rocks now frighteningly close below. He did not like the view one bit, hauled himself back from the edge of the abyss and vowed never to glimpse the scene again. With typical Yorkshire pride and grit, his subsequent career has proved that relentless persistence, competence and professionalism will in the end reap its just reward.

The extraordinary length of his career has been much discussed of late with due reference being given to the natural physical advantages accorded to him by his wiry frame. However, I have always felt his longevity was as much due to his love of the jockey's life as to his physique.

Since moving back to Yorkshire from Newmarket, the typical Duffield schedule on a Tuesday or a Friday (workdays at Heath House) is very demanding. He leaves home at 3.45am, drives to Newmarket, rides out one or two lots – including galloping three to six different horses – prior to motoring on to an afternoon meeting followed by an evening meeting, and thence back to Yorkshire.

Whilst reading the paper in the car park at Southwell, prior to an evening meeting last summer, a car skidded to a halt in an adjacent parking bay, disgorging a babbling, giggling group of various young jockeys and apprentices, who then sprinted towards the weighing room making as much noise as a team of overexcited schoolgirls playing their first away from home hockey match. Leading the charge was the ancient Duffield, still as enthralled by the sport and its camaraderie as he had been when I first knew him 35 years before.

Unlike a freelance jockey who is booked to ride on a daily basis as 'the best available', a stable jockey requires many more enduring attributes, such as loyalty, honesty, reliability, consistency, discretion and an eye for the future. As much as anything, he also requires enthusiasm. Enthusiasm imparts itself to owners and staff alike. It eases the long drives to distant meetings. It overcomes the inevitable bad patches that bedevil all stables from time to time and, most importantly of all, it transmits itself to the horse.

George Duffield has all of these qualities to the full.

With the exception of his whip action, now more restricted than the overhead smash of the 80s which found little favour with the Stewards of the 90s, his style has remained locked in that of his youth. Less aerodynamic and more upright than his counterparts (except for Kieren Fallon) with his feet firmly into the stirrup iron (as opposed to only the toe), he rides with a shorter hold of his horse's head than most, which probably accounts for his greater success with horses that require driving, rather than free-running horses who require settling.

Brilliant in his youth at the old tape starting gate, he had developed to an art bringing his mount in slightly sideways and just ahead of the line, only straightening it as the starter pulled the lever – thus gaining a precious length on all his rivals and slightly hampering at least two of them! Fearless at the stalls, if at times impatient with any misbehaviour on the part of his mount, he is particularly adept at sitting down to drive any horse slow into its stride: in the first four or five strides, peeling off two or three sharp backhanders to get it motivated, racing and into its stride.

Tactically he has grown more astute with age, but has always preferred having horses handy, or in front, to holding one up for a last-stride dash to the line. One of the strongest finishers in the game for the last 30 years, he is equally effective with his whip in either hand – surprisingly, an attribute not shared by all top jockeys today. His greatest moments have come when rallying a recently headed front-runner to get back up in front on the line.

He will no doubt choose his own 'finest rides', but my vote would go to his handling of User Friendly in the Irish Oaks at the Curragh. In front some way out, tracked by Kevin Manning who appeared to be going the better, Duffield, with his stick in his left hand, half a horse's width off the rail, ensured that enough of a gap remained to entice poor Kevin into thinking User Friendly must drift off the rail without ever allowing it to happen. The gap never did materialise and User Friendly won.

For Heath House, I would single out Brave Act (in the Solario at Sandown) and Pelion (in a Catterick maiden) as his finest 'power-drive' rides, together with Alborada's second Champion Stakes win as his finest tactical ride. In the latter race, he broke fast, chased the filly up to track the Godolphin pacemaker, himself a useful horse who was sure to be able to carry her into the Dip at least, thus denying Godolphin's premier runner a chance of a lead and the cover he required.

However, perhaps it is George, the man, who is of more interest than any of the horses he rode. Having been his principal employer now for almost 30 years, I shall be as interested as any reader to see how much the following pages may reveal of the clues to his character that have enabled his unusual career to link the days of Scobie Breasley to those of Frankie Dettori and dear old 'Ally Pally' to the international racing scene of today.

Sir Mark Prescott, Bt.
Heath House,
Newmarket,
May 2002

PROLOGUE

None of us is one-dimensional. From the moment I first sat down with George Duffield to begin numerous hours of interrogation and conversation, it was made abundantly clear George intended his story to portray the other, hidden, darker side of his personality. Hence the insertion of that crucial question mark at the end of our title.

At times George was honest to the point of brutality. Owners, trainers, jockeys and racing officials the length and breadth of the land, however, can rest pretty easy since George reserves his most withering comments for himself. When the jungle drums began beating with news of this book, there can be no doubt that one or two sets of knees would have begun knocking at the prospect of what George was, or was not, going to say about them. I think it's fair to say that where people other than himself are concerned, George has erred on the side of generosity instead of brutality. I suspect James Fanshawe, to name but one, may count himself lucky that he has escaped so lightly. And Sir Mark Prescott may rest easy in his bed, safe in the knowledge that some secrets of Heath House are still firmly under lock and key!

Reading these pages, it will soon become clear that George is not someone who sets out consciously to win friends and influence people. Shades of grey do not exist in the Duffield scheme of things. There is invariably a right way and a wrong way; truth and falsehood; honesty and dishonesty; good and bad. You can be sure that George will favour one extreme or the other, never being caught sitting on the fence or falling between two stools. The Duffield palette, you see, is dominated by black and white.

In such circumstances, therefore, the fact that he has got to the top of his chosen profession and stayed there for over 30 years is as much unequivocal testimony to his stubborn singlemindedness as it is to his unquestioned skill in the saddle.

This book is not one of those flimsy volumes where the subject is barely out of nappies or has lived a life hardly worth a second thought. To claim that, as both a man and a jockey, George Duffield has lived a life which merits the telling is no extravagance. Nor, I believe, is it a jockey's autobiography in the purely routine sense, for this is the story of a man who just happens to earn his living as a jockey. It is not unusual nowadays for autobiographies to claim surprising revelations lurk between their covers. In the main, these disclosures merely add light or shade to the features of a portrait that we are already conversant with – for example the 'obsessive' streak within Richard Dunwoody. What elevates George's revelations onto a different plane is the simple fact that they release skeletons from cupboards only a select few knew ever existed. For George not only to enter the confessional booth but also don a hair shirt on emerging – each entirely at his own volition – can only be viewed as a characteristically forthright Duffield declaration of intent which, I trust, will not be deemed misguided.

The heartbeat of any sportsman's book is the collection of

reminiscences and memories provided by his scrapbooks. George and I have been obliged to do without the scrapbooks covering the majority of his career, since they reside in the possession of his first wife, who, I'm assured, denied access to them unless money changed hands. Hopefully, George and I have managed to overcome this substantial obstacle placed (unnecessarily I feel) in our path. By means of compensation, the meticulous and copious scrapbooks of Sir Mark Prescott, whose career is so inextricably linked with George's own, were absolutely invaluable. George and I extend our most sincere thanks to Sir Mark for lengthy access to them, in addition to the provision of a typically stylish foreword.

The appearance of the name G Duffield alongside a runner at any racetrack in Britain guarantees its owner, trainer and the public value for money. I am confident the appearance of the name G Duffield on the cover of this book assures the reader similar value for money. If some of the language and depth of factual recall within these pages does strike some of George's many friends as being in any way out of character, the blame must rest with me. But, in my defence, however appetising the 'skeletons', every now and then some flesh must be put on the bones to ensure the tastiest possible meal!

George's life and career, it seems to me, has been characterised by a compulsive need to prove himself. To prove he was tough; to prove he was honest and trustworthy; to prove he was a grafter; to prove he was worthy of his job; to prove he could still be good at his job. George, you no longer need to prove anything. You've long since won over the jury.

Michael Tanner,
Sleaford,
Lincolnshire
May 2002

1

STANDING UP TO JIMMY THE SKUNK

There is much, much more to G Duffield than the courteous 'Gentleman George' who occasionally crops up in television interviews, that amiable old soul who politely answers each and every question to the accompaniment of a genial smile. You see, this affability conceals a multitude of sins. There is a darker side to my character the public never sees. I've always possessed a right old temper and when I'm riled the red mists descend with a vengeance. One summer's day in 1991 they became especially impenetrable. I lost it big-time and proceeded to place my very livelihood in jeopardy by punching one of the most powerful men in British racing. I did what a lot of folk would probably quite like to do: I whacked Peter Savill.

Although Savill was still some eight years away from becoming chairman of the British Horseracing Board he was already one of the biggest fish in the pond. He'd made millions from publishing magazines for cruise ships, aircraft and the like. According to one newspaper survey of the day this resident of the Cayman Islands was worth £40 million and the proud possessor of additional homes in Miami, London, Scotland and Ireland. Not bad for the son of a Scarborough antique dealer. Owning racehorses was one of his passions and he had horses with a number of Northern trainers, such as Mick and Peter Easterby, Jack Berry, Mary Reveley and Lynda Ramsden. Why, even I had ridden a winner or two for him.

But, and it's a bloody big but, besides his undoubted ability to make money Savill possessed an uncanny knack for rubbing people up the wrong way. He was an abrasive personality, confrontational and, according to any number of people who had every reason to know how he operated, he was not averse to adopting strong-arm tactics if he thought they would help him get his own way. One award-winning journalist described him in print as having 'a damaging penchant for conflict and prone to losing self-control...Savill's disputes tend to have an acrimonious edge.' Another wrote: 'His capacity for gratuitous offence has been noted amongst the very individuals he needs to impress.' For instance, after Savill – known to us all as 'Jimmy' on account of the TV personality Jimmy Savile – eventually parted company with Jack Berry, Jack named one of his horses Jimmy The Skunk on account of his antics.

On Wednesday, 12 June 1991, I got some first-hand experience of 'Jimmy' at work. The day had promised nothing more than a typical midsummer double shift, kicking off at Beverley in the afternoon before flying up to Hamilton for an evening meeting. I had just the two rides booked at Beverley, Rose Alto for James Fanshawe in the 3.30 and a rank outsider in the 4.30 for Brian Murray called Fort-Galas Pride but four in the evening, including another of James's which was fancied to win the two-year-old maiden, Franny Lee's Regal Romper that looked likely to start favourite for the handicap at 8.30 and Neville Callaghan's Majed which was certain to be sent off odds-on for the 7.30. Nothing special, just a run-of-the-mill day, really, but a fair old trek that made a plane essential.

Two planes were making the trip, a single-engined plane and a larger twin-engined job which would obviously be much faster and knock 20 minutes or so off your journey. Kevin Darley, Peter Savill's retained jockey at the time, and Mark Birch had done the organising. Just to be on the safe side, before I left home for Beverley I got off Brian Murray's outsider in the later race so that I'd have plenty of time to make the ride on Majed, probably my 'banker' of the day. I never like doing this kind of thing to a trainer but I'd little option. Riding the best chance of a winner is always a jockey's priority and I couldn't afford to be late. 'Nasty Nev' is not a man to antagonise unnecessarily. Ask Seb Sanders who once memorably dropped his hands on a Callaghan horse and got caught on the line!

It was arranged for me to fly up straight after the 3.30 in the larger plane; Kieren Fallon and Michael Tebbutt would be finished at Beverley by then, so they were to accompany me. Trainer Mark Johnston would come with us. So would Peter Savill. Kevin and Mark were going to take the smaller plane and come up later since they were not riding until the 8 o'clock race.

Rose Alto won her race nicely, beating Tebby's mount Dovale (which was his only ride of the afternoon) and we're ready to leave as arranged when Kevin informs us that Peter Savill wants to stay and watch another race. 'We can't do that, Kev,' I said to him. 'If we wait too much longer we'll struggle to reach Hamilton in time to ride and it's just not fair on the people who've booked us.' All Kevin could say was 'You know what he's like. That's what he wants to do. You'd better speak to him.'

I told Tebby and Kieren what the situation was and said that I was going to have a word with Savill to see what the score is. I put out a message over the public address asking Peter Savill to please come to the weighing room. The first person to bump into him is Tebby who asks him whether he is going to stay because we have commitments at Hamilton. For his pains he gets a serious flea in his ear. 'You rude, insignificant little man – who the hell do you little bastards think you are?'

I'm next in line. 'It was me that broadcast for you,' I say. 'If we stay for you to watch another race it's going to tighten-up our schedule and we'll struggle to make Hamilton in time. It's not fair on us or the people we're meant to be riding for.'

Savill is fuming. 'Is it your fucking plane?'

'No, it isn't. Is it yours?'

'Well, it is, actually!'

'Oh, I didn't know.' In fact, the pilot, Peter Johnson, later told me Savill owned just 10 per cent, but never mind the details. 'All we want to do is leave,' I said to him.

So, Savill starts shouting 'Where's Darley? I want to see Darley!' and when Kevin comes out of the jockeys' room he starts off: 'These little bastards here,' meaning me and Tebby, and I'm thinking, 'Hang on, what little bastard? You can't just call me a little bastard.' I go to grab hold of him but see sense and change my mind because this was no time nor place to be having a fracas with Peter Savill. Anyway, the entire scene is played out under the eyes and ears of the Clerk of the Scales, Martin Wright, who immediately says to me: 'Do you want me to take this further? I heard the abuse you were just subjected to. I'm prepared to take it in front of the stewards if you want me to.' Of course, that would only delay our departure even more. 'No,' I said. 'Just leave it. Thanks, but forget it.'

Nevertheless, my temper is coming into play and I'm starting to lose the plot. 'This is not on, Kev,' I say. 'We've all agreed to share the costs of this plane – Tebby's even had to bring a cheque with him to get on the plane – and out of the blue Peter Savill decides he wants to stay. Peter Savill hasn't got any riding commitments at Hamilton but we have! Kev, this is not the way to conduct business and I'm not happy!'

Peter Savill gets my final shot: 'And you, Mr Savill, can stick that fucking plane where the sun doesn't shine! We'll go on the other plane!'

Now, while the bigger and faster plane would have handled the journey between the 3.30 at Beverley and the 7.30 at Hamilton without a problem, it's going to be a closer call in the smaller and slower plane. And with a hot-pot to ride in the 7.30 for 'Nasty Nev' I'm in no mood to hang about.

Tebby, Kieren and me pile into the back of a taxi, with Mark Johnston in the front alongside the driver, and we head for the strip which is at Pocklington, about 20 minutes away from Beverley racecourse. Before we had gone a mile or two, who do we spot through the rear window but Peter Savill following us in his own car. Now, this is the man who a few minutes earlier had wanted to stay at Beverley to watch another race, but all of a sudden he's decided to leave the course and pursue us for some reason or another. Arriving at the strip, we jump out and me and Tebby are in the process of paying the taxi driver, while Kieren is getting his kit out of the boot, when Savill's car pulls up beside us. Savill climbs out of his car and makes straight for me, waving his mobile phone. Under no provocation whatsoever he launched into another tirade, swearing and cursing at me.

This was the cue for the fur to start flying and some really serious verbals to kick off. A few nasty insinuations are made and plenty of juicy insults traded. I was trying to give as good as I got but Savill was relentless. All the while he was right in my face, half-shoving his mobile phone up my nose. Now, Savill is a stockily built guy and considerably taller than any jockey. There was no doubt in my mind that he was trying to strong-arm me. But he'd picked on the wrong fella. Whether he appreciated it or not, he had pushed me to the limit – and then some. I swung a right-hander and clocked him smack in the kisser.

I was immediately dragged away by Tebby, Kieren and the taxi driver, although I couldn't help noticing that the biggest man present, who you'd expect to step in to split up a fight – namely Mark Johnston – looked the other way. Me? I had no regrets, other than I'd not hit Savill hard enough. I should have decked him and made a proper job of it.

Still Savill refused to leave me alone and he continued having a go at me. 'I didn't get where I am today by not knowing how to deal with fucking people like you!' he ranted.

All I could summon up by way of retaliation on the spur of the moment was to call him 'an ugly fat bastard,' because I was already coming to terms with the possible repercussions of that right-hander. I could lose my licence if I was ever convicted of a criminal offence.

As I tried to contain myself, and come to terms with the possible repercussions of that right hook at one and the same time, Savill hurled insult after insult in my direction. He accused me of once deliberately keeping my hands in my pockets when I'd shared a taxi with a mate of his, the Scottish bookmaker Alex Farquhar, known as 'MacBet'. As it happened, I'd offered Farquhar a contribution and he refused to accept it.

'How much was it?' I yelled at Savill. 'A tenner? Here,' I said, taking a tenner out of my wallet, 'take this tenner and stick it right up your arse because it'll make me feel better – you seem to need it more than I do!'

To make matters worse neither plane was even at the strip. We didn't take off in the slower plane until 5.10 and only touched down at Cumbernauld – the best part of half an hour from Hamilton – at 6.50: head winds had put 15 minutes on our flight time. Savill landed soon afterwards in the faster plane. I was pleased to learn from Peter Johnson later on that his principal passenger hadn't exactly enjoyed his flight. Savill was so hot and bothered and in such a muck sweat after our altercation that in spite of it being a very warm evening the man somehow still managed to steam up the windows!

We finally got to the track too late for me to weigh out for the ride on Majed (which got beat with John Carroll deputising for me) and later on I was out of luck on the two favourites I did ride. It just wasn't my day.

My troubles were far from over. The next thing I know the police want to see me 'in connection with an incident at the Pocklington airstrip'. Apparently, Savill had obtained a doctor's certificate stating the bruise on the side of his face was 'consistent' with someone thumping him. The police took statements from all of us. It soon became quite obvious that Savill was not going to let the matter drop. At the time he had a filly in training with Sir Mark Prescott, who was my number one employer. He rang Sir Mark to complain that he had suffered all manner of abuse from his stable jockey and what was Sir Mark going to do about it. In 1991 I had been riding for Sir Mark for 19 years. Our association was – and still is – based on trust. One of Sir Mark's oft-quoted remarks is 'If the whole world told me X and George told me Y, I would believe George – and I wouldn't ask him to tell me again. His word will always be good enough for me. I have never known him to tell me a lie in all our time together. He is the most honest man I've met.'

So, Savill was unlikely to get any change out of Sir Mark. 'Well, Mr Savill,' Sir Mark informed him, 'if G Duffield thinks it was right to give you a thump in the ear, he must have had due cause to do so because he's not the sort of man who goes round thumping people for no good reason.' End of story ... and in 1992 there were no Savill horses in Sir Mark's care!

The police decided not to press charges. In fact, I can chuckle now at the memory of the policeman who interviewed me because he said: 'After speaking with Mr Savill I can fully understand why you hit him – you must have been greatly provoked!' The decision not to prosecute could not have gone down well with Peter Savill because he then threatened to take out a private summons against me. Fortunately, Sir Mark had already found me a solicitor, Martin Blakemore, who specialised in GBH cases of this kind and the whole thing came to nothing.

I've not spoken a word to Peter Savill since. If our paths ever cross, I ignore the man. I wouldn't give him the time of day. The whole affair had dragged on for almost a year and there's no escaping the fact that it had been a worrying period. I could have lost my licence. And I'd have had myself partly to blame. I hadn't started the row but my fierce temper had certainly finished it.

2

'You're Not Worth Two-bob, You'

I often wonder whether my temper in some way owes anything to the fact that my father dropped me on my head when I was only two years of age, fracturing my skull! Or it may stem from the years of frustration when my lack of size ensured I was regularly on the receiving end of hidings from the bigger kids at school. And every kid was bigger than me!

Dad was walking home from the Victoria Working Men's Club in Stanley, where he was on the committee, with me perched on his shoulders. He tipped me off backwards in the belief there was someone behind him waiting to catch me. No such luck, I'm afraid, and I took a nose dive into the pavement. I can't remember much about staying in hospital other than it wasn't very pleasant, but I still retain the memory of my dad sat beside my bed crying like a baby. Although an accident, it was his fault and he felt terribly guilty. At any rate, I certainly grew up with the violent temper of a right little psychopath, not averse to throwing my toys at doors in a tantrum or even hurling things at kids who incurred my wrath!

Anything at all could cause me to blow a gasket and result in me receiving a serious kick up the backside from dad or a slap from mum. Without question, I was a funny old kid.

George Peter Duffield came into the world on Saturday, 30 November 1946, upstairs at 5 Spa Fold, Lime Pit Lane, in the West Yorkshire mining village of Stanley, just to the north of Wakefield, where my parents, Charles and Elsie, lived with my mum's widowed mother. I was their first-born. My brother Michael arrived 11 years later.

In those days it was common for working class families to share housing. Money and housing was tight and there was seldom little choice. On the plus side was the fact that the extended family worked well. Dad was the eldest of six, while mum was the eldest of five. She had a sister, Margaret, and three brothers, after one of whom I was named. Strange, but I never grew so close to dad's side of the family as to mum's. I have loads of cousins on dad's side I've never seen and I wouldn't know them if I fell over them in the street. On mum's side it's quite the reverse. I was the first grandchild but within 15 months or so along came my cousins Ray, Chris, Lynn and Graham and I was brought up alongside all of them. When I was five we got a house of our own at 51 Bevin Crescent, on the new council estate in Outwood, where we remained until mum and dad agreed to a house exchange which brought us back to 17 Lime Pit Lane when I was nine or ten. Mum and dad still live there today.

My dad had been a miner at the Roundwood pit, between Ossett and Wakefield, from the age of 14. Like a lot of that ilk he was small – slightly larger than me now, an inch or two maybe – and squat with broad shoulders and slightly bow-legs: very powerfully built, hard fit-and just as tough a character as you can get. Had he kept his weight under control as a young man he might have made a jockey but he was more interested in backing horses than riding them or going down the pub or club for a pint. He also kept greyhounds. His own father had been involved with horses in a working capacity but what dad was really mad about was racing. Once I'd started school I noticed he'd always go for a pint in the pub at lunchtime and leave a slip with all his bets on, his trebles and accumulators, for mum to take round to the bookies. Only a few shillings, mind, he never had enough money to gamble heavily. Charlie showed all the characteristics of a bad punter: dad hated losing money to the bookies and his losses usually outstripped his winnings by a mile! Mum was forever moaning about him losing all his money.

Despite never having sat on a horse himself, let alone ride one in a race, his knowledge of individual races and jockeys was extremely good and he would assume the role of armchair critic par excellence. Eventually he was to follow my own riding career with equal passion but we rarely discussed it. Although he was probably one of my sternest critics, any points tended to come to me second hand via mum, which I found rather irritating. Perhaps he was talking through his pockets or on behalf of other punters in the betting shop. Or, maybe it was because I was doing what he'd have loved to do for a living and he was a little jealous. I really don't know. It would rub me up the wrong way, though. If he'd talked to me face to face it wouldn't have been so bad. This way was all so frustrating.

My relationship with dad was indifferent. I don't doubt his love for me, but, aside from the fractured skull incident, his character would never allow him to show any real emotion. In those days it just wasn't the 'done thing' to do so. He would have thought it a bit 'soft'. It's a sad fact of life that when you are unable to be free and open with your feelings you miss out on so much warmth. It has taken me the best part of 50 years to realise this: life can pass you by and so much can remain unsaid and unknown.

I enjoyed a far closer relationship with my mum, although she was as strict as my dad. We may only have been a working class family but manners were drummed into me like there was no tomorrow. At mealtimes, for example, I was made to eat everything on my plate – whether I liked it or not – or else I had nothing at all. And if my table manners weren't perfect, if I ate with my mouth open, smacking my lips, I'd be walloped by one or other of them. Dad would soon have his belt off and there were no half measures if I'd misbehaved badly – and mum could deliver as hard as dad! I wouldn't have been the easiest kid in the world. I was pretty wilful and if I set my mind on doing something, I did it and took the consequences. As I got older and began to want to stay out playing, they always imposed a curfew, usually between seven and eight, which I frequently broke and resulted in me being 'grounded' from time to time. The very thought of my parents' shame and disgust ensured I never indulged in petty crime beyond 'scrumping' apples. Nicking from shops, for instance, was a definite no-no. I never had the guts to try because I was petrified of the consequences at home. I had no idea what life had in store for me at this stage, but the irony of my disciplined upbringing preparing me for a life of discipline at the behest of the Jockey Club would be amusing if it weren't so bloody infuriating!

Sad to say, my relationship with my parents has foundered of late and we've not spoken for two years. One of those family tiffs that seems daft to outsiders. First of all dad became seriously ill and was admitted to hospital, where he lost seven or eight pints of blood from a perforated ulcer, and, because the doctors were frightened of bringing about brain damage if he was brought round too soon, they left him sedated for a week. Then my mum fell off the couch at home and broke her hip. So the pair of them are in adjoining wards at Pinderfield Hospital! Once they were well enough to return home things began to go pear-shaped. Michael accused me of not visiting them or pulling my weight, which was untrue. I'd taken four days off racing at one stage to be with them and I was always popping in to see them on the way to, or on the way home from racing; and I'd offered to pay for home improvements like central heating. There was a major fall-out and the last time we tried to patch it up dad put the phone down.

We were still living at Spa Fold when I got my very first experience of riding a horse at the age of two. Besides a few cattle and pigs, the local farmer had a huge shire horse which he used to bring down Lime Pit Lane every day. I would stand at the bottom of the lane waiting for him. I adored this horse. One day the farmer put me up on its harness and I sat there pleased as punch while he slowly walked a couple of hundred yards down the lane. Once we reached the top of the lane, the farmer gently pulled me off the shire's back and I toddled home thrilled to bits. I'd acquired the taste.

I was truly besotted with any kind of horse. On our day trips to Blackpool or Scarborough I made a beeline for the donkeys on the beach. I always tried to make them go further along the beach than they were supposed to go – which was an impossibility because each donkey was programmed to turn at exactly the same spot every time. I'd also attempt to make them go faster, which was equally impossible!

Riding ponies was soon all I ever thought about. By the age of nine or ten I was forever wagging off school to find a pony somewhere – it didn't matter who it belonged to – so I could ride it until I fell off or it threw me off. Stanley wasn't very big when I was a child and I didn't need to travel far to be in the countryside. Behind Spa Fold was Stanley Marsh and the old slag heaps known to us as 'The Black Hills.' There'd always be some horse tethered in a field or on a patch of spare ground, attached by a collar to a stake so it could wander about. My best friend at junior school was Keith Slater, who shared my love of the outdoor life and was equally keen to bunk off school, although he was never that keen on ponies. Even so, Keith happily joined me in my quest to find some pony to ride. Once we'd discovered one, we'd keep going back. It didn't matter to me whether or not it had been broken. I just wanted to get up onto their backs and ride them. All of them. Every single one I came across.

Riding the roughest pony was better than school, which held no appeal for me whatsoever. Apart from schoolwork I also had to face John Beaumont and his gang of four mates. I was much smaller than everyone else in junior school – I was still only four feet seven and four-and-a half stone when I finally left school at fifteen – and these lads used to pummel me on a regular basis. I was easy meat for bullies. The situation began to get out of hand. Then my dad intervened.

Being a hard man himself, dad knew I had to make a stand and deal with this myself. Dad had a serious temper. I'd seen him have one or two scraps in the club. Even though he wasn't over-big, he could handle himself. He wouldn't go looking for it but if it came his way, then watch out. He appreciated that even if you were going to get a good hiding you had to put a brave face on it and get stuck in to ensure you didn't get picked on the next day. If you bowed down to it, a good hiding became the norm. But my dad ensured my stand would be on level terms.

'What's going on?' he asked one evening after I'd come in from school for the umpteenth occasion looking as if I'd been dragged through a hedge backwards.

'It's John Beaumont and his gang. They beat me up on the way home every night. There's five of them, dad.'

All he said was: 'That's too many.'

The next day dad came along to meet me and when my tormentors duly made their appearance he said to them: 'He'll fight each and every one of you. But one at a time. He's only small and there's five of you – do you think those odds are fair?'

John Beaumont – known as 'Birdy' – held no fears for me on a one-to-one basis. I was not frightened of him. We fought it out alone. And I gave HIM a good hiding. I had no problems after that.

Mum could be as fiery as dad. She took no nonsense from anyone and I've seen her have the odd punch-up, which is unusual for women. One day, some woman who was quite a bit bigger – she'd give mum two or three stone – had been picking on me and she sorted her out with a punch, right there in the street. She was a tough cookie, was mum. I think all the family were. It was the way they were brought up in those days. Fight your own battles.

It was mum who helped me confront another bully who continually made my life hell. He was twice my size and trying to fight back seemed both fruitless and hopeless. Every night he took great pleasure in punching me in the ribs or pushing me into a ditch. Then mum got wind of it.

'You!' she shouted at him, 'Coat Off!'

And then she turned to me. 'You! Coat Off!' she repeated.

I can remember thinking to myself: 'Shit! He's gonna kill me! Why is she making me fight him?'

'Get stuck in,' she said to him. 'Don't worry how small he is.' I couldn't believe what I was hearing!

This lad couldn't get his coat off quick enough, could he. He flung me to the ground, sat on top of me and knocked seven bells out of me until mum put a stop to it by saying 'OK! He's had enough!'

And that boy never bothered me again. The fact that mum had told me to get stuck in and I'd tried my best to do so must have changed this brute's opinion of me. Either that or my mum had put the fear of Christ into him.

This attitude has stayed with me to this day. I was always a determined little bugger and I still am. Whether or not I've been any good at anything I've always been very competitive and willing to have a go, to TRY. I've always maintained a positive attitude.

Not surprisingly Keith and me both failed the 11-Plus! At Stanley Secondary we made a new friend in Howard Rainbow, whose parents owned a smallholding where they kept pigs and hens...and they also had a pony! We'd muck out the pigs and collect the eggs before Howard and me took turns on the pony while Keith, who still didn't fancy it, stood watching. We even used to try and ride the pigs! Take it from one who knows, don't try it. They are the hardest beasts to sit on. And then we had to help Howard's dad castrate the piglets. The job entailed holding the piglet's head and front feet between your legs while holding their back legs apart so that he could slice off their testicles with a razor blade. Mr Rainbow's party piece was to rub the severed testicles on our faces while we were preoccupied with the next squealing piglet. Neither Howard nor I shared his amusement.

During the holidays me and Keith would head off to Sharratt's bungalow at the bottom of Lime Pit Lane. The Sharratt family included numerous kids who were friends of ours, but the biggest attraction was a donkey. All the kids were allowed to ride him in the summer and I couldn't wait to jump on him. In the years to come I would often push something for one and a half miles and then think to myself that certainly wasn't the only donkey I've ever ridden!

We also befriended a wily old Irishman who tethered his black pony on Ferry Lane, near the canal. The old boy used to take us for rides in his pony and trap, and promised us a pony each – as long as we helped him with chores. We spent all the hours God sent mucking out, helping him gather and stack his hay and what-have-you. Of course it was all a ruse to get us to work for nothing and his promises vanished into thin air: the ponies never materialised. Another valuable lesson learned the hard way!

We'd also go along to Arthur Hopkinson's riding school in

Outwood. Arthur only had one arm. The horse we all wanted to ride was Mickey because he was the biggest and strongest but only Arthur, one-armed or not, could handle him. Howard was a far better rider than me at this stage and he taught me a fair bit. Eventually his parents bought him a proper horse and we'd go out together with me on the pony. One day this almost led to disaster. We were going down this rough dirt track when I fell off out the side door but as I was wearing a pair of boots far too big for the irons one of my feet got stuck. I was dragged along on my back as the spooked pony headed toward home and a tarmac road. After being frightened to death for 200 yards or so, my foot came loose. I didn't ride for six months after that.

Keith and me continued to skive off school. Academic qualifications were not considered important by Charlie or Elsie, and their son was not one to disagree. I never attended school much. Every report used to say that I'd do better if I attended more often. I'd pick and choose my days according to the timetable. If it was gym or games, art, history, woodwork or metalwork, I'd pay school a flying visit. I wasn't a great athlete. I didn't like tennis, didn't like cricket, I wasn't awfully keen on football but I loved rugby. Dad had played on the wing for Wakefield Trinity but my light weight and small frame was always a drawback.

What I did excel at was climbing the ropes in gym. I went up them like a monkey! I especially liked art and got on famously with the art master Mr Davenport, who encouraged me to stay on in order to take my exam as he thought I had possibilities. Maths, on the other hand, could be unbearable. The master had a metal plate in his head from a war wound, and this caused him to experience violent mood swings. Many's the day a board duster came whizzing past my head, I can tell you, and the slipper, stick or cane became very familiar with the Duffield posterior! So, if none of my favourite subjects featured in the day's lessons I'd be off wandering round the countryside in search of a pony. Mum was a real soft touch as far as attending school was concerned. She'd always take pity on me when I'd say I was unwell. Then, as soon as the clock passed nine I was up in a flash and gone. I could wrap mum round my little finger, just like most kids!

Qualifications meant nowt because it was assumed I would follow in dad's footsteps by going down the pit. However, what my parents didn't appreciate was that the mines were the last place on earth you were going to find G Duffield.

By the time I was ready to leave Stanley Secondary School everybody was telling me I should become a jockey. 'You should be a jockey, you. You're just the right size.' They thought it was as easy as that. You just went out and became a jockey. I was to learn otherwise. When I left school aged 15 at Christmas 1961 it was no racing stable I entered as a budding jockey but Willie Lamb's clogs and footwear factory down the road as a general dogsbody.

From the outset the thing I hated most about my new job was the confinement. The factory was a small, grey, miserable building with tiny windows down by the River Calder. As you can see, I didn't exactly fall in love with the place. The words dull, dingy and gloomy don't do it justice! The 'Boss'was a man in his fifties of medium height, slim with sharp, weasel features. He was very much the hard-nosed businessman whom we seldom saw. His son, on the other hand, was always around. Taller and timid, he seemed overshadowed by his father and, probably because it was his role to oversee the day-to-day running of the factory, he was not particularly popular with the workforce of about 30 people. My duties, such as they were, revolved around carrying leather, moulds, studs etc to whoever needed them but, far more importantly, making the tea and getting the fish and chips at lunchtime. Although the workers were a fantastic bunch who took me, as the youngest and smallest, under their wing, the daily routine bored me to tears. It was purgatory working in that factory. The smell of the leather and the glue was almost overpowering at times and the constant drumming of the machinery was mind-numbing. I ached to escape to the countryside and its fresh air.

Salvation duly arrived in the form of a chance meeting with a girl I'd gone to school with. I can't, I'm afraid, remember her name but she was to change the direction of my life. She had got a job as secretary to Jimmy Walsh who trained racehorses at Nostell Priory, a stately home on the other side of Wakefield. 'Why don't you come and see him?' she said. 'You're always riding ponies, come and see what a racing yard looks like.' I wasn't sure whether racing was for me but the idea of spending time with horses certainly appealed, as did the opportunity to get back out into the open air. 'OK. Ask him if he wants any staff.' The message came back that Mr Walsh didn't need any permanent staff but, if I wanted to, it was all right for me to go over on a Saturday, stay the night and return home on Sunday. If I wanted to! I jumped at the opportunity.

So every Saturday morning I'd get up early and pedal my bike the eight miles or so to Nostell Priory. The yard was an old-fashioned one, set around a courtyard, with the estate grounds providing the gallops. Mr Walsh was a very nice man who had a wonderful, wonderful wife who was – and still is – very attractive. His string was very small and not of the highest quality. A lad named Kenny taught me how to muck-out, dress a horse over correctly and grease its feet. I swept the yard and cleaned the tack. I loved each and every minute. Naturally, I longed for the chance to sit on one of the racehorses.

Eventually the great day came. I was so chuffed when Mr Walsh legged me up on this old horse. 'Trot him up the lane,' he instructed. 'Yes, Mr Walsh, right sir.' Unfortunately, I was not yet up to the job. The old horse bolted with me. 'That's enough for you, mate,' he said. 'You'd best stay in the yard.'

Mr Walsh could not have thought too badly of me because it was he who put me on the first rung of the ladder which ultimately led to where I am today. He offered to ring a friend of his in Newmarket on the off chance that he might need young staff. That man was Mr Jack Waugh of Heath House. Mr Waugh said he was happy for me to come down as an apprentice on a one-month trial basis. Whether being a jockey or a stable lad was the future for me, I didn't know. That had never been my dream. I'd only ever been to one race meeting (an Ebor day at York) and I'd not bothered to watch a single race. Being involved with horses and becoming completely independent of home, on the other hand, definitely would be a dream come true. I accepted Mr Waugh's offer.

All that remained was to hand in my notice at the factory. Willie Lamb could be an awkward old bugger and I feared the worst as I went in on the Friday night to collect my wages and hand in my notice at one and the same time.

'I'm going to Newmarket and I'm going to be a jockey,' I blurted out.

He slowly looked me up and down, obviously searching for the most scathing put-down he could muster.

'You'll never be a jockey,' he hissed. 'You're not worth two-bob, you!'

'You'd better believe it!' I countered, picking up my pay-packet. 'I'll show you!'

Silly words, I know, from a young lad as unremarkable as I was. However, I was determined to prove him wrong and make him eat those words. All that remains, I thought as I walked out of Willie Lamb's office, is for you to get on and put your money where your mouth is.

3

GREASE POTS AND MUCK HEAPS

The night before I left Lime Pit Lane for Newmarket in September 1962 I'm afraid to say I lay in my bed and cried my eyes out. I'd never been anywhere on my jacksy in my life. How was I going to cope? The journey alone was frightening me to death. Mum had found out the train times for me and the journey involved any number of changes. I could see me never reaching Newmarket. All I could visualise as I struggled to get to sleep was the sight of me, suitcase in hand, wandering up and down a platform at Doncaster or March on the verge of tears because I couldn't find my train and I was going to find myself in a lot of trouble when I failed to turn up on time at Heath House.

Somehow I managed to get on all the right trains and arrived safely in Newmarket. There to meet me at the station were three lads from Heath House – the three most recent arrivals – Tommy Dickey, Johnny Morgan and Sandy Cairns, who'd come down from Ayrshire only a few weeks previously. Sandy and me were destined to share a room and he became my best mate. They escorted me up the road to make the acquaintance of what was to be both my home and place of work for the foreseeable future. It's unbelievable to think that 40 years later I still turn up there for work!

Heath House lies at the bottom of Long Hill, in the fork between the Bury and Moulton roads. But first it was to Osborne House, just down and across the Moulton Road from Heath House, where all the lads lived. This was the yard built for Tom Chaloner in the mid 19th century and named in honour of his wife's family, the famous Osbornes of Ashgill in Middleham. Nellie Chaloner actually took over the training after her husband's early death and lived to the grand old age of 97. The house was a fair bit different to what I'd imagined, being three-storeyed and quite pleasant inside with a small kitchen, a large dining room, TV room and plenty of bedrooms and bathrooms, although from the outside it reminded me of the Bates house in the film 'Psycho.' About fifteen lads lived there, aged from about 15 like myself into the mid 20s. We were looked after by a large bespectacled lady called Mrs Jay, who had her own private quarters on the second floor. Mrs Jay proved to be a decent cook and there was never any shortage of grub. Chips, mash, mince, roasts, huge breakfast fry-ups, cream cakes delivered daily fresh from the bakery – everything a 15-year-old boy could possibly want. The only question that came to mind was how on earth was I going to stay light enough to become a jockey if I ate like this every day!

Before I could get my feet under the table – literally as well as metaphorically – I was taken to see my new employer in Heath House. This was probably not the same Heath House in which the great Mat Dawson had lived while training St Simon and no fewer than 18 Victorian Classic winners in only 15 years (that had stood next door on the site of what is now the Heath Court Hotel), but the one built during the 1880s for his nephew George (who sent out a further ten Classic winners) after Mat himself had moved to

Exning. Heath House Cottage does remain from Mat's day. The three downstairs rooms commandeered by Fred Archer – one to sweat, one to cool and the third to change – during his spell as Heath House's most renowned stable jockey, are now three separate boxes, although the doorways from one to another are still clearly visible under the brickwork. In the wake of the Dawsons, Heath House had acted as the base for the likes of Harry Sadler, Fred Butters and Basil Jarvis, but in spite of continuing to be associated with countless top-class animals, the yard had not housed an English Classic winner since Volodyvoski won the Derby for the American John Huggins in 1901.

I can't recall whether my knees were knocking at my introduction to Mr Waugh but if they weren't they should have been. I was a weedy little specimen of barely five and a half stone wet through, standing less than five feet. Before me towered this six feet four inch-figure immaculately attired in shiny, sturdy, rubber-soled shoes, sharply-creased flannel trousers, crisp shirt and woollen tie, snazzy Fair Isle pullover and a tweed jacket. A pair of piercing blue eyes fixed me from beneath the rim of a flat cap. I'd never seen anyone like this in my life and when a voice beckoned me to come closer my natural inclination was to take a terrified step in entirely the opposite direction.

'How are you, boy?' were the giant's first words. 'I'm sure you'll enjoy it here. See how you get on. You're here on a month's trial and if you're still happy after that you can sign on for a five-year apprenticeship. You'll be staying with all the other boys, who'll look after you, and Mr Button, the head lad, will tell you what you should be doing in the yard. Now, be off with you.'

That first month was a 'trial' in more senses than one. I never really got homesick but I did get heartily fed up with all the pranks and good hidings I received at the hands of the senior lads, the older apprentices who were not going to make it as jockeys. My saving grace was the fact that I'd been used to this treatment all my life. If that's the worst that's going to happen to me, I reasoned, it's not that bad – so just get on with it. I was determined to stick it out.

These senior lads could be right cruel bastards. The initiation rites were many and varied. Sandy Cairns reeled off a few favourites. You might be tied up, stripped, covered in grease, your private parts boot-polished or dusted with itching powder; buried in the muck-heap up to your neck; dropped down the hay chute; or possibly dunked fully-clothed in a cold bath if you were a scruffy Herbert who didn't keep himself clean. By fair means or foul – mostly the latter – they ensured everyone toed the line through a combination of vigilante justice and kangaroo courts. And further indignity was always only just around the corner. Mr Waugh employed a lot of girls – and they'd join in the fun as well!

Nothing happened. 'They're just giving you a week to settle in,' said Sandy reassuringly. True enough, after a week a glint began to appear in the eyes of the torturers-in-chief, Tom Dickey, Graham Buckley, Mick Valentine, Tony Shaw, Tommy Rattley, Kevin McGuinness and Geoff Thompson. I just wanted to get it over and done with. The suspense was killing me.

My mental agony was soon relieved. One lunchtime they cornered me in the saddle room. Jamming a head collar over my head and under my arms, they stuck me up on a bridle hook, removed my jodhpurs and underpants and left me hanging there, spinning round on this hook, till evening stables at 4.30. Mr Waugh turned a blind eye. Although he'd intervene if someone was being seriously abused, he knew how the law of the jungle worked.

I was to suffer the full repertoire in due course. Some were less physical, but no less embarrassing. You'd be dispatched to the dry cleaners in the High Street with a big brown paper bag with the instructions 'Get these cleaned and re-texed'. The bag invariably contained dirty muck sacks. I was once told to go down to the ironmongers for 'some of those special rubber nails' – and I went! Another priceless prank was set up in the saddle room. 'See those colours up there?' someone would say. 'You realise you've got to get measured for your colours. We've all got a set each. You'd best get straight down to Goldings in the High Street and tell them you've come to be measured up.' The staff in Goldings didn't know whether to laugh or cry when I marched in and said: 'I've come to be measured for my colours.'

I weathered the storm and signed on for my five years. And, as always seems to be the way in life, I became one of the boys and grew to be as bad as the next.

Anyone could become a target. Heath House had a wonderful old stableman called Don Yarnle. He was a proper stableman of the old school, who didn't ride out. He'd start dressing over his horses earlier than us and they always looked magnificent. Consequently, he tended to get the best horses. What Don didn't know about the job wasn't worth talking about but he could be a miserable old sod. He was forever on our backs. In Don's eyes we couldn't do right for doing wrong. One afternoon we decided to pay him back. In those days there was a large muck heap in the centre of the main yard enclosed by a low wall with one entrance at the front. Some of us went back early one afternoon and dug out a hole just inside the entrance, about three feet deep, just big enough for someone to fall down. We filled the hole with water and lay sticks across the top, which we covered with straw. Come evening stables we're all crouching behind the doors of our own boxes waiting for Don to arrive, because we know he'll be first in as usual and then first to the muck heap. Sure enough, out goes Don to the muck heap, muck sack over his shoulder. And down he goes, just his head and shoulders sticking out of this hole, water everywhere, and plastered in muck. We are all absolutely howling! And poor old Don is trapped there covered from head to toe in water and horseshit cursing us. 'You fucking bastards! I'll get you for this! I'll fucking kill every one of you little sods!'

All the pranks and good hidings could drive you crazy but, looking back, it was all so much fun and I've no doubt the stable staff of my era were far worse behaved than they are today. Certainly, we lived under pretty Spartan conditions in our version of Dotheboys Hall but we were well fed. My first weekly wage was 18 shillings and six pence in old money, about 92p today, but as we lived 'all-found' – including the free haircuts you dodged unless you were the kind of idiot who fancied the unflattering short-back-and-sides, pudding-basin style of a monk – that mattered less than it should. And I could earn a few extra coppers from the others by ironing shirts or running their washing through the laundrette. What you couldn't pay for, 'Simba' used to nick. Simba was a black lad, whose real name I can't recall, who hadn't cut the mustard as an apprentice and had been passed over to Mrs Jay as an odd-job man and helper. Simba's real talents, however, lay in thieving. 'Do you need some socks?' he'd say, 'I'm going down to Woolies this afternoon.' He was a tremendous tea-leaf, was Simba, and he tried every scam going. One day he cut the outline of a pound note out of a newspaper and went across the Moulton Road to the shop run by a short-sighted old lady. Simba used it to buy something for tuppence and pocketed all the change from a pound!

In those days, during the 1960s, a lad only had two horses in his care, unlike three or more today, so no one could say they were overworked. For example, Mr Waugh employed a loft-man, a tack-man, a hack-man, a yard-man. No wonder we apprentices had plenty of surplus energy. Nowadays they work so much harder and probably want their sleep a lot more than we did. Bullying and Dickensian living quarters aside, Osborne House was a holiday camp as far as we were concerned.

Not that Newmarket in the Sixties was exactly 'swinging' like the rest of the country was supposed to be. But there were girls. Although Mr Waugh employed more girls than most – six or seven – at that time, females were not exactly thick on the ground in Newmarket. There were ten of us to one of them which meant just finding a girl was a tough task. My first encounter was with a girl whom the lads used to fix up with any new boy because she was a bit of a 'raver', a bit warm if you catch my meaning. They'd let her loose on all the young kids. The plan was simplicity itself and as old as the hills. The older lads took you out on a Friday or Saturday night after you'd got your wages and proceeded to take great pleasure in getting you absolutely arseholed – which didn't require much effort when you were 15 or 16. The pub crawl began in The Horseshoes at the bottom of the Moulton Road near Osborne House and it wasn't long before you were completely plastered and barely conscious.

If you survived and it was a Saturday, there was a dance at the Memorial Hall – which is where the 'raver' would be lying in wait for fresh meat. 'She really fancies you, George,' they said. 'She's the girl for you, no mistake.' She was not the greatest looking girl in the world but, boy, was she a man-eater. She was far too much woman for 16-year-old G Duffield, I can assure you! I wasn't ready for someone like her. I couldn't handle her at all. She frightened the life out of me, which only gave the lads even greater pleasure. There'd be other nights for me.

Our favourite haunt was the cinema. No one cared what the picture was, it was just a way of passing the time. Newmarket had two in those days, the Doric and the Kingsway on opposite sides of the High Street beyond the Jockey Club, both of them converted to night clubs now. Having next to no spare cash for pursuits like the cinema could pose a problem, which was solved in the traditional manner. We'd wait till the lights had dimmed and the picture had started before bunking in through the toilet window and creeping up the aisle under the cover of darkness in search of empty seats. Some of us would have torn tickets from previous visits that had been paid for, and these would be handed around in case an usherette challenged us. It was the sheer thrill of getting in for nothing that made the evening. I remember getting back to Osborne House the night we'd bunked in to see 'Psycho'. Still half-terrified, I went for a pee, not knowing someone had decided to hide behind the long drapes at the bathroom window, ready to impersonate 'Mrs Bates'. I'd just started to pee when I felt this hand rest on my shoulder – I jumped so much my pee shot all over the bathroom!

Every now and again, of course, we'd be slung out of the cinema, and if you'd got a date with a girl it was always a case of 'I've got to work late – I'll see you in there' because there was no way you could, or would, pay for her. Once we tried to get upstairs at the Doric by forcing the fire doors. We calculated that if one was pushed and one was pulled simultaneously, they would spring open. They opened as sweet as a nut, but in so doing they knocked for six the usherette who was leaning against them on the other side! We had to scarper pretty damn quick.

Mr Waugh had so many good lads who could all ride well – Lawrie Thorpe, Peter Bonney, Eric Apter and Ginger Craig besides all the younger brigade – that you were hard pushed to get started if you weren't up to scratch and it was into 1963 before I even got to ride out. I spent nearly all my time with Fred Webb, the hack-man, looking after the Guv'nor's hacks. Fred Webb, who was a lovely old guy in his 60s and even smaller than I was, took care of Bee Wallah, who was a ten-year-old chestnut, and I attended to an old bay called Quilt, formerly a stayer, who was two years older. Mr Waugh tended to ride Bee Wallah and Jack Button would use Quilt. Fred also taught me dressing-over and mucking-out when I wasn't on duty sweeping or raking the yards and picking grass from between the stones. Mr Waugh did not want a piece of straw or a weed anywhere to be seen. 'I think you need to do that again, boy,' he'd say if he ever found anything. All this grew to be quite boring, particularly if I was so occupied when the rest were riding out.

After my first Christmas I was at last allowed to sit on a horse – old Quilt! He and I went for a canter. And I couldn't pull him up! It didn't take more than a second or two for him to rumble the fact that I couldn't ride for toffee. Even though he was so bloody old and so bloody slow, I had neither the strength nor technique to handle him. Needless to say, this did not stop me from constantly badgering Jack Button as to when I was going to be allowed to ride out properly with the string. 'You carry on, son,' he'd keep replying. 'When the Guv'nor thinks you're ready, you'll ride out. And when the Guv'nor thinks you're up to it, you'll ride in a race.'

I loved Jack Button to bits. As I grew more and more despondent at my slow progress – or lack of it – he would keep my spirits up with 'It'll come, it'll come.' If I was going to succeed it was clear I was going to have to be a late developer, but I was determined that whatever the outcome of my five-year apprenticeship, I was going to look back at the end of it able to say I'd given it my best shot. In the meantime I loved being with Jack Button, whether in the yard or, eventually, riding out. Watching him or talking to him taught me so much and I couldn't get enough of his company. Always impeccably attired for whatever the occasion demanded, Jack stood about five feet five inches tall with twinkly-eyes and sparrow-legs, the physique of a jockey although he never made it in the job himself. But, by God, he was the most fantastic horseman you ever saw. You often find that superb horsemen don't make jockeys: you're either one or the other. If the two come in the same package you've a rare find. Jack had served his time at Heath House under Basil Jarvis before the war when Mr Waugh had been assistant trainer and returned after the war (during which he had acted as batman to Bob Crowhurst, the famous Newmarket vet) to be reunited with Mr Waugh. There was nothing in the string Jack Button couldn't ride. He had the most wonderful hands which were able to settle and relax the most badly behaved horse. He taught me an awful lot about riding and I shall always be eternally grateful to him. Jack is still with us and I occasionally see him to this day.

It took nearly four years before the Guv'nor considered I was 'up to it' but eventually the great day duly arrived. On Saturday, 21 May, 1966, Mr Waugh in his wisdom put me up on a two-year-old filly in a five-furlong race for first-timers, the Blue Peter Stakes, on the Rowley Mile. He ran two in the race. Paul Tulk partnered Cheek To Cheek and I rode a grey filly by Persian Gulf called Tiara III. Us pair of 'first-timers' went off at 25/1 and managed to beat just one of our 18 rivals. I can barely remember anything of the experience, even though I'd waited so long for it. Nothing registered. It didn't have the impact on me it should have done. Did I dream it? It's completely blacked out, as if it never happened. I don't know why. Perhaps it just didn't come up to expectations.

Tiara III certainly failed to come up to expectations. She was no bloody good, never ran again and was sent to the Sales. Whether I was any bloody good was also open to question. What can be said without fear of contradiction is that my first ride could not have impressed Mr Waugh very much because I had to wait 11 months and another season before I got a second one.

4

I OWE THIS MAN EVERYTHING

I suppose you could say I've had three mentors. My dad put me on the straight and narrow. Jack Button taught me so, so much about horses and how to ride them. And Jack Waugh taught me how to conduct myself. He was like a second father to me. He turned the little boy into a man.

Training racehorses was in Mr Waugh's blood. There had been Waughs training in Newmarket since 1880 after Mr Waugh's grandfather James opened a stable at Middleton Cottage before later establishing himself at Meynell House on the Fordham Road. The family hailed from the Scottish borders and claimed descent from no less than Rob Roy MacGregor, and Jimmy Waugh's only Classic winner was fittingly a colt called Macgregor who won the 2000 Guineas of 1870. Tom, one of his many sons who went on to train horses, became the father of my new boss Jack and younger brother Tom. Their mother, Eleanor, was the daughter of Alfred Hayhoe, whose four Classic successes as a trainer included St

Amant in the Derby of 1904. Both Toms trained a Guineas winner: senior won the 1920 1000 with Cinna and junior the 2000 of 1962 with Privy Councillor.

Apparently, Mr Waugh disliked his schooldays (at Framlingham College) almost as much as me and left at the age of 15 to assist his father at Meynell House (renamed Hurworth House after World War II, it was a yard I came to know painfully well). After moving on to Basil Jarvis at Green Lodge, he saw war service with the Royal Artillery until invalided out of the army in 1942 as a result of the wounds he received in the ill-fated raid on Dieppe, a practice run of sorts for the D-Day landings two years later. As Mr Waugh also escaped the earlier fiasco at Dunkirk, some may consider he had used up life's ration of luck by the time he commenced training at Heath House in 1945.

One thing's for sure, Mr Waugh never enjoyed any luck in the Classics and never could settle the family score. The closest he had come to Classic success before I arrived at Heath House in 1962 was Arabian Night's second place behind Never Say Die in the 1954 Derby and the filly Sanlinea's third in the St Leger of 1950. The best horse he had trained thus far was probably the sprinter Matador, who won the July Cup followed by the Stewards' Cup, under a record weight for a three-year-old, in 1956 and the Cork and Orrery a year later. During my time at Heath House the fillies Ostrya and Almiranta won the Ribblesdale and Park Hill respectively and in my first full season of 1963 the colt Star Moss finished second to Ragusa (beaten six lengths, though) in the St Leger after an interrupted preparation. That Star Moss got to Doncaster at all was a testament to Mr Waugh's skill as a trainer because the colt only managed to visit the racecourse on five occasions in his entire career.

The two real stars in my time at Heath House were Oncidium and Lucasland. Oncidium was a handsome bay half brother to Ostrya belonging to Lord Howard de Walden who, after winning the Lingfield Derby Trial by five lengths, started 9/2 second favourite for the 1964 Derby. Unfortunately for Mr Waugh, he became increasingly difficult at home and at Epsom he refused to settle for Eph Smith. After Oncidium had led into the straight only to fade into eighth behind the 15/8 favourite Santa Claus (who beat Indiana by a length compared to the six-length beating Oncidium had given him earlier in the season), Mr Waugh wisely did what was best for the horse and recommended to Lord Howard he be given a change of scenery in the hope this would revitalise him. Accordingly, the colt was sent to George Todd at Manton, for whom he won the Jockey Club Cup and the following year's Coronation Cup.

I never got near Oncidium, but I was once allowed the privilege of partnering Lucasland on the gallops. She was a lovely big bay filly who improved with age to win the July Cup and the Diadem as a four-year-old in 1966 and prove herself just about the best sprinter in training that season. Anyway, I rode her one morning upsides a pair of old sprinters and she was so strong I couldn't hold one side of her! She could really pull and we ended up going right round the top of the gallop to the top of the High Street!

When Mr Waugh entered my life he was still only 50-years-old. In attitude, manner and deed he was a product of the age that moulded him. People were brought up to know their place. There was order and punctuality; protocol and proprieties to be observed. Emotional self-restraint was the norm. No sportsmen cried in victory or defeat. There was more than a trace of the parade ground in all this, as there was in Mr Waugh's application of discipline: firmness and fairness in equal measure. Shades of grey did not exist in Mr Waugh's thinking. What was the point of 50 years of accumulated wisdom if you didn't enforce to the hilt the lessons it had taught you?

So, it may have been the liberated 'Swinging Sixties' everywhere else in England during my time at Heath House but, to Mr Waugh, Heath House was still cocooned somewhere between the two world wars. And though we'd occasionally gripe, all of us young lads were the better for it. We dressed like Mr Waugh told us to dress, we behaved like Mr Waugh told us to behave and we did what Mr Waugh told us to do and at the precise time he told us to do it – everything to the exact letter or we paid the price.

And that applied to everyone at Heath House. When Sir Mark Prescott came to Heath House as Mr Waugh's assistant in 1968 he was advised not to bother finding a flat to live in because 'bed and breakfast will do you, no one could last with that bugger for more than a week. The man's a madman!' The first job Mr Waugh entrusted to his apprehensive new 20-year-old assistant was the task of writing out a list of forthcoming entries, 'in pencil', to be on his desk by 5am the following morning. Sir Mark toiled throughout his first night in Newmarket to accomplish the task – only to suffer the mortification of discovering the fruits of his nocturnal labours torn into small pieces. Why? Because he had written them in biro! 'I said, do them in pencil,' explained the hardest taskmaster in Newmarket, looking up from his morning newspaper. 'You do exactly as I say and we'll get on fine.'

Newmarket's racing fraternity divided the town's numerous Waughs into the 'hard' Waughs and the 'soft' Waughs. I'll leave you to guess which category included Jack Waugh!

Mr Waugh didn't spare himself and he spared nobody else. Of a bitterly cold February morning when the horses would be restricted to trotting endlessly round a straw circle laid out in the paddock, it was Mr Waugh who stood on top of the muck heap in the centre, picking out the usable straw and throwing it onto the barer sections as they appeared. He'd as like stay up on his hill-top throughout all three lots, gradually peeling off layer after layer of protective clothing, seemingly oblivious to the nip in the air which might inconvenience a brass monkey. If you could do it, he could do it.

Mr Waugh left the day-to-day running of Osborne House to Mrs Jay but this did not mean to say he was not averse to occasionally making his presence felt in order to ensure our tomfoolery did not get out of hand. Normally we'd get up at six o'clock to be in the yard by 6.30, but every now and again he would be on the prowl to rouse us 15 minutes earlier. The first you'd know about it was having the blankets ripped off the bed, and if you were still clinging to them you wound up on the floor along with them, staring up at the most frightening alarm clock in Newmarket.

I well remember the first occasion I was hauled over the coals by Mr Waugh. How could I forget it! Every lunchtime we used to have cream cakes fresh from the bakery. On one of my early days I walked into the kitchen and Tommy Rattley says, 'Would you like one of these cream cakes, son?' In my reet Yorkshire accent, I replied 'Ooh, aye, I'd love one,' and was immediately met with one splattered right in my face. I wiped off the mess, picked up another cream cake and pushed it into Tommy's face. Then we really got stuck into each other, rolling on the floor fighting, and cream cakes flying everywhere. Mrs Jay eventually managed to pull us apart and, of course, she reported us to Mr Waugh. Later that day, at evening stables, I'm in one of my boxes mucking out with my back to the door when I suddenly feel this almighty thud in my back. I'm literally lifted off the ground.

'Now then, boy. You haven't been here very long and you're fighting already! You've come from Yorkshire. You've got no criminal offences against you. You've never been in trouble with the police. As far as I'm concerned you seem to be a nice sort of lad. But I will not tolerate all this fighting and messing about in the house. Do I make myself clear?'

So, any misguided soul working at Heath House today who thinks Sir Mark Prescott is a tough cookie should have worked for Mr

Waugh. He makes Sir Mark look like a nun.

Dress and conduct came under constant scrutiny. Every one of us lads had to be kitted out just right in brown corduroy jodhpurs which were obtained through Mr Waugh. Proper manners were to be observed at all times in the yard. It was tip your cap and 'Good Morning, Sir' or else. In fact, I continued to address Mr Waugh as 'Sir' until the day he died. If you lost your cap, another had to be bought before you could ride out. The penalty for being discovered minus your cap was a large rubber-soled boot up your arse that lifted you ten yards down the path. The same standards applied when you attended Newmarket races to find out for yourself how things ticked, watch how the top jocks rode and how they conducted themselves with their trainers and owners in the paddock. The uniform for those occasions was trilby, a nice pair of slacks, collar and tie, clean shoes. Woe betide anyone found without one item of the regulation garb. We weren't keen on trilbies but God forbid Mr Waugh spotting you at the races minus your trilby because there'd be hell to pay. And, somehow or other, he would spot you! That man did not miss a thing.

Evening stables was a daily examination worse than any 11-Plus. Head collars were inspected every night to check they had been soaped and polished and every brass buckle and fitting had to gleam. No trace of white polish was permissible on any leather. Transgression as likely meant the culprit being locked in the box till supper time. All our tools – curry comb, dandy brush, hoof pick etc – had to be laid out on a clean white stable rubber on top of a little pile of straw we'd built into a box shape in one corner. The horse had to stand on a layer of freshly flicked straw, which was twisted over at the door like a rolled carpet, facing three quarters to the left. And there we'd wait, horse and lad, for Mr Waugh to make his entrance like a hospital consultant on his ward rounds.

He'd start by feeling the animal's front legs, then its back, ribs and, finally, its hind legs. If all was well with your horse's health and the state of your equipment passed muster, the final test came as Mr Waugh prepared to leave the box. He'd run his hand the wrong way up the horse's back which would leave grease or white dirt on it if the animal was not clean. If he did find dirt ... oh dear! He'd say nothing, just walk out of the box, and return carrying a bucketful of water – which he'd proceed to throw over the horse.

'You stay here till you dry it all off,' he said to me one evening after I'd failed the test. 'I'll be back at eight.' With that, he locked me in the box and disappeared. 'You won't do that again, will you?' he said, once my second attempt had met with his approval. And I didn't. That's the way Mr Waugh operated. You knew what he expected and you did it. Or you paid the price.

You didn't receive any detailed riding tuition from Mr Waugh until you were riding in races, but one thing we did learn very early on was that he wouldn't tolerate misuse of the whip. So much so that he would never let us carry a whip riding out unless he was convinced we could use it properly. If you tried to sneak past him with one tucked up the side of your arm, there'd be a stentorian 'Drop that whip, boy!' before you got out of the yard. Sandy Cairns and myself, however, would often go back to the saddle room half-an-hour before evening stables began to practice riding a finish. We'd put a bridle on one end of this seven or eight-feet long saddle horse, stick a saddle across it and take it in turns – while the other gave a pretend race commentary. We'd practise changing our hands, pulling the whip through, waving your stick or giving it a backhander. We did this for months virtually every night, although we made quite certain we finished and put everything away again before the other lads arrived or else we'd get the piss taken out of us something chronic.

Once you were riding proper work Mr Waugh might jump into a gallop if it was over a distance of ground and give you instruction, which was quite a common practice in those days. For instance, I can remember three of us working ten furlongs one morning on the Flat and after we'd straightened up, he joined in on his hack for the final two and a half furlongs. 'Sit on your arse, boy!' he shouted at me. 'Get behind it! You're pushing it like a big girl! Get hold of it, boy! What are you doing? Give it a kick!' He'd really instil some enthusiasm into you. They do say that the only thing more catching than enthusiasm is lack of enthusiasm, and Mr Waugh did his level best to ensure the former held sway at Heath House.

Nevertheless, in the aftermath of my experience aboard Tiara III, I became increasingly despondent. I even approached my Uncle Ken, who was a foreman with the contractors near home that built coolers for power stations like Goole and Ferrybridge, as to whether there might be a job for me should my five years at Heath House and my hopes of becoming a jockey all end in tears. Why wasn't I given another ride? I kept asking myself this question but could not come up with a sensible answer.

Now, with the benefit of hindsight and the acquisition of some sort of maturity, the reason why I was treading water in 1966 is as plain as a pikestaff. I still hadn't grown up. Mr Waugh recognised the fact but I didn't. Messing about in Osborne House and giving Mrs Jay grief at every opportunity still seemed tremendous fun but I was now approaching my 20th birthday and I should have known better. I should have been setting a better example to the younger lads and providing them with a suitable role model.

This may have been as galling to Mr Waugh as it was to me because he knew my riding had improved sufficiently for him to be capitalising on it. Apparently, one morning as he watched me work a horse between the Ditches, he said to his companion 'Every horse goes significantly better for that boy and he can't even ride properly yet.' But until such time as I'd shown him I'd grown up, matured a bit and was a responsible adult worthy of his trust I was going to be left kicking my heels in frustration on the sidelines.

I should have learned my lesson from Tommy Rattley. Tommy was probably the most gifted rider among us, but he was a rebellious little bugger. He'd always want to buck the system. He alone refused to get his hair cut in line with Mr Waugh's wishes. Tommy's urge to be a long-haired 'Child of the Sixties', complete with beads and scooter, guaranteed Mr Waugh's displeasure – which manifested itself by no rides going Tommy's way. If Tommy had conformed to Mr Waugh's regime it would have been him and not me who ultimately got the opportunity to ride Mr Waugh's horses. His rebellious streak cost Tommy the position I took.

By the beginning of 1967 I must have got my act together because Mr Waugh finally gave me my second ride in public. On Saturday, 25 March, I rode a four-year-old filly called Peep of Dawn in a five-furlong handicap at Kempton Park. Mr Waugh had two in the race and his number-one jockey Eric Eldin was on Passport, sent off the 9/2 favourite. My filly, who only had 7st 1lb to carry, drifted from early 5s to 13/2, but I suspect Eric may have fancied her. He spent an awful lot of time tutoring me for the ride and proceeded to look after me at the gate, which, of course, in those days was the old-fashioned tape that could lead to you getting a race-losing slow start if you weren't sufficiently on the ball. Perhaps Eric knew something I didn't and had invested a few quid on Peep of Dawn. Without a shadow of doubt I should have won, but after I had taken it up a furlong from home, Bill Williamson outrode me inside the last 50 yards to beat me half a length on St Alphage – who later proved himself to be a decent horse. Had I 40 or so rides under my belt at that time, I'd have won the race hands down. Basically, I did nothing wrong, I just lacked strength and 'Weary Willie' rode me out of it. On the day I was on the best horse but the best man on the day was Bill Williamson.

Even so, it had given me a great thrill to ride in a race against the likes of Bill Williamson, Jimmy Lindley (whom I beat into third), Joe Mercer and Ron Hutchinson, and mix with others in the weighing room such as Scobie Breasley and Frankie Durr. Making the experience even more memorable was the fact that Mr Waugh was over the moon with my performance, and even Eric Eldin was kind to me – a considerable boost to my ego for someone of his calibre to say I'd done well, especially if he had backed my filly and lost his money! I was floating on cloud nine until it gradually sank in that I'd given away a race I should have won.

Over the next two months I relived the excitement with four more rides, which included another on Peep of Dawn when I was beaten in a tight finish at Newbury by Messrs Breasley and Williamson – each old enough to be my father! This really did seem like being thrown to the wolves, because these two were not run-of-the-mill jockeys. Scobie and 'Weary Willie' genuinely were exceptional, and to be competing with them in a finish was truly awe-inspiring. My 7lb allowance meant nothing pitted against jockeys who in reality were easily 12-15lb my superior at that stage of my development. You don't realise what you're up against at the time. It's only later in your career that it sinks in and you sit back in wonder, appreciating just how good the jockeys were in that era and that you, a raw little kid, were slung in the middle of them and left to sink or swim. This pair were proper jockeys and to get that close to them was quite a feat from my point of view. And for Mr Waugh to pitch me in the deep end against them suggested he must have been starting to think that I might, after all, just have something.

My other mounts were on Rodeo (at Sandown and Kempton) and a three-year-old chestnut filly called Syllable in a one and a quarter mile handicap at Newbury. Syllable showed some early speed that day, and a month later Mr Waugh brought her back to seven furlongs for the Burgesses Apprentice Handicap, the first race on the card at Yarmouth on Thursday, 15 June. Syllable was a big, uncomplicated filly whom I'd ridden work at home and knew pretty well. She had 7st 1lb to carry and I weighed 5st 12lb in my colours! Along with four of my six rivals, I was allowed 5lb in this apprentices' contest while the other two were on levels. We practically made all to win by a length and mere words cannot describe how I felt on pulling-up. After nearly five years of mucking-out and dressing-over and after five years of frustration and occasional bouts of despondency I had finally realised my dream and ridden a winner. 'You've done it!' I kept telling myself. 'You've ridden a winner! You've only actually gone and ridden a winner!' I came in beaming from ear to ear and I can't believe any winning horse ever received more pats than I gave poor Syllable.

There was to be a sting in the tail. After weighing-in, I came back out to speak to some pressmen on account of it being my first winner. Mr Waugh pulled me aside. 'You were bloody hopeless there,' he said, puncturing my inflated ego in the blink of an eye. 'The horse won on its own. You were a bloody passenger. You just went with it. It was a good job the horse had a bit in hand otherwise you'd have lost. You laid up its neck and were all over the place. By no means are you a jockey or look like being one, at the moment.'

I was dumbstruck. My world collapsed around me. How could Mr Waugh be so harsh? What I failed to understand was that this was his way of keeping my feet firmly on the ground before I had a chance of getting carried away with any grand ideas of my worth.

But I was on my way. I won again on Syllable, at Catterick in July; aboard Rodeo at Yarmouth the following month; and made it four on Fearless Lady, a filly trained by Mr Waugh's younger brother Tom, at Leicester on 26 August. She was owned and bred by Major Gerald Glover, a Jockey Club steward, and was the horse that really got me started. Every jockey needs one horse to put him in the limelight and, although I'd won twice on Syllable, this bay daughter of Major Glover's 2000 Guineas winner Privy Councillor was the animal that worked the oracle for me. Up to this point Mr Waugh had kept me well away from other trainers' horses but now, thanks to Fearless Lady, he began to relent. Of my last 43 rides in 1967, 29 were for other trainers, and of my remaining six winners (numbering another on Fearless Lady plus Ruddy Duck, St Cuthbert and National Trust for Mr Waugh) I partnered Penetentiary for Mr Combes and Major Glover's Pytchley Princess for Mr Reg Day. I completed the season with ten winners, six seconds and eight thirds from just 64 rides, for a winning percentage of 15.6 that only 12 jockeys could beat – and above the likes of Willie Carson, Eddie Hide and even Eric Eldin.

For this breakthrough I had one man to thank: Mr Waugh. He had seen something in me and I was overjoyed at being able to repay his faith because I had so much respect for him. He had spent increasing amounts of time with me as the season progressed, finding ten minutes or so each day, as the horses were taking a pick of grass after exercise, to run through my races, explain raceriding tactics or how to conduct myself with owners. He also took charge of my money, opening an account with the Halifax Building Society for me. I'd already given him ample evidence that I couldn't handle the little bit of money I had begun to earn. For instance, I bought myself a new £50 suit from the Co-Op in the High Street, which I was to pay off on a weekly basis. Because I was away racing so much and the shop was never open when I was around, I gave my paying-in book to another lad along with a pound note each week, to make the payments for me. The next thing I know, is I receive a letter from the Co-Op asking when I intended to start paying for the suit. This lad – I can't remember his name – had only been pocketing the money every week, hadn't he. I confronted him, gave him a good hiding and made him pay me back out of his wages.

Mr Waugh knew full well that if he did not keep an eye on my finances I would waste my money buying all manner of stupid things. He got me my first car, a white Vauxhall Viva with two flashy aerials on the back, for £350 from a garage in the High Street. I was like a dog with two tails. Later on, when I'd accumulated a fair bit of money in the Halifax, I blew £1,200 on a brand new yellow MGB Sports with a black top, but I was too terrified of Mr Waugh's reaction to dare park it where he could spot me getting in or out of it. One day I arrived at Heath House later than usual and had no alternative but to leave it in the yard. As I walked back to the car after work, I sensed Mr Waugh coming up behind me. I braced myself for the ticking-off I felt must be coming. 'Lovely car, George,' he said. 'I used to have one of those myself. They're beautiful cars.' What a relief!

I'd love to report the MGB helped G Duffield pull the birds but I can't! The car proved to be no 'babe magnet'. Years after I sold it, I spotted it in a showroom window in London. Naturally, I had to go in and check it out to confirm it was mine. It was – but the mileage had obviously been 'clocked'. The salesman gave me the 'Are-you-interested-in-buying-this-car' spiel and was aghast when I replied: 'No. It used to be mine and I think you'll find the mileage is a bit dodgy – I did twice as much as that myself!' Boy, did his jaw drop.

It came as a great surprise to all of us at Heath House when we found out that Mr Waugh had decided to retire at the end of 1970. He was, after all, only 59 and we'd no inkling of him being fed up with the job. He didn't stray that far from Heath House, living in Paddocks Drive, and he went on to manage the Lordship and Egerton Studs belonging to Sir Reginald and Lady Macdonald-Buchanan, for whom he had trained for many years.

Mr Waugh's influence on me was profound, both during my apprenticeship and beyond. He was a father figure to me. Before he retired he was on hand to oversee my appointment as stable jockey to John Oxley, and if ever I needed any advice throughout my subsequent career, it was his advice that I sought and held in the highest regard. He got me started and he got Sir Mark Prescott started, so when his two Heath House proteges looked as if they might split on account of G Duffield being offered a more remunerative retainer, I went to see him. One of Patrick Haslam's owners, the Chrysalis record boss Terry Ellis, offered me £250,000 over three years to ride his horses. This was a serious amount of money to earn before even throwing a leg across a horse, so the offer had to be given due consideration. It drove me crazy, wondering what to do. I couldn't sleep for thinking about it. The one man who will point me in the right direction, I thought, is Mr Waugh. It made his day that I took the time to go and see him and that I still had such respect for his opinion. Money wasn't everything, we decided, quality of horses is far more important. Stay where you are.

I'll never forget that day. That meeting and that conversation meant so much to each of us, two grown men who tended to keep their emotions on a very tight rein and their innermost feelings very well hidden. Mr Waugh was a big man, a tough man. But when we said our goodbyes, he actually cried.

Mr Waugh died in 1999 at the age of 87. I had contemplated visiting him at the time of my marriage break-up, to explain my situation, but I'm ashamed to say I was too petrified to go through with the idea. You see, I was afraid he'd be disappointed in me.

I had so much respect for the man. I shall never forget him, or forget what he did for me. If it wasn't for him I wouldn't be where I am today. I like to think every big winner I rode made him proud. After I won the 1992 Oaks on User Friendly, for example, Mr Waugh rang to offer his congratulations on my first Classic victory. 'You know, George, my only regret is not having trained a Classic winner,' he said. 'Sir,' I always called him Sir, never Guv'nor or even Mr Waugh, 'Yes you did. Me.'

He always used to say 'I am only a professional trainer but I am proud to be one.' I am enormously proud to say that I was one boy he made into a man.

5

MIXING WITH THE BIG BOYS

After riding those ten winners in 1967 I decided to sign on for another two years with Mr Waugh. I could ride as second jockey to Eric Eldin and eventually received a retainer of £1,000. As is invariably the case once a young rider makes the breakthrough, other trainers became increasingly keen to capitalise on my apprentice allowance – soon reduced to 5lb – and my total of winners rose to 39 in 1968 which put me just one behind David Coates and Richard Dicey in the race for the title of champion apprentice.

I also won my first quality race, the Cecil Frail at Haydock, on a horse called Charlie's Pal for Ryan Jarvis. I felt this was a very significant success because Ryan Jarvis was a Classic-winning trainer and if someone of his repute was prepared to put his faith in me I must be making progress. The following season I did manage to win my first award, the TV Times Flat-Race Trophy for Apprentices (based on a points system for televised races), pipping a certain Patrick Eddery. But 1969 held something in store for me that was far, far sweeter. Despite a further reduction in my allowance to 3lb, I consolidated my progress with a further 35 winners to finally ride out my claim – and actually finished the season with a couple of wins without poundage up my sleeve, which was a massive boost to my confidence. After seven years of toil and sweat, at long last I had reached the promised land. I was a fully-fledged jockey. If only Willie Lamb could see me now!

G Duffield was now mixing with the big boys. On level terms. And the weighing room I'd entered in the late 1960s was packed full of big boys. Gazing along the line of pegs was both daunting and awe-inspiring at one and the same time. There were the young Turks already clawing their way up the ladder, such as Sandy Barclay, Ernie Johnson, Tony Murray and, especially, Willie Carson, who would win his first jockeys' championship in 1972; then there were the established top-notchers, like Geoff Lewis, Jimmy Lindley, Joe Mercer (a jockey so perfect to look at you felt he'd been born on a horse), Eddie Hide, Frank Durr and Brian Taylor – not to mention Heath House's own Eric Eldin; crack visitors, like the Aussies Ron Hutchinson, Bill Williamson and George Moore, and John Gorton from South Africa; and, top of the shop, the senior men Scobie Breasley and Doug Smith, multiple champions both. Finally, there was Lester Keith Piggott at his most ruthless and most brilliant.

I accept that youthful impressions can assume mythical proportions with the passage of time but that list contains five individual British champions who between them won 26 titles. And let's not delude ourselves, jockeys like Scobie Breasley and Doug Smith had cut their teeth competing against Gordon Richards, Harry Wragg, Rae Johnstone and even Steve Donoghue. That's some pedigree, some CV, some lineage. These were premier jockeys by the standards of any era you care to name. Their reputations have stood the test of time. Let's be honest, the present day weighing room – as full of talent as it is – has a far different feel to it compared to when I started as a kid. It was a different world. A very serious place. You looked and learned.

The two elder statesmen were Doug Smith and Scobie Breasley. Since their respective careers were to end in 1967 and 1968 I saw relatively little of them and certainly nothing whatsoever of them in their prime, but to a youngster like me they were gods – and they frequently behaved like them. I first rode against Doug Smith at Newbury when me and Peep of Dawn were third to Scobie and 'Weary Willie', yet my abiding memory was of him bringing into the weighing room his own flask of coffee and supply of sandwiches – with the crusts neatly cut off – inside a little case. No common-or-garden weighing room fodder for Mr Smith! Scobie used to travel to the races in his chauffeur-driven Rolls Royce and this grand image was maintained by his seemingly cultured habit of washing his hands after every race. In point of fact, Scobie had no option because, believe it or not, he suffered an allergy to horses.

Scobie and me had a few rare old tussles after that first Newbury clash. I usually came off second best! Riding Ruddy Duck for Mr Waugh one day at Alexandra Park I thought I had him beat but the wily old bugger had kept something up his sleeve and beat us a head. Mind you, we did get our own back at Windsor the following month when Ruddy Duck foiled a big gamble on Scobie's mount My Advice, backed from 6s down to 5/2 as if it was unbeatable.

Scobie was an absolute wizard round Ally Pally, which was amazing when you consider his seniority and the quality of horse available to him. Why someone of his age (he was 53 in 1967), calibre and class would want to risk riding moderate animals round the infamous 'frying pan' is beyond me. The track was a nightmare. Every race bar a five-furlong sprint was run the reverse way, starting by the winning post and running right-handed round the loop to complete the 'circle' of the pan before finishing up its 'handle'. All the cambers ran the wrong way for a start, the going was always firm and when it rained horses fell for fun. And, for whatever reason, there always seemed to be a shower of rain on the Monday or Tuesday night when Ally Pally invariably raced. I went round there one night in a 20-runner seller and there were seven fallers on the bottom loop. They were going down in all directions. I just closed my eyes, dropped my hands and prayed I'd come out the other side. Plenty of jockeys refused to ride there, and those that did, seldom enjoyed the experience.

I actually won the very last race run at Ally Pally, the St Albans Handicap over one mile five, aboard Acrostole on 8 September 1970. The 'funeral' was attended by 2,400 mourners, an insignificant turn-out compared to the 12,000 that gathered for its first evening meeting in 1955. Apparently, the place was losing five grand a year toward the finish. Occasionally there are calls for Ally Pally to be revived but you'll not find me at the head of the queue for rides if it is! Stockton – or Teesside Park as it was later known – would be a track I'd welcome back with open arms as it was a lovely, flowing track far superior to its near neighbour Redcar, but Lanark – another lethal place where I did once come a cropper – and especially Alexandra Park, no thank you. Good riddance to the place. I never fell at Ally Pally, thank God, but plenty did – including Scobie who suffered paralysis of the eyes and loss of balance after a crash in 1954. The doctors told him he would never ride again – and possibly not even walk – yet ten years later he'd still turn up at Ally Pally of a Tuesday evening, whizzing round with all the other lunatics and risking life and limb.

He wasn't half-bad at Brighton either. It's a tricky enough track to ride now – all downhill, on the turn and usually bone hard – but in those days there was insufficient camera patrol so you could get away with a lot more in running. It was often a case of dog eat dog. Scobie, of course, was the maestro at producing his mount very late and very fast from way off the pace. He had obviously wound one up for a flying finish one afternoon and nothing was going to stop him. I just happened to be in his way. Scobie won, all right, after he'd knocked me out of the way and almost through the rails. Scobie copped a suspension. He was not best pleased with young Master Duffield! But what a jockey that man was. He was, I feel, the best of the Australians and what a jockey to measure yourself against.

The resident comedians of the weighing room were Geoff Lewis and Brian Taylor. The humour was verbal in those days, not the kind of puerile antics and stupid practical jokes more common today. Geoff was full of quips, so dry and so quick, and that little stammer of his just seemed to make them sound funnier still. Geoff also possessed a bit of a temper, which made him good value at times. I caught him right on the line one night at Ally Pally in a one and a half-mile race, and as I got there I shouted 'Gotchya' across at him. Geoff was not about to put up with that! 'F-F-Fucking gotchya!' he yelled back, 'You l-l-little f-f-fucker, I'll g-g-give you f-f-fucking g-g-gotchya!' and he chased me up the hill, where you used to pull up, right up to the hedge at the end. 'You ch-ch-cheeky l-l-little f-f-fucker! You c-c-cocky l-l-little f-f-fucker!'

Brian Taylor's big mate was Lester and he would take the piss out of Lester mercilessly. 'And who are you going to rob today, you old gangster you?' he'd say as soon as he spotted Lester in the weighing room. He and Lester were very contrasting characters and I suppose that's why they got on so well. No one else was ever able – or allowed – to bait Lester as successfully as Brian.

Lester was a law unto himself. Winning was all that mattered. It didn't matter to Lester how he came by it. For instance, back then they still raced at Liverpool on the Flat and everyone looked forward to going there on Grand National day. We'd get to watch the race from Lord Derby's private box and ride in a couple of races. The Flat course was a pretty good one, the turns maybe a bit sharp, but a good racing surface. The main problem, as I found to my cost, was the lack of a photo-finish camera. After seeing Gay Trip win the 1970 National, I went out to ride Leo Lad for Les Barratt in the Cunard Handicap over a mile. I took up the running a furlong out, only to catch sight of Lester on a horse of Bill Marshall's called Northern Wizard making ground on me hand over fist as the line approached. I reckoned I'd held Lester comfortably, by half a length. Unfortunately, Lester was on the side nearest the judge and he and Northern Wizard were given the verdict by a neck. I could not believe it. 'That's a shame, innit?' he mumbled with a huge grin all over his face.

Lester's riding was just out of this world during this purple period of his career. A lot of the kids were not impressed with Lester when he came back in 1990 after his five-year absence, but they didn't see Lester Piggott at his very best. They got the occasional glimpse during those last few seasons but it was left to us older guys to put them straight: 'You're not actually seeing the Lester Piggott we saw. That Lester Piggott would eat you for breakfast! You're seeing a man who is enjoying what he's doing. He's just as focused, but he hasn't got the vicious streak any more toward the rest of us. Whether you like it or not, you're looking at a genius, though not the genius he once was.'

Nothing got in Lester's way, on or off the track. He knew what he wanted and tried very hard to get it. Most of the time he did. He'd jock anybody off. No one was safe. He even got a rider of the calibre of Yves Saint-Martin off on the day to ride Rheingold in the 1973 Benson & Hedges at York. The only time Lester had a conversation with you was when he wanted to pick your brain about a horse. He'd sidle up next to you, pick up a paper and pretend to be reading it – but then you'd hear: 'Do you fancy that? That can win, you know.' At that, he'd be gone, without even looking at you. If it was going to benefit Lester, he'd chat to you. Otherwise, forget it.

But when Lester came back he was much more fun. Locking the

guy up for that short period of time must have made him realise what life was all about. He'd never really sampled life before. Prison gave him a chance to think about life in general and about other people in particular. Prison changed him, mellowed him. Lester had time for all of us during that final handful of seasons in the 1990s.

The trainers of the day were as fearsome as the jocks. Most of them were poured from the same authoritative mould as Jack Waugh, adopting a brusque – some might say rude – no-nonsense approach to one and all that brooked no interference or argument. If the senior jockeys like Scobie and Doug Smith were little gods, the senior trainers were larger than life and infinitely louder. The top brass at Newmarket when I began were people like Jack Jarvis, Captain Boyd-Rochfort, and Sam Armstrong, trainers who had been in the job since the 1920s or earlier, although currently the most successful was Noel Murless who had worked his way into a position where he wouldn't bother training anything other than quality horses. That became his policy, which ensured he remained a quality trainer.

The Heath tended to resemble a parade ground in those days. Strings in single file, riders impeccably dressed – no jeans or dirty wellies anywhere to be seen. You had to keep an eye open for Sam Armstrong. He was one of the toughest and was hard on his staff, taking no prisoners whatsoever. His horses had a tendency to be a mite 'fresh' on the Heath, which could lead to the odd mishap. One frosty, sleety morning in February, his string was out on Bury Hill with Sam, resplendent in red-russet jodhpurs, gaiters, highly-polished boots and sheepskin jacket, inspecting it from aboard his hack as each animal passed him one by one. All Sam's apprentices, and there were a few of them because Sam had a deservedly high reputation as a producer of young riders, came along at the rear. As the last kid went by, his little filly skidded on the slippery chalky surface. Her legs splayed out like Bambi's on the icy pond and down she went – with this poor kid eventually trapped beneath her. She proceeded to roll on him and, as she got back to her feet, gave him a kick for good luck before galloping off into the wide blue yonder. Having sat through this pantomime utterly speechless, Sam, a man unable to pronounce the letter R, looks down at his motionless, rag doll of an apprentice and summoning up all the sympathy he is capable of mustering, says: 'Well done, you stupid child! You've been twying to fall off all morning and now you've fwightened the poor thing to death!'

I never fell foul of Sam Armstrong, though I certainly knew where I stood with Doug Marks. 'Sir Doug', as we called him (who only retired in 2001 after holding a licence for more than half a century), was as mad as a bloody hatter. He once instructed his work-riders to circle a tree on the gallops and await his arrival. When their Guv'nor failed to appear, the swearing and cursing kicked off! Whereupon 'Sir Doug' jumped down from the branches of the tree and greeted them with a broad grin on his face said: 'I've heard everything you've said about me!'

The day I was due to ride some old sprinter for him at Ally Pally, the doorman on the weighing room comes over and tells me there's someone outside waiting to see me.

'Now then, Duffield!' he barks. 'Doug Marks! You ride for me today. They tell me you can hit one very bloody hard. If you hit my horse at all today I'll have your legs broken.'

'Right, Sir. Anything you say, Sir.'

I was terrified. I got beat on the horse – but I didn't pick up my stick once. I dared not! I did eventually ride a winner for him before he retired. He was an absolute star was 'Sir Doug'.

Trainers like Doug Marks were always on the lookout for competent apprentices whose claims might convert a handicap 'good thing' into a 'sure thing'. I well remember Richmond trainer

Jack Ormston legging me up on a chestnut filly called Elderberry that had a row of six duck eggs beside her name, for a five-furlong handicap at Redcar in 1968. The only words he said to me were 'Son, just go down and come back in the right direction, kick her in the belly and we'll collect.' And they did. I also landed touches for other astute handlers who liked to use boys, such as George Todd and Cyril Mitchell.

Mr Todd had a decent handicapper called Picture Boy on whom I won twice in 1968, the first on the July Course after he'd been well supported down to 9/2. Bruce Raymond, who wasn't riding in the race, came up to me beforehand and said he'd seen it run last time at Kempton, where it had enjoyed a 'quiet' race. 'If it's 'off', you'll win,' he said. 'Has anyone said anything to you?' I assured him no one had said a word to me about today. 'If Mr Todd tells me it's going to win, I'll pull my boots up like this,' I say to him, 'and if nothing's said I won't go near them.' Mr Todd gave me my orders and ended by saying the magic words: 'This'll definitely win.' So I gave Bruce the signal and I imagine he went off to get his money on. Three years later Picture Boy won the Royal Hunt Cup with Jock Wilson riding.

Cyril Mitchell's horse was called Bar Fly and it trotted up at odds of 25/1 in a seven-furlong Newmarket handicap. Geoff Lewis had been riding it and he confirmed it was a cert. 'Do what Mr Mitchell tells you and it should win.' At 25/1, can't be, I thought. But they knew something all right because it delivered just like they said it would. Geoff certainly looked happy afterwards.

The weighing rooms were full of eager beavers like me desperate to make an impression on every trainer from Sam Armstrong to Doug Marks. My best mate was Ray Still, a Londoner who was attached to Sam Armstrong. We both started in Newmarket in 1962 (Stilly was a mere four-and-a-half stone stripling!), although Stilly got off the mark two seasons before me in 1965, and, eventually, after completing our time, we shared the same house in St Philip's Road, Newmarket, where Mrs Jones, wife of Bob Jones the jockey, ruled the roost. Mrs Jones was an astute woman. It was she who dragged me down to the Midlands Bank to open my very first current account complete with my very first cheque book. Stilly and me would travel to the races together and the obvious incentive was to compete with each other. Consequently, it was only toward the end of 1968 and 1969 that the possibility of becoming champion apprentice ever remotely crossed my mind.

Although I finished 1968 only one winner behind David Coates and Richard Dicey (but thankfully one ahead of Stilly!), David would have won the title comfortably had he not been injured late on. Four years younger than me at 18 years of age, he was attached to Taffy Williams up north at Ferryhill, and was a real down-to-earth, rough-and-ready Northern lad. Dicey was a year older than Coates and very much his opposite, a quiet sort of lad who kept himself to himself and he was with Epsom trainer Herbert Smyth, who brought on Duncan Keith and Brian Rouse, and, later, Alan Bond. In 1969 Clive Eccleston took the title with 41 winners (though Tony Murray was the real champion with 44 because although riding without an allowance he was still officially apprenticed to Frenchie Nicholson), six more than I could manage.

Being a fashionable or successful apprentice, however, is no guarantee of you making the transition to fully-fledged jockey successfully. How much do you really want the job becomes the ultimate question. Once you've lost your claim and you're left on your own, you discover what you are made of: 95 per cent or more go through the post-apprenticeship blues. No one does you any favours. It's all down to you and that's when you realise what life is all about and what kind of character you are. In those days you had to fix your own rides, and it's never easy ringing trainers. They prefer ringing you. Everything tended to be fixed on a Sunday morning, so I'd be sat by the phone with a book and pen to hand praying for it to ring with the offer of a good ride. Actually, it was a challenge I enjoyed each week. I always remained positive. I never thought I was going backwards. It was always tomorrow-is-another-day.

To my eyes, none of my contemporaries in the weighing room (though you had to be an idiot not to spot a future star in Pat Eddery coming up fast behind us) stood out as possessing the crucial X factor that raised them head and shoulders above the rest of us. Being a natural lightweight enabled Stilly to win some big handicaps – the Bunbury Cup, Victoria Cup (for Sir Mark Prescott no less!), the November Handicap, Zetland Gold Cup and the Ebor, for example – and he also did well for himself out in India, where he won all five Classics on a filly called Air Express in 1973-74. A fall at Bangalore five years later nearly finished him, but he didn't finally pack it in until 1989. Eventually, he found his way back to the St Gatien stables of his old boss, as a work rider to begin with and then assistant trainer to Sam's son Robert until he too retired at the end of the 2000 season. But you can't keep a good man down! Stilly's just been hired as a stand-in on the new Harry Potter movie, 'Harry Potter and the Chamber of Secrets', doubling – along with fellow ex jock Richard Fox – for Harry and his mate Ron Weasley! Stilly and me remain close friends. Neither David Coates nor Richard Dicey really made it in the game. Coates left for Scandinavia in 1970 and did win a Danish Derby, but his career petered out. He died in 2001. Weight was always going to catch up with Richard Dicey (as with the sad case of Tony Murray who died aged only 41 in 1992) and he rode his last British winner the season following his apprentice championship before having spells in Holland and India. In the end he was living on one meal a week! I read recently that he now lives in Queensland, Australia, where he runs various businesses.

Of course, I always hoped I'd be the one of us to go onwards and upwards! Maybe I have. At least I've outlasted them all!

However, I am sure about one thing. There is no shadow of doubt in my mind that the old apprenticeship system was far superior to today's methods of producing jockeys. Perhaps a five-year apprenticeship was too long, but I served seven and that didn't do me any harm. In fact, it was beneficial being tied to one trainer. Nowadays, as soon as a kid starts riding a few winners, they think the grass is greener on the other side of the fence and begin to move around like yo-yos. The kid will be claiming his seven and before he knows it he'll find a trainer tapping him on the shoulder, saying 'I've got more horses than the man you're working for – why don't you come over to me?' This is such a falsehood. This new trainer will use the boy until he's exhausted his claim and then he'll chuck him in favour of another kid. If you tie the kid down – maybe three years not five would be long enough – the system might improve.

I do hold very strong views on this issue. It drives me crazy to see these kids hopping around like frogs from one trainer to another. You can't expect trainers to give kids a break and teach them as much as they can when they know in 12 months time that kid will be poached by some other trainer with false promises – and bugger off. Especially when trainers have less and less time to spend with kids. They're fully occupied by so many horses and too few staff. It's the kids who suffer in the long run. A trainer like Reg Hollinshead (and before him, Frenchie Nicholson and Sam Armstrong) is a genius with kids, but Reg is the last of a dying breed. Greville Starkey first rode a horse at Reg's place; Paul Eddery, Tony Ives, Walter Swinburn, Willie Ryan, Kevin Darley all served time with Reg, and he's got young Graham Gibbons today. Yet Reg is now 78-years-old and no one looks like assuming Reg's mantle. You can't expect the top trainers to get too involved. The trainers with top-class horses – the Michael Stoutes, the John

Dunlops and the Henry Cecils – have no time to be messing around with kids because their job is to train 100 or more quality horses, not apprentices.

Too many of these kids have no one to guide them, neither a master nor an agent. Any agent worth his salt would tell a kid to stay put with the man who starts him off. Yet most kids do exactly the opposite. Adrian McCarthy is a prime example of a kid who has not fulfilled his potential as a result. Jamie Mackay, on the other hand, has a father, Alan, and a grandfather, Eric Eldin, who were jockeys (and Eric was also a trainer and an instructor at the apprentices' school out in Singapore for six years) and they are able to give him the best tuition possible. Alan would be the first to admit he was often his own worst enemy, a jockey who enjoyed the trappings of the job but committed too many indiscretions and never completely bowed to the demands of the regime. He can say to Jamie with genuine conviction: 'Don't do what I did. Do not make the same mistakes as me.' Jamie has two excellent mentors within his family, and his Guv'nor, Michael Bell, has helped further by not rushing him too much.

Whenever I'm asked to speak to apprentices at the two schools in Newmarket and Doncaster (and I've had dealings with both), the one thing I try to drum into them is: 'Do not move from yard to yard because you'll finish up at the end of the day mucking-out and doing your two or three or more until your dying day. You will disappear up your own arse. Establish yourself somewhere and stay there! Do not hop around like a fucking frog!'

A few years ago I agreed to take six kids from the Northern school under my wing and tried to instil the right things into them. I thought all six of them were pretty good, but I'm afraid to say all six of them did precisely what I told them not to do. It was a complete waste of time and effort. The bosses of the school employed me to educate them about the pitfalls of the job – and that was the outcome. It drove me demented. One or two with this kind of attitude may make it if they're lucky, but I doubt it. Most will drift from trainer to trainer and get nowhere. The system is letting them down. It's a crying shame.

All of which leads me to harbour grave concerns for the future of British jockeys and jockeyship. With hand on heart, I look back now and can honestly say that I couldn't have wished for a better grounding than the baptism of fire I received at the hands of my elders and betters in the 1960s, masters and role models alike.

6

BRICKS, BULLETS AND BATTERIES IN JAMAICA

Since I had never so much as been out of the country let alone flown on an aeroplane for ten hours, I was a mite anxious boarding the flight due to convey Ray Still and myself across the Atlantic. Our destination was Jamaica, where each of us had a three-month contract to ride during the winter of 1969-70. These three months were to provide some of the most unusual and hilarious memories of my entire career. If dodging bricks and bullets weren't sufficiently novel and hair-raising racecourse experiences, I was to strike such a rich vein of form – winning 36 to finish fourth in the jockeys table – that the punters became convinced I was enlisting the help of the local 'booster', namely a battery-powered whip!

The trip was set up by Newmarket trainer Gerry Blum, for whom I'd ridden a few winners. Gerry trained for a guy called Lucien Chen, who was a big punter and bookie in Jamaica, and he arranged the job for me with his friend Eddie Lai, a Kingston hotel-owner. Eddie Lai's horses were trained by Bobby Hale, a balding, good-looking white Jamaican, who was very amusing company and a real practical-joker. Stilly and me stayed at one of Eddie Lai's hotels, the Courtley Manor in New Kingston, occupying one of the apartments in the annexe at the back. We had access to all the hotel's facilities and only had to sign for anything we wanted. After the damp and cold of an English winter, the tropical feel was marvellous and we couldn't wait to get cracking.

We turned up for work at Caymanas Park on the first morning as if it was Newmarket Heath, resplendent in short-sleeved shirts, jodhpurs, boots and helmets to be met by a motley workforce – dressed in jeans, American top-boots and a colourful array of shirts – who openly sniggered at us. To say that we two little white boys stuck out like sore thumbs is an understatement.

Bobby Hale had around two dozen horses in his care and proved to be a talented trainer, in the top three on the island. Stilly was going to work for the champion Jamaican trainer A.E. Williams, whose yard was adjacent to Bobby Hale's in the compound at Caymanas Park, a large sugar cane plantation which was home to all the local trainers – about 15 of them – as well as the racetrack itself, the only one on the island.

Bobby's lads lived in the horse crates that had been used to ship in horses from overseas. He had one tiny Indian lad, who looked no older than eight, whose party piece was to kill rats with his teeth. We had to see this to believe it. So, at around 4 to 4.30 in the morning before it got light, we went down to the feed room to watch him. This kid opened the door and shot across the floor under the bins with the speed of a terrier to emerge with this rat which he promptly bit in the neck!

These lads were something else. They were always fighting amongst themselves, but not with fists or anything simple like that – they favoured machetes. One morning we were hurriedly called down to the crates to have a look at 'Rat Boy' and found him shivering under an old sack. Lifting this sack, we found he'd been opened up from neck to dick as if he'd been unzipped. The flesh was so neatly parted you could see his ribs. We rushed him off to hospital to be stitched up. He was back working inside a week.

The old racetrack had been in New Kingston until the site was redeveloped and had supermarkets and hotels built on it. Unlike that old track, the new one at Caymanas Park was dirt and modelled along American lines, with a five-furlong straight and seven-furlong and mile chutes in the back stretch, and it rode very well. The horses – a mix of English, American and homebreds – were of quite acceptable calibre, the A and B Class sprinters, for example, perfectly capable of clocking 58.2 seconds for the five furlongs. However, the track and our mounts were to be the least of our problems.

The facilities at the track should have given the game away. The place looked more like a POW camp than a racetrack. 'The Great Escape' could easily have been shot on location here, no problem! The enclosure for the winner and placed horses was a mesh cage, the paddock was surrounded by a tall mesh fence topped with curled barbed wire, as was the weighing room which amounted to a primitive concrete blockhouse containing benches, a chilled-water container and a couple of showers. The only missing ingredient was a machine-gun tower. Although racing only took place once a week, on a Saturday (plus the holidays such as Boxing Day and New Year's Day), it did not take Stilly or I much time to work out why Caymanas Park was defended like a fortress. The local punters were fanatical gamblers and defeat was not something they accepted with anything approaching good grace. To put it bluntly, on occasions they greeted defeat with downright hostility!

Salvos of coke bottles might bounce noisily off the mesh, and sometimes the projectiles graduated to really heavy duty ammunition. For example, in order to reach the track the horses passed through an arch beneath the grandstand, and one day an unsuspecting animal had the skin ripped off the tops of its hind legs as it emerged into the sunshine thanks to a large litter bin being hurled down on it from the top of the stand.

On another occasion, after I'd been beaten on one, this guy cursed me all the way back to the weighing room, pressing his face right up against the wire-mesh fencing. Eventually I ran out of patience, stopped and punched him in the face, straight through the mesh. It was a shot in a million! And it cost me a 500-dollar fine for 'conduct unbecoming of a foreign jockey.'

Then there was the day when an irate punter started spitting and throwing orange peel at me through the fence before he made the monumental error of sticking his head through some railing to get even closer to me. Sadly, for him, his ears got caught and his head became trapped momentarily, making it an easy target for a smack with a whip!

It was not really advisable to get involved, however. Guns were everywhere. Stilly and I were parking the car one Saturday and found ourselves unwittingly in the middle of a gunfight. Bullets came whizzing from all directions, kicking up the dust at our feet, forcing us to take cover under the car. Then it stopped as suddenly as it had started. We never did discover what it was all about.

Winning did not necessarily guarantee your safety. Two or three lengths clear coming into the straight one day, I felt this almighty thud in the chest. I thought: 'Shit! Somebody's shot me!' I collapsed onto the horse's neck but I was winning so far that it didn't matter because it was winning without me. The replay of the race showed a guy in the middle of the track had thrown a brick at me!

Raceriding was pretty clean in the main, probably because the camera-patrol system was good enough to catch most things, but you still had to look after yourself. Apart from ourselves and the odd Panamanian, all the jocks were coloured locals and they could make a nuisance of themselves. I had a bit of a set-to with a local called Sammy Hislop, who reckoned I had 'done him' in the early part of a race, and when I was preoccupied undoing the girths of my horse after the race, he came up behind me and punched me in the ribs, dropping me to my knees. I wasn't having that so, after I'd pulled myself together, I chased after him and jumped on his back. No sooner had I got a couple of good thumps into him, the next thing I know is the feel of a gun being shoved in my back and someone saying quite quietly but menacingly, 'No, man! Don't do that!' It must have been one of Sammy's henchmen. As it happens, Sammy and me got on like a house on fire after that!

Stilly caused a riot once by doing something similar. He got flattened in a race and exacted revenge on the perpetrator by busting his nose open as we were cantering back after the race. Unfortunately, this was in full view of the crowd and in an instant there are people coming over the fences from every conceivable direction. All the white jocks needed a police escort to make the weighing room and Stilly eventually exited the course under police guard. It was nothing to do with me, but anyone who was white was in trouble.

I started slowly compared to Stilly and, consequently, received plenty of stick of the 'white-man-go-home!' variety that quickly made me grateful for the protection of the cage. However, once I had worked out the track and the pace at which the races were being run, everything suddenly clicked into place and I could not stop riding winners. I quickly became flavour of the month. Calypsos were made up about me and Stilly and we appeared on the TV sports show. It was unreal.

Now, because I began winning lots of the races, the punters assumed I was using a battery-powered whip, which were common-place in Jamaica. These whips had a battery in the handle, and as the horse sweated, the battery was rubbed on its neck to administer a shock. There were confiscated examples of these whips hung up in the Jockey Club Rooms in Kingston, and you always suspected when one had been used because horses would beat you too far on the book – a horse could find an extra three lengths. You finally put two and two together when, once he'd beaten you using one, the jockey would go all the way round the back straight so he could throw the battery away into the undergrowth. If the jockey wasn't caught, quite literally, red-handed, he escaped scot-free.

Every now and again the stewards made a concerted effort to catch somebody out. We'd be sat in the stalls waiting to jump and the starter would get a phone call to hold the race because a steward was coming down in the car to conduct a body search. He'd look up your sleeves and under the saddle, anywhere the battery might be concealed until required. I only saw one instance of a successful raid. This guy near me refused to vacate his stall for the inspection and was sat there sweating profusely, practically shitting himself. He was a jockey who got very few rides and he's acting very suspiciously. He stood out a mile, and they found a battery on him.

This did nothing to convince some people of my innocence in this regard because my whips were always being nicked and stripped down by punters searching for the battery that was enabling me to ride two, three and occasionally four winners of a meeting. I'd be riding work in the morning, trotting down the track before giving my horse a spin, and someone would rush out of the bushes, drag the whip from my hand and disappear back where he'd come from. I kissed goodbye to five whips like that!

I'm also pretty positive that a fair bit of doping, 'stoppers and goers', went on. It was all too easy to bribe a groom with 100 bucks, which would be a fortune to them. Horses were tested, and winners were disqualified, but that didn't get to the root of the problem. Prizemoney was negligible, it was the betting aspect that counted and by the time a horse had the race taken away from it, the winning bets would have been settled. I've no doubt that the real big-hitters had their own jockeys whom they could buy and sell.

Bobby Hale proved to be a very talented trainer and was really good to me. He wound up being more like my manager or agent than a boss because he'd always let me off one of his if I received the offer of a better mount. He was exceptionally shrewd and knew the Jamaican racing scene inside out. We became good friends. He'd take me and Stilly out and about, cook us English breakfasts and see that we were entertained. There was plenty of scope for the latter. We rode out each morning at four to avoid the heat of the day, so we were finished by eight or nine with the prospect of a full day at leisure in front of us. We'd laze by the hotel pool, drinking coke and consuming a few Club sandwiches, or go shopping. Neither of us drank much, so the only temptation was the 'ganja' which the locals would give to you as soon as sell it. It wasn't my scene and I can honestly say that I never gave it a try.

The one thing Stilly and I did succumb to was hypnotism! The hotel cabaret one week was a hypnotist. He was a tiny little chap of about five feet, smaller than us. He was always on the lookout for volunteers for his act, individuals prepared to get up on stage where he could assess whether they were the type of person who'd consciously fight his hidden powers of persuasion or whether they'd relax and co-operate with him. Stilly and I thought we'll have a piece of this!

'You're going into a deep sleep, and when I click my fingers you'll open your eyes and listen to what I tell you,' he said to the ten of us he lured onto the stage. He found four suitable candidates, of whom G Duffield was one. I opened my eyes. I knew exactly what he was saying – and I could not stop myself from doing exactly what he told me to do.

'George, do you smoke?'

'Yeh.'

'George, go to the bar for a drink and ask for a cigarette. But, I must tell you, you've never smoked in your life and you're going to hate it.'

Like a Zombie I went over to the bar and obediently asked for a cigarette, lit it and took a drag. Now, at the time I was a 20-a-day man but the habit didn't save me. I began coughing and retching and was almost sick on the spot!

He got some of the others to limbo-dance and act the fool in all sorts of stupid ways, utterly daft behaviour in front of 200 complete strangers but we were all powerless to stop ourselves. Unfortunately, he hadn't finished with me just yet.

'George,' he said matter-of-factly, 'You're the best stripper in the world. You are going to stand up here now, listen to the music – and take all your clothes off.'

'Yeh. OK. Great.'

On comes the music – and off comes my shirt, shoes, socks, trousers. The Full Monty had nothing on me. I'm dancing to the music, playing to the audience, giving it plenty of welly. I'm on the verge of whipping off my underpants…

'That's enough, George. You can stop now.'

I'd never believed in hypnotism, but Stilly and me were such a roaring success this guy asked us to go on again later in the week!

I returned to Jamaica for further stints with Bobby Hale the following two winters but neither visit was as remotely successful as the first and each in its own way was as fraught a period as ever I've experienced in my entire life.

7

FLAT ON MY ARSE

In 1970 my prospects looked rosy. The future seemed to hold so much promise. I was out of my time at Heath House. I was a fully fledged jockey. I was handed the job of stable jockey to one of Newmarket's most high-profile yards, that of John Oxley. And I had found a girl I wanted to marry. What could possibly go wrong?

I first set eyes on Gillian Hughes at Goodwood in the summer of 1970. She was watching the races with a friend up in the grandstand. Small and slim with her long hair dyed blonde, she may not have been a 'stunner' in the conventional manner but the mini skirt she was wearing made the most of her legs and I was definitely interested. Gill hailed from Liverpool, but after working for Tarporley trainer Eric Cousins she came south to work as a stable lass for Gordon Smyth, who trained at Lewes close by Goodwood. Luckily for me, David Maitland, one of my apprentice contemporaries, had served his time at Lewes and knew her. At my instigation David arranged an introduction. I took her out for the day to Brighton and, later on, she came up to Newmarket. We got on like a house on fire and by the time I left for my second stint in Jamaica our relationship had reached the 'going steady' stage. We were married on 6 November, 1971 at Stanley Church, with Ray Still as my best man, and set up home in Moulton, just outside Newmarket. Later on, we'd move to Cedar Cottage in Borough Green.

It didn't take long for me to find out what could 'go wrong'. did it? The Oxley job proved a disaster. Within three years I was knocked flat on my arse. Bereft of confidence and self esteem, I was left staring down into a professional abyss that would swallow me up forever if I didn't somehow manage to stop myself from slowly teetering over the edge.

The position at Hurworth House should have been the professional making of me. Instead it was almost professional suicide. I was not mentally tough enough to handle the demands of the post, dealing with high-powered owners and controlling the work-riders. It was a job for a stronger character than I was at that particular time. I wound up riding like a complete prat, and I knew I was riding like a complete prat. It quickly reached the stage where I said to myself: 'George, your arse is grass and John Oxley is a fucking lawnmower! You're gone from this job!'

Nevertheless, the predicament in which I found myself was not entirely of my own making. Though one couldn't have realised it at the time I accepted the post, John Oxley's fortunes were beginning to dip. The number of horses in the yard hovered around the 40 mark, and the winners only amounted to 18, 13 and 24 during my three seasons, 1970-72. Of that aggregate of 55 my grand total was 23, made up of 14, six and three. Just three races of Pattern status were won, all in 1970 (the Pattern wasn't introduced until 1971), two of which involved me.

An Old Etonian and another ex-Army man, Oxley had assisted Geoffrey Brooke and George Colling before taking control of Hurworth House on the latter's death in 1959. Still a comparatively young man at the age of 40 and boasting a roster of owners that included Lord and Lady Halifax, Dick Hollingsworth, Lord Manton, and former senior steward General Sir Randle Feilden, Oxley seemed to possess all the necessary ingredients for maintaining the level of success achieved in his first 11 seasons. For instance, he'd won the 1964 Oaks and Yorkshire Oaks with Homeward Bound, the 1968 Lincoln with Lady Halifax's Frankincense (at odds of 100/8 which, so the story goes, enabled travelling head lad Barry Hills to win sufficient money to finance his own training operation) plus a whole stack of top-quality races such as the Coronation Stakes, Dante, Great Voltigeur, King Edward VII, Craven, Princess of Wales's and Yorkshire Cup with the progeny of Mr Hollingsworth's famous Arches Hall Stud. But things weren't all they seemed at Hurworth House and as it turned out G Duffield was about to play the roll of fall-guy.

Greville Starkey had been Oxley's stable jockey virtually throughout this successful period, but then a young and ambitious Henry Cecil came calling and Greville immediately, and wisely, jumped ship for Warren Place in time for the 1970 season. The vacant position came my way thanks to Captain John Macdonald-Buchanan, the son of Mr Waugh's long-standing owners Sir Reginald and Lady Macdonald Buchanan, who had horses in training with John Oxley. Apparently, the Captain pushed my name forward, but the first I knew of the offer was Mr Waugh informing me one morning. The retainer was only a smallish one of £2,000 or so, but the position represented a step up to a higher-profile yard supposedly full of quality animals. I went round to Hurworth House for a brief meeting with John Oxley, who told me to have a word with Greville, resting at home after an injury. Greville didn't say an awful lot. An omen?

Perhaps I should have spotted the warning signs. My first season of 1970 seemed to begin well but, significantly as it transpired, the first Oxley winner of the year was not partnered by me. Furthermore, it was a winner in a big race, Torpid in the John Porter Stakes at Newbury. Brian Taylor rode Dick Hollingsworth's five-year-old, who had won the Jockey Club Stakes the previous season. I can only imagine Mr Hollingsworth wanted a stronger, more high profile jockey on the horse because I never got an explanation. I suppose I expected that sort of thing to happen to start with on the bigger occasions. I just hoped I'd get on one or two of the good ones as time went by.

The weeks passed and not a single winner did I ride for my new boss. The chance I'd been waiting for finally came at the York May meeting. Mr Hollingsworth's most promising three-year-old was an attractive grey filly by Grey Sovereign called Fluke, who was closely related to Torpid since she also descended from the famous foundation mare Felucca. As a juvenile, Fluke had won her first two races, both at Yarmouth, before running fourth in the Cheveley Park to Humble Duty, the season's premier filly. This was top-class form. Fluke had dwelt in the stalls that day but she was beaten only three and a half lengths. She was always blindfolded for stalls entry, but you had to whip it off as she was halfway in. If the blind was left on too long she'd play up, which is what had happened in the Cheveley Park. Fluke received 8st 5lb in the Free Handicap and was obviously one of my big hopes for 1970.

Fluke's half sister Anchor (by Major Portion) had been well beaten in the 1969 1000 Guineas after starting favourite on the strength of winning the Nell Gwyn over seven furlongs, and as Fluke was by a sire noted for even speedier produce she was never likely to contest the Guineas – which Humble Duty won by seven lengths. She had worked like a good horse throughout the spring, though, and it was decided to start her off in the Duke of York Stakes (now a Group III) over six furlongs at York on 14 May.

Only three ran. In effect Fluke had one to beat, the four-year-old colt Balidar, trained by John Winter at Newmarket, to be ridden by Lester. Balidar had looked useful in 1969 until intestinal trouble sidelined him, and he returned full of beans to run fourth in the Abernant before shouldering top weight successfully in the Bretby Handicap on the 1000 Guineas card. Even though he was required to give Fluke 9lb more than weight-for-age and sex, Balidar was made 3/1 on to accomplish the task. He wasn't up to the job. We made every yard. Lester was content to let me bowl along in front but Fluke was blessed with loads of natural speed and was probably a lot better than he – and probably we also – thought she was. We held off Balidar quite easily to win by a length. Subsequently, only four other animals were to finish in front of Balidar as he won Chantilly's Prix du Gros-Chene, the Prix de Meautry at Deauville and the Prix de l'Abbaye de Longchamp to establish himself the joint best sprinter in Europe alongside Amber Rama and Huntercombe.

Since I also won the previous race on Colonel John Chandos-Pole's three-year-old filly Shady to complete a Hurworth House double that York afternoon, I could be forgiven for thinking everything in the garden was coming up roses. Hurworth winners continued to flow steadily at the minor meetings until Fluke's next target, the Jersey Stakes (now a Group III) over seven furlongs at Royal Ascot on 17 June. I'd one other ride on the card, Calpurnius for Bill Watts in the Royal Hunt Cup. What a day this turned out to be! They both won. If only there had been more days like this.

Fluke was made the 9/4 favourite and she once more dared anyone to stay with her. The firm ground again suited her and though the extra furlong did see her beginning to tire slightly up the Ascot hill, she still had three lengths to spare over the American import Zingari, who was having his first run in this country. Zingari belonged to Charles Engelhard of Indiana, Ribocco, Ribero and Nijinsky Classic-winning fame, the multi millionaire precious metals baron who at one time virtually cornered the world gold market, thus inspiring Ian Fleming to create his Goldfinger character. It was lucky for me that in real life Mr Engelhard was more of a jolly, roly-poly, fruity-voiced Orson Welles figure instead of the ruthless, power-crazed adversary of James Bond type, for I'd done him no favours in the Jersey – but two races later I was to redress the balance because he was also the owner of Calpurnius.

Most of the Engelhard horses not trained by Vincent O'Brien in Ireland were lodged with Fulke Johnson Houghton or Jeremy Tree, but Jack Watts had won the 1964 St Leger for Mr Engelhard with Indiana, which ensured one or two also found their way into his son Bill's care at Pegasus House, not too far from Hurworth in the Snailwell Road. Calpurnius was a chestnut four-year-old by the Derby and Leger winner St Paddy who was lucky to be alive. After running in the previous year's Lingfield Derby Trial he developed a serious internal complaint and he wasn't seen on the racetrack again until winning a Newmarket handicap under top weight on his seasonal reappearance. Normally the Engelhard horses were earmarked for Lester, but Calpurnius was set to carry a mere 7st 13lb in the Royal Hunt Cup which left the ride up for grabs – and I eagerly grabbed the opportunity with both hands. Lester contented himself with the ride on the former Austrian Derby winner Brabant who had a record of two from two for the season.

Although Calpurnius started at 33/1, I felt the odds were extremely over generous. I'd partnered him in his last serious piece of work, with two others over seven furlongs on Racecourse Side, and he'd shown every sign he could win a handicap of even this competitiveness off a low weight like 7st 13lb. In the race itself I held him up until the final furlong and he finished with a right rattle to win by one and a half lengths. And who had I passed to relegate to second place? Why, poor old Lester on Brabant! That made it all the sweeter still! And I received some encouraging headlines in *The Sporting Life*: 'Big Ascot race victory for young Duffield – a young rider of high ability.' Years later, after Bill Watts had moved up to Hurgill Lodge, in Richmond, we combined to win another of the Royal Meeting's major handicaps with the 7/1 shot Atlantic Traveller in the 1981 Ascot Stakes.

I'd driven to Ascot for two fancied – as far as I was concerned – rides, and to deliver the goods on both horses was a great feeling. I began to think I was starting to achieve something. I was on the road to somewhere at last. And yet lurking round the corner was that great kick up the arse which told me in no uncertain manner 'It's not as easy as that, buddy!'

The 1970 season finished with me on the 51-winner mark – obviously a personal best – and as I'd partnered 14 of John Oxley's 18 winners I had to be a contented man. And I was. The only slight disappointment surrounded the remainder of Fluke's season. She failed to win again. The mile of the Falmouth Stakes on ground softer than she liked proved too far for her and she finished third to Caprera, to whom she was giving a stone. Reverting to sprinting trips, she gave me my first ride in France when running sixth in the Prix Maurice de Gheest at Deauville, and then found a couple too good for her in the Diadem Stakes, her final race before joining Mr Hollingsworth's band of broodmares.

Life at Hurworth House soon conspired to lower my spirits. The yard had to wait until 12 June for its first winner of the 1971 season – and Lester rode it. John Oxley's total dropped to just 13, but far more critical from my point of view as the stable jockey was the fact that I'd ridden only six of them. My own score included just one decent winner – Tom Waugh's Tartar Prince in the Great Met – and plummeted to a pathetic total of 16 for the season. My career was in free-fall.

What had gone wrong? The calibre of horses and owners at Hurworth House was not, as it turned out, any different to those I'd left at Heath House. The trainer, on the other hand, was different.

Mr Oxley may have been almost 20 years younger than Mr Waugh but he was not so good at getting out of bed in the morning. Often one of us would have to go back into the yard and shout: 'Come on, Guv'nor! We're out on The Severals taking a turn! Are you coming out this morning?'

After a while I came to appreciate that all the work was controlled by the paid lads, the senior lads, who'd been there quite a few years. Me? I was just a new face, fresh and had no power behind me. I'm still a kid, just out of my time, trying to keep a low profile, getting on with the job and learning as much as possible as I go along. If I'd had the same job later in my career, I'd have been more forceful, controlled the work better and discussed matters with Mr Oxley in greater depth. I'd have grasped the nettle.

As it was, the lads didn't go out of their way to help me a great deal and I was left in limbo land – doing what I thought was right. If Mr Oxley said go a certain speed in a gallop, I'd go that speed but the others would go flat out. The result was he'd say 'That worked bad' and I'd reply 'It didn't actually, Sir. You said half-pace and pick it up quietly. They all went flat out from the moment we set off. I've been taught by Mr Waugh that what I was doing was half-pace.' Just about every work morning ended with a conversation like that and eventually it became a waste of time. I wasn't a big enough name to dictate to the lads. It was no good trying to change the system to suit me or what I believed was correct. They'd been doing it this way for several years with success, so you play safe, go with the flow and merely look after the horse you're on.

Of course, once a few of the horses didn't run up to scratch someone had to take the bullet. Being the last piece in the wheel made me hot favourite and I've no doubt the odd disgruntled lad contributed his two-pennorth behind my back, especially if he'd backed one and done his money. Every Sunday morning I had to go and see Mr Oxley in the office at Hurworth House to discuss the past week and running-plans for the next. Each Sunday got worse.

I was not doing this right. I was not doing that right. I got no reassurance whatsoever. It was criticism after criticism. There's only so much you can take. The last thing anyone needs is criticism 100 per cent of the time. Your confidence goes and everything begins to unravel. It's the domino effect, isn't it?

The inevitable outcome was that I began to ride like a complete novice and started winning fewer and fewer races. I knew the responsibility for this idiotic state of affairs did not lie entirely at my door but the whole thing was snowballing out of my control. I was doing all the wrong things in a race. If I was drawn on the inside, for example, Mr Oxley would instruct me to drag the horse back and come round them, instead of doing what I knew to be best, which was staying on the inner and fiddling my way through. He didn't want me stuck on the inside because he had lost confidence in me. And that cut both ways. Through making me ride them arse backwards I also lost confidence in him.

Looking back, the prudent move would have been to pack the job in at the end of 1971. But I wasn't – and never have been – a quitter and I was determined to give it another shot, even if the only way I was going was downhill at a mighty rate of knots.

The rot truly set in. Every jockey bar Fred Archer began riding the horses. To see Willie Carson, Eddie Hide, Eric Eldin, Frank Durr, Brian Taylor, Greville and Lester winning on Hurworth House animals was bad enough but being made to sit and watch youngsters like Tony Murray and Pat Eddery win on my mounts was a cruel kick in the bollocks.

By Royal Ascot I was at my wits' end. One afternoon, I had a long chat with Frank Durr, a man whose opinion I respected enormously. If ever I wanted to know anything I'd go to Frank. He was very approachable and knowledgeable. You asked Frank questions and you got answers and, I always thought, the right answers. I had bundles and bundles of respect for him. 'I'm for the boot, Frank,' I told him. His advice was straight to the point: walk away from the job now, on my own terms, rather than wait for the sack, which was surely a stone-cold certainty. It would be far more tactful, he reasoned, if I were to write to all the owners, thank them for their support and to say things aren't working out so it's best if I move on. That way, Frank suggested, I could slip out of the job quietly mid-season and try to build bridges for 1973. 'And get it put in the newspapers what you're doing before they put something in saying you're sacked,' Frank concluded by saying. 'It'll look more respectable and better for you.'

So that's what I did. My third, and final, winner for Mr Oxley in 1972 was King Top at York on 31 August. Two months later King Top won the Manchester November Handicap with Willie Carson in the saddle. Que Sera, Sera?

Mr Oxley asked me if I was prepared to still come and ride out. I was determined not to be tied down to one yard any more. I needed to spread my wings, develop contacts. I told him I'd only come two days a week and it would cost him. He paid me £800 a season for going in to ride twice a week. We didn't fall out, though, and the split was perfectly amicable. The position of stable jockey I'd vacated never was filled. Given the yard appeared to be in decline, I don't suppose anyone wanted the job. Mr Oxley only trained for three more seasons, relinquishing his licence at the end of 1975 'on account of increasing overheads in the poor economic situation' and selling Hurworth House to Tom Jones. He died in 1986 at the young age of 55 after a long illness.

The short-term objective was to regain some confidence. Mentally I was totally fucked up. After being sheltered and guided by Mr Waugh for so long, these past three years had been a shock to my system and I hadn't coped. I'd not sought Mr Waugh's advice on this occasion. He had done his bit to put me on the ladder. It was up to me to climb up on my own, and if I fell off it was up to me to clamber back on again. I began riding out for Johnny Winter – the nicest man in Newmarket – who promised me nothing. But it was a start. I managed to get back up off the floor and had ridden 33 winners by the close of the 1972 season, a respectable score for a freelance. Unless you happened to be Lester Piggott it was terribly difficult going out on your own. Basically, I was riding for small trainers in small races but it was nothing to have a ride taken off you the night before a race and you didn't know whether you were coming or going. In the circumstances, to ride 33 winners was a substantial boost to my ego.

When you go through a situation like these three years had provoked, you do tend to find out what you're made of. You either lie down and die or you get back up on your feet and fight. I've seen quite a few lie down in such situations. They had the ability but not the character. If my life has had a defining moment this was it. I refocused and identified what really mattered in life and what didn't.

I'm not pretending those three years didn't shake me to the core – because they did. However, they also taught me the truest meaning of that old line 'Nothing concentrates a man's mind so much as the knowledge he is to be hanged in the morning.' I had indeed stepped onto the scaffold and almost had my head in the noose, staring into oblivion, before inching my way back off the trap. I was granted a reprieve. What's more, and crucially so for my battered state of mind, I had been saved by my own efforts.

And further salvation was only just over the horizon courtesy of a most surprising source.

8

ME AND SIR MARK

'That's our new assistant trainer,' Sandy Cairns said to me one morning in August 1968. Sandy was motioning in the direction of the slight, bespectacled figure, leaning against the bonnet of an old grey Austin A40 van parked on the grass verge, who was watching us intently as we crossed the Moulton Road on the way back to Heath House after third lot.

That was my first glimpse of Sir Mark Prescott Bt., a man who was to play a not inconsequential role in my life for the next 30-odd years. Just consider the statistics. I've been assured by those who know about these things that I've ridden 744 winners for Sir Mark in this country (to the start of 2002), amounting to 62.8 per cent of his grand total and 31.4 per cent of mine; in addition, we've shared winners in Ireland (six, all bar one at Group level), France (three, all of them Group III) and Belgium (nine, thanks to our regular forays to Ostend in the 1970s). Nineteen of my 43 European Pattern-race winners have been trained by Sir Mark, which accounts for all bar four of his own total. Last, but by no means least, our association as trainer and stable jockey entered its 29th season in 2002, which constitutes a record of its kind.

In such happy circumstances as these, you may be surprised to learn that we instantly took a mutual dislike to each other! I was a jack-the-lad and, as he thought he was a bit special as well, we didn't see eye to eye. It was probably more my fault than his because I really did believe I'd arrived and was pretty good – which I clearly wasn't. It was a period in my career when, like most kids starting to get rides and a few winners, I began to get a bit cocky, a bit arrogant, and always had plenty to say for myself. I didn't realise this at the time, of course, but that would have been me to a tee, a right cocky little shit. I always felt Sir Mark could rub me up the wrong way and bring out the worst in me. It had nothing to do with me being the son of a miner and him being a baronet. Class didn't come into it. Sir Mark was never that 'sort'. Nor were there any incidents of him pulling rank and giving me a bollocking. We just didn't spare the rod with each other. He'd call me 'an arrogant little shit' and I'd retaliate with 'and who the fuck are you, nothing but a jumped-up fucking jump-jockey.' He wasn't in love with me and I wasn't in love with him. Full stop. And when I left Heath House to take the job with John Oxley we were glad to see the back of each other. End of story.

None of us at Heath House knew Sir Mark Prescott from a bar of soap at this point in time. Why he'd arrived, nobody knew. We weren't even aware he had a title. He was just 'Mark' to us, one of the boys who had a job to do like the rest of us, which in his case was overseeing all of us in the yard when Mr Waugh wasn't around. He never made a point of stressing his title, and I don't think it played on anyone's mind at Heath House – it certainly didn't mine.

Nor did he cut the urbane, authoritative figure we've become accustomed to. This was well before the makeover brought about by contact lenses and the switch to combing his hair back over that increasingly domed head of his. Sporting a side parting and a pair of heavyish, half horn-rimmed spectacles did very little for his looks!

We gradually pieced together the track record of our new 20-year-old assistant trainer. He was the third baronet whose home was near the village of Ipplepen in south Devon. His grandfather, the first baronet, was Colonel Sir William Prescott, a barrister and Conservative MP for North Tottenham, and his father, Major William Stanley Prescott (the younger of two sons), was also a barrister and an MP for the Lancashire constituency of Darwen. He was 14 when his father died in 1962, by which time his parents had long divorced and his mother, Gwendolen, had remarried Daniel Orme, a stepfather who exerted considerable influence upon him – not least in the area of punctuality, as many a Heath House employee and visitor will testify. Sir Mark's standing promise to all his staff is that if ever he is more than two minutes late for work they can all take three weeks off on full wages! They're still waiting in hope.

In 1965, his uncle, Sir Richard Stanley Prescott, the second baronet, also died – without an heir. At the age of 17 Mark thus inherited the title. School was already a thing of the past. Prep schools, one gathers, had been attended on a here-today-gone-tomorrow basis ('You could say I was difficult to train,' he says by way of explanation) until he finally took root with three years at Harrow. It's no surprise at all to learn that the adolescent Prescott was no duffer. In 1963 he won the school's prestigious Winston Churchill Essay Prize, named in honour of the most renowned Old Harrovian of them all, and received his prize of a Dictionary of Quotations from the hands of the great man himself. The distinct possibility – however unlikely it seems today – of entering theological college was briefly entertained but racing had by now started to get under his skin and into his blood.

A family friend called Frances Selley had introduced him to the pleasures and excitement of riding and racing by taking him along to Newton Abbot when he was 13. This visit proved to be the Road to Damascus as far as the teenage Prescott was concerned. His vision materialised in the unlikely guise of Tim Brookshaw. Standing beside the final fence to savour the atmosphere of a steeplechase at close quarters, the schoolboy saw the leader come a right cropper and its jockey, the teak-hard former champion Brookshaw, receive a dreadful kicking as the rest of the field galloped all over him. He was convinced no man alive could possibly survive such punishment and that Brookshaw had to be dead. When the jockey just got to his feet, hurled his whip into the turf and snarled 'Fucking Hell!' the impressionable teenager was hooked. What a man! The clergy had lost the soul of Mark Prescott to the glory of the racetrack. Becoming a jump jockey was now the only ambition firing his thoughts.

During the school holidays he began cycling the seven miles from his home to the stables of Sid Kernick, near Kingsteignton, to learn his trade. Kernick's yard housed nothing but four-legged problems. One of them, the unlikely conveyance of a twelve-year-old novice chaser called Monarain, provided its 16-year-old amateur rider with his first victory in a three-horse race at Wincanton in September, 1964, at odds of 100/7 after the odds-on favourite had slipped up on the flat. 'I've always thought the Almighty played a big hand in that winning ride,' Sir Mark explains, 'primarily because he was rather anxious not to have me on his team.'

Nevertheless, Sir Mark maintains a working relationship of sorts with his maker since he is a churchwarden at All Saints in Newmarket – although he does tend to draw the line at the blind acceptance of modern church practices. Apparently, when a new trendy vicar came to All Saints he asked the congregation to express its love for mankind by turning round and kissing the person in the pew directly behind them. Doubtless hoping to find some stunning creature awaiting him with puckered lips, Sir Mark executed an about-face only to be greeted by the less kissable features of John Waugh, Jack's cousin. So much for that idea!

After spending two and a half years with Kernick, Sir Mark – as he'd now become – moved to the far grander yard of Frank Cundell at Aston Tirrold in Berkshire. Cundell had 50 horses in his care, mostly jumpers trying to fill the shoes of the marvellous Crudwell whom he had expertly placed to win no fewer than 50 races (seven of them on the Flat). Even toward the end of Crudwell's 11-season career, Cundell chose his races with such care and astuteness that few detected the old horse's declining powers and many went out of their way to avoid him, thus presenting the veteran with bloodless victories. Cundell also advertised his Flat-race skills with horses like the tip-top sprint handicapper Welshman who won 14 between the age of two and 10. Although Sir Mark never struck up quite the same rapport with Frank Cundell as he did with Sid Kernick, it's plain to see where and how he acquired his methodical approach to placing his horses to their best advantage.

The moment triggering the chain of events that led to Sir Mark's fortunes becoming inextricably linked with those of Heath House was not a pleasant one. In May 1968 a crashing fall from a horse called Pike's Fancy at the now defunct course of Wye, in Kent, resulted in a broken back and a lengthy spell in hospital. Sir Mark never returned to Aston Tirrold and was recuperating at home in Devon when Mary Alderman, daughter-in-law of the Newmarket trainer Reg Day and a former girlfriend of his stepfather, paid a house-visit along with her current escort, Jack Leach, the noted jockey, trainer and, ultimately, author of the popular book 'Sods I Have Cut on the Turf' – not to mention a man-about-town who counted Fred Astaire among his friends. Leach knew Mr Waugh hadn't been too well of late and was looking for an assistant to take some of the workload off his shoulders. Accordingly, Leach brokered a meeting. After a brief five-minute interview with Mr Waugh at Newbury races Sir Mark was given the post on a six-month trial basis and told to report for duty 48 hours later.

Naturally, our first opinion of Sir Mark wasn't especially high. We didn't have an awful lot to do with him – other than insult him! We didn't go in for conversations and saw nothing of the legendary Prescott wit or humour. He had his own set of friends and watering holes in Newmarket. We wouldn't have thought him up to much as a rider simply because in our eyes he was nothing but an amateur jump jockey.

Sir Mark did ride out with us, however, which provided occasional support for our low opinion of his riding abilities. A horse I'd 'done' at one point was a big, raw-boned grey called Grandtully who was a complete firecracker and, consequently, hadn't seen a racecourse as a juvenile. Anything at all could spook him and away he'd go into the distance. Sir Mark, along with Jack Button, was given the task of teaching him to settle through the following winter. One frosty morning, to our great delight, Grandtully carted Sir Mark round and round the tarmaced perimeter of the yard while the rest of us were trotting nicely across the straw bed laid out in the centre. Sir Mark completed an undignified four laps before he managed to pull him up!

Better was to come. Grandtully was, needless to say, a law unto himself in the starting stalls, which had only recently been introduced. He'd go in but wouldn't come out. Mr Waugh decided to solve the problem by encouraging him with an electric cattle prod. So, one freezing, rainy morning – described drily by Jack Button as 'Real funeral weather' – Sir Mark and Grandtully were loaded into the practice stalls, which were positioned facing up the hill away from the Bury Road and towards the Moulton Road. Suffice to say, the prod worked a treat. Sir Mark and Grandtully left those stalls so quick it looked as if they'd jump straight across the Moulton Road and be in Cambridge for lunch. Somehow Sir Mark got this runaway nutcase to turn right and head down Long Hill toward Heath House, at which point they executed another right-hander to arrive back at the stalls where a despairing Mr Waugh and Jack Button made unavailing efforts to stop them. Eventually Grandtully ran out of steam and slowed to a walk, Sir Mark slumped dejected and soaked to the skin in the saddle. How we loved that! The fact that the outcome would have been the same whoever had ridden Grandtully – he'd already run off with Eric Eldin – mattered not one jot. Grandtully never did get to see a racecourse. He became so dangerous Mr Waugh had him shot.

Funny though it was to watch our esteemed assistant trainer lapping Long Hill, his efforts that cold, wet morning earnt him some respect. It took a lot of bottle to stay with Grandtully and he must have been scared stiff. Once you get to know him a little, however, you cease to be surprised by displays of guts like that. Sir Mark greatly admires courage in all its forms, moral and physical (the Prescott family motto is 'He conquers who endures'), and regards the true test of courage to be man confronting himself. His heroes are people like Captain Oates, who went out into the blizzard and certain death during Scott's Antarctic expedition rather than risk the lives of his companions, or Gordon Wilson, the father who lost his daughter in the IRA bomb outrage at Enniskillen but subsequently announced he bore no grudge. Sir Mark has no time for that modern form of hero worship which puts on pedestals footballers who cry or whatever.

Other things jostle for Sir Mark's affections besides horses. He is both an opera and a film buff. Lines from *Citizen Kane* or any Marx Brothers film you care to name are recited at the drop of a hat. Come to that, any quotations! That dictionary Sir Winston presented to him has definitely been put to good use! His love of field sports is well documented and, eccentric as it sounds, the story that he has reserved three plots in Newmarket cemetery 'so I don't have to lie there for eternity next to some fucker who doesn't like field sports' is perfectly true. He revitalised the ailing Waterloo Cup, the Olympics of greyhound coursing – and co-wrote its history – and he has his own menagerie of Old English gamefowl at Heath House, which down the years has brought him into conflict with bands of gypsies and travellers intent on making off with one or two of them. Heath House is chock-a-block with paintings and sculptures of gamebirds, greyhounds like Mick The Miller and the great 19th century coursing champion Master M'Grath, and bare-knuckle contests of yesteryear.

Most of all, though, Sir Mark loves bullfighting (in his view 'a blend of beauty and courage and most stimulating if you're interested in animal behaviour') and the courage it highlights in both man and bull. As a young man of 16, he trekked south through France by bus for the 'running' of the bulls through the streets of Pamplona and was immediately smitten. The conservatory at Heath House is a mini shrine to Sir Mark's passion. On one wall is a collection of wonderfully evocative photographs he has taken of action in the ring and on another are the mounted heads of two fighting bulls. One of the bulls, Pinitefco, fought so well that he was accorded the rare honour of being allowed to leave the ring at Arles in one piece, and he went on to become a seed bull siring more of his kind. Every time Sir Mark gazes up at those magnificent creatures in death he is reminded of the meaning of courage and the price occasionally paid for demonstrating it.

There is no denying that Sir Mark has had a somewhat patrician Edwardian air about him for as long as I've known him. He insists, for instance, that he has never had any desire to be champion trainer, that he trains only for his own pleasure and that he'd 'rather train a bad horse for someone I like than a good horse for someone

I don't like because in a couple of years the good horse will be gone and I'm stuck with someone I can't stand!'

One particular story he tells of a Yuletide visit to an owner's property speaks volumes. Out in a snow-covered field he identified a former inmate of Heath House looking cold and forlorn. 'Is your grandmother coming for Christmas?' he enquired of the owner. 'If she is, you might as well keep her in a tent out there and chuck her a can of beans now and again like that poor horse!'

Frankly, you either like him or lump him. I don't think he minds either way. At least he is now nearer the age he has always acted, because he's always been beyond his years, giving the impression he's 20 years older than he is.

Marriage has never looked an option. He's never been short of female company down the years, mind, but I could never see him tying himself to one woman. He's far too set in his ways for a woman to occupy a permanent place in his life. Mention marriage to him and he'll mutter the GK Chesterton line – 'The ever widening chasm by the fireside' – in self-defence. All he's ever wanted out of life, he says, is a cigar (he has a cushion embroidered with the motif 'If I cannot smoke cigars in heaven then I shall not go!'), to go and see a bullfight and the freedom to turn up the heating when he wants to. No wife would last five minutes in Heath House. Everything has to be laid out properly, everything put away in its proper place, everything done just right. He'd be hell to live with! A monster! And he's none too keen on kids either!

Mr Waugh saw through the youthful façade and recognised something in Sir Mark that caused him to give freely of his knowledge, a generosity not exactly characteristic of all trainers. When he saw that Sir Mark was really willing to learn, he was really willing to teach him. For instance, every Sunday he used to stand him in the yard blindfolded, and bring out a series of horses for him to identify by feeling their front legs. This was Mr Waugh's way of conveying how important it was to feel a horse's legs with minute care every day of the week. One Sunday Sir Mark disgraced himself by getting three wrong. 'Train?' Mr Waugh muttered to Jack Button, 'Never!'

Sir Mark had to be good at his job, though, or he'd not have lasted the six months' trial let alone almost two and a half years. He was there to learn and he'd make mistakes but he must have got things right more than wrong to have won over Mr Waugh. There was an incident early on which I'm sure must have tipped the scales in his favour. One hot summer's night Newmarket was struck by a tremendous thunderstorm and, realising the rain might be blown into the boxes, Sir Mark hurried in from his Exning flat to close the box-shutters. Having commenced operations from one end of the yard, who does the drenched assistant meet in the middle but an equally drenched Mr Waugh closing them from the other end. 'Ah, there you are! I see I've made you as mad as I am!' said Mr Waugh. That degree of thought and willingness would have registered with Mr Waugh.

There's no doubt in my mind that Mr Waugh made as great an impression on Sir Mark as he did on me. Mr Waugh was kind enough to take each of us under his wing and, I like to think, each of us has repaid the faith he had in our potential abilities. Certainly, Mr Waugh quickly demonstrated his faith in Sir Mark when he arranged for him to take over Heath House at the end of 1970. None of us had any inkling that Mr Waugh was going to pack in training. He was only 59 and appeared to be in good health. But one morning early that season, he just turned to Sir Mark and said: 'I'm fed up with this. It's a young man's game. You better train these horses next year. I'll have a word with the owners.' In August he informed Sir Mark everything was cut and dried. The owners were happy with the proposal and had bought the yard for him on an interest-free loan. Sir Mark was 22 years-old. It was all a bit sudden for him, but he could hardly look a gift horse in the mouth. No wonder Sir Mark always resorts to that 'I always gagged on the silver spoon' line Orson Welles used to describe his own youthful triumph in *Citizen Kane* when recalling how he inherited Heath House.

It did not take long for Mr Waugh's protégé to open his account. Lady Macdonald-Buchanan's four-year-old filly Belle Royale justified odds-on favouritism at Teesside Park on 23 April, 1971, in the hands of Eric Eldin – though she had to survive an objection to do so. There seemed no likelihood of me ever getting a ride. I was retained by John Oxley, of course, but me and Sir Mark were perfectly happy to stay out of each other's way. If our paths ever crossed on the Heath of a morning we'd give each other a cursory grunt, no more than that. I was too concerned with my own job to wonder how he was getting on at Heath House. I wasn't interested in Sir Mark Prescott or his horses. I even advised Stilly to try for the yard's lightweights – which led to him getting the winning ride on Heave To in the 1972 Victoria Cup after Eric Eldin had taken a fall on the gallops the morning of the race.

By that summer of 1972 the Oxley job was going down in flames and I was interested in riding anybody's horses. Most articles mentioning the beginnings of my association with Sir Mark state that my first ride for him was a winner, at Warwick on the Easter Monday of either 1972 or 1973. In fact, my first ride for Sir Mark was at Yarmouth on 19 July 1972 on a two-year-old filly called Sirmio, owned by Mr Hugo Morriss, making its debut in the Jellicoe Maiden Plate over six furlongs. Starting at 25/1, we finished sixth to one of Johnny Winter's ridden by Willie Carson. Sod's Law decreed that the day Sirmio won at Warwick I was not on her because I rode the favourite for John Oxley! That same season of 1972 I also had three unplaced rides on Kentucky Robin, a two-year-old filly belonging to Lady Macdonald-Buchanan. At the start of the 1973 season I'd already partnered Kentucky Robin and Clairvoyance (also owned by Lady Macdonald-Buchanan) for Sir Mark before I got a call from him asking me to ride a two-year-old filly called So Valiant (owned by Percy Parnell) who was to make her debut in the five-furlong Gog Brook Maiden Stakes at Warwick on Easter Monday, 23 April.

Finding a jockey on a Bank Holiday is headache enough but finding jockeys you want to employ is an absolute nightmare. Eric Eldin now had a retainer with Doug Smith and he was required at the main meeting, Kempton Park. Sir Mark's phone call came as a bit of a shock – he had to be desperate! But I was only too pleased to ride for him, regardless of anything that had gone on between us in the past, because my career was starting to go the wrong way. I knew nothing about the filly whatsoever, other than the fact that she was by the 1968 July Cup and Nunthorpe winner So Blessed which meant she ought to be able to go a bit. Sir Mark told me all I needed to know in the paddock. Although So Valiant turned out to be leggy and still rather unfurnished, she won her race well, taking up the running a furlong out to win by one and a half lengths at odds of 10/1. Sir Mark (and Mr Waugh) seemed very pleased. So was I, particularly after I made it a double for the day aboard Wyntac in the next.

I expected this to be nothing more than a one-off, but with Doug Smith's claim on Eric Eldin causing him to become increasingly unavailable, I rode Celestial Fire (only eighth of 12) for Sir Mark up at Thirsk on 19 May, and, pretty soon, one thing led to another. Four days later I went up to Ripon for him (it was my only ride of the day) and got the two-year-old filly Lapis Lazuli home by a short head. By the end of the year I'd ridden ten more to contribute 12 winners toward Sir Mark's total of 32 and mine of 30. Ten of those wins came courtesy of eight different juveniles which I was lucky enough to get my leg across. Sir Mark had clearly acquired the knack of training precociously fast two-year-olds from Mr Waugh because they knew their job and were spot on first time out. Good old Kentucky Robin provided one of the other two wins in a Catterick handicap.

From being two people who couldn't stand the sight of each other, Sir Mark and me began to get on big time. We suddenly found we could communicate when once immaturity and arrogance had stopped us. We had both grown up. And been forced to do so very quickly, which served to bond us together. He'd grown up because he was handed Heath House far sooner than he wanted – or felt he was ready to take it on – and I'd grown up 12 years in two because the Oxley job had made me realise I wasn't as clever as I thought I was. Sir Mark threw me a lifeline and I was more than happy to grab it. Halfway through 1973 he said to me 'You're riding most of these two-year-olds, you'd better come in and ride them work' and at the end of the season he offered me a small retainer – about £500 I think – for 1974. I was over the moon to be back in a steady job again, and we've been together ever since.

Like all the best marriages we don't talk too often! In fact, we're seldom in each other's company nowadays and don't socialise. I don't want to play croquet on Sir Mark's lawn and I'm sure he doesn't want me there. We're both firm believers in familiarity breeding contempt. Most stable jockeys, for instance, would have breakfast with their trainer after riding work. In the 29 seasons I've been the retained jockey at Heath House I've had one breakfast. One was enough! It was way back in 1974 – or possibly even 1973 before I was actually retained.

Me and Stilly were taken into the kitchen and given our orders. 'Now then, Still and Duffield,' says Sir Mark, 'There's the teapot, there's the tea, there's the cups and the milk, there's the cornflakes, there's the bread if you want some toast. Right? When you have finished, the teapot goes back there, the cups go back there, the cornflakes go back there. Leave the table nice and clean – don't forget to wipe it down when you've finished. And don't forget to wash up and put everything away.'

Me and Stilly can't help but start to grin. Major mistake! 'I'm serious!' intones Sir Mark. 'I'm serious!'

Anyway, Stilly and me sit down to partake of our first ever breakfast at Heath House, conspicuous by the lack of eggs, bacon, sausages etc, when this cat comes staggering through the cat-flap into the kitchen. It's a big, black tom-cat that could obviously fight and fuck for England, which by the state it's in – chewed ear, runny nose, blood and snot all over its face – was exactly what it had been doing all night. Not that we knew it, but this cat, Ashley, meant more to Sir Mark than any other animal in the yard, and definitely was more important to him than a pair of jockeys.

I'm just raising a spoonful of cornflakes to my mouth when Ashley jumps onto the kitchen table and shakes himself, sending blood, snot and God knows what flying everywhere, before proceeding to tread in the bowl right in front of me. Naturally, I go to give him a flick to shoo him away, and that's when I hear this voice from behind me.

'Don't you dare, Duffield! You'll find yourself without a fucking job if you hit that cat!'

Animated car journeys to and from the races are also figments of the imagination. The last shared car I can recall was back from Hamilton to Newmarket about 12 years ago. I think my car had broken down so Sir Mark gave me a lift back to Burrough Green. The 400-mile journey took something around four to five hours and the entire conversation went something like:

Leaving car park at Hamilton: Sir Mark – 'That ran badly.' Me – 'Yes.'

Filling station at Scotch Corner: Sir Mark – 'I'll get the petrol, you get the sandwiches.' Me – 'Right.'

Newmarket: Sir Mark – 'Don't be late in the morning.' Me –

'No.'

That was it.

However, I would not want to paint Sir Mark as some sort of cold fish. For instance, he was back home in Newmarket for the October Sales one year when I had a terrible fall at Bath, damaging my neck and back, and even though the horse was not one of his, he immediately rushed all the way down to Bath to check on my condition. He arrived very late at night to discover me being wheeled along a corridor on a trolley wearing a neck brace and covered with a flimsy white sheet. 'What am I doing here? Where am I going?' I asked, obviously completely ga-ga. Sir Mark couldn't resist milking the situation, could he? 'I don't know whether it's good news or bad, George,' he said, 'but you're going from critical assessment to intensive care!'

Later on, in the ward, I found myself in a bed next to an old ex-Army type. I was in such agony from my neck I was whingeing and moaning, begging for a shot to kill the pain and all I could hear was 'Fucking wimp, fucking shut up and fucking grow up you fucking wimp!' coming from this old boy in the next bed.

However amusing that Bath incident seems in hindsight, it was nothing compared to the events surrounding my ride on Lily Augusta at Carlisle on 10 July 1976 – the date is seared into my brain – which in turn were acutely painful, riotously funny and downright excruciating. I can laugh at it now, but believe you me, it was no joke at the time.

It was a blazing-hot summer's day, and Sir Mark and me had driven all the way up for the Saturday evening meeting in company with one of our owners, David Hicks, whose Doublette I was to partner in the first. Doublette finished second in a three-horse race. Lily Augusta was due to contest the 8.05, a little nine-furlong handicap. Sir Mark had a soft spot for her because she was a half-sister to one of the decent animals who had got him started, the miler Dawn Review who won seven races for him. I was far less enamoured with her. She was a big, horrible, scatty bay thing, always fly-lepping and what-not. I'd won a couple of races on her as a two-year-old but she had lost her way since then and had not won in ten attempts at three and four. She was becoming more and more of a handful at home let alone on the racetrack and a lowly contest such as this one was likely to be her last chance.

Sir Mark led us out of the paddock and down the walk-way onto the track to stop her fly-lepping but as soon as Lily Augusta catches sight of the wide open spaces she takes off out of his hands, shooting through the air as if catapulted. Usually when a fly-lepper does this it will automatically put in a second one. Not Lily Augusta. When she hit the ground, she threw her head back – meeting my head as it was coming forward! There was an almighty crack which they said could be heard in the stands. Sir Mark likened it to a 'ping-pong bat falling onto lino.'

The long and the short of it was I met the filly's head right between the eyes with my mouth. Two of my front teeth are embedded in Lily Augusta's head and mane. I'm just sat there holding my hand to my mouth, with blood oozing between my fingers and pouring down my silks, as Sir Mark grabs hold of her again and steadies me by gripping my leg. 'How are you, George?' I can remember him saying, though I've no recollection of him maintaining: 'You'll be all right. Just ride this one and then we'll get you down the hospital. This filly can win.'

I aint that tough! I can't speak and I'm concussed! I've left two front teeth in Lily Augusta's head, two others are pushed right back into the roof of my mouth and I've bitten deep into my lower lip. No, Sir Mark, I don't think I'm fit to ride this filly.

Still in my boots, breeches and bloodstained silks, I'm ferried to Carlisle Infirmary by Sir Mark, and we head for the casualty department. Well, you can imagine what the scene is like on a Saturday night as, by now, the pubs are beginning to close. There's knife wounds, 'bottled' faces, broken arms...the lot! Every time we got toward the front of the queue some fresh life-or-death case would come through the doors and push us back.

Then, as we're nearly there, a mother comes in with this little kid who's got a saucepan stuck on his head! He'd been playing soldiers, she tells the nurse, and had wedged this pot on his head for a helmet and now he can't get it off! Well, Sir Mark is rolling about laughing, isn't he, tears rolling down his cheeks – and he starts me off! My teeth are killing me but it's so ludicrously funny! The more I laugh, the more I keep touching the bare nerves of these broken teeth and the more it hurts. But I can't stop myself from laughing even though I'm in so much pain.

'All right, George,' says Sir Mark, 'Hold on. Won't be long now. It's our turn next.'

Just as he says that, the double-doors swing open and in staggers this old tramp wearing one of those huge, thick overcoats that street-dwellers never seem to be without whatever the weather – and this is one of the hottest days of the year, remember – and as he ricochets past us off the walls we can see a bloody great kitchen knife sticking out from between his shoulder blades.

'Sorry, George,' mutters Sir Mark, 'It looks as if we've just lost a bit of ground.'

It's 1.30 in the morning before we get away. All they could do for me was give me a tetanus jab and stitch my lip. And that jab felt as if the nurse had thrown this huge needle at me from the other side of the cubicle! Sir Mark phoned Gill to forewarn her that her husband would not look a pretty sight when he finally came home (at five in the morning!), and he arranged for me to see a dentist, who lived in Burrough Green himself, the following morning. Heath House had two 'good things' running at Edinburgh on the Monday and Sir Mark wanted me patched up to ride if at all possible. 'It's only bust teeth and a few stitches in your lip, George. See what the dentist thinks.'

Philip Laver, the dentist, picks me up at 10am on the Sunday and drives me to his surgery. 'Oh dear, that looks a mess,' he starts by saying. 'I'll take an X-ray of your upper gum to assess the damage and we'll go from there. OK, George?'

He takes the X-ray and after he's studied it he says: 'You've broken two bones in your gum and I'll try to splint them. It may work, it may not. But there's bad news. I can't give you anything to numb the pain because your face is so swollen and you've so many stitches in your mouth that there's nowhere to insert a needle. It's really going to hurt, I'm afraid. If you want to scream, scream. If you want to cry, cry. Just don't hit me!' He wasn't kidding. When he said pain he meant pain. He had to extract the two teeth that were smashed backwards, put temporary caps on two others to protect the stumps in addition to inserting the splints.

Sir Mark rang that evening and I told him I was prepared to ride at Edinburgh the next afternoon. Besides three of Sir Mark's, I was also riding a couple for Derek Weedon and he drove us up in his car. Of course, I'd never be allowed to ride in that state today, I'd be signed-off, but in those days you could get away with murder. I couldn't speak or eat – I just took some liquid through a straw. I also made myself a protective mask, out of a stocking, to go over my head and stop any dirt from getting into my mouth.

Our two-year-old filly Linguistic trotted-up in the first at odds-on as did our juvenile colt, Bushy Pieces, in the last. Mission accomplished. I'm completely whacked after five rides and close to flaking out. Sir Mark got me dressed and walked me to Derek Weedon's car for the long journey back to Newmarket. 'You'll fucking kill him, you know,' Derek says to Sir Mark. 'You'll never kill him, he's too fucking tough!', Sir Mark replies.

'Fucking tough' or not, I needed most of the next fortnight to recuperate after that little escapade and only rode the odd one or two for Sir Mark. Lily Augusta was sold to go to Australia.

You see, our association has worked because we've never made a big deal about anything and because we're honest with each other. We try to keep everything very simple and don't get too technical. We put together what he sees and what I feel. He has faith in the way I ride. I have faith in the way he trains. We don't regard it necessary to exchange many words and there's no fuss in getting the job done. Our relationship is not one of the buddy-buddy variety but one of the business-like variety that is based on mutual trust and respect. I trust him to have the horse ready and he trusts me to ride it as he wishes.

From the outset, the one thing Sir Mark liked about me was that when he legged me up on a horse he knew I'd do my utmost to follow his instructions. He is not a trainer who says 'ride it as you find it' because 70 per cent of the time he'll have gone through the race with a fine-tooth comb – 'horse X will make the running, we're drawn here, you can come across there' and so on and so forth. And then he'll say: 'Does that make sense? If you get beat I'll tell you where you went wrong.' If he wanted a horse ridden in a certain way he knew I would ride it that way if humanly possible. He could trust me to do what he wanted, and as long as I had carried out his orders there was no way I'd be criticised whatever the outcome of the race. If I made a cock-up it did not become an issue, there was no blasting or ear bashing. I'd be told quietly, with no one in earshot, and it would then be forgotten. It gives a jockey confidence when you know you're not going to get a bollocking in front of half the racecourse if something goes wrong. Consequently, you make fewer mistakes anyway because you are less tense.

I can count on the fingers of one hand the disagreements we've had in 30 years. I can remember one instance from 1981 when I was getting close to achieving my maiden century. I was so desperate to reach the 100-winner mark at long last that my increasing anxiety began to make me ride out of character. I was on this filly called Reem in a race at Folkestone and got boxed-in. I should have stayed there, finished fourth or so, and saved Reem for another day the following week – in due Heath House fashion – but, no, I pulled her out, set about her and finished second. The net result was I still didn't win and the filly had endured such a tough race she couldn't run for weeks. I was, quite rightly, not popular. And I still failed by six to reach the century.

Only one thing has seriously – and I mean seriously – upset me concerning a lost ride. I'd been everywhere to ride old Wizard King but when he got an invitation to run in Hong Kong in 1997 I was not asked to go over there. That wonderful trip – at Hong Kong's expense not the owner's – would have been some sort of reward, and it took a fair few days for me to get this out of my system.

If we ever disagree over a horse, the one who is eventually proved wrong always owns up. He's the trainer, I'm the jockey. Ask a question and give the answer – hopefully, the right one. That's how we conduct our business.

During the winter we keep ourselves to ourselves but sometime in the spring the phone will ring and it'll be 'Now then, GP' – he always calls me GP – 'How are you? Wintered well? Right, about time you got yourself down here and got one or two of these horses going. They're ready for you now. Pull out ten to seven, Tuesday morning.' And toward the end of the season it'll be 'Same again next year?' That's all, not even a handshake.

So, if there is a magic formula behind one of the longest – if not THE longest – trainer-jockey partnerships in racing history, that just about sums it up. Perhaps I should let Sir Mark have the last word on the subject.

'With people in key jobs at Heath House, such as head lad, assistant trainer, secretary, stable jockey, I work on the principle "I trust you implicitly. I'll tell you everything, and, as a result, the job is very, very interesting. But, in return, I've got to be able to trust you. I'll never, ever, let you down in public. But, in return, I expect the same from you." Trust comes from me first of all. I give them that to start with. It's a contract until broken by an untruth. If you know the truth, you can always deal with it.

'I've never known George or Colin Nutter, my head lad, to tell a lie. Consequently, if the whole world told me one thing and George or Colin told me the other, I'd unhesitatingly believe George and Colin – and I suspect it would be the same for them. I would trust them both with my life. It wouldn't matter how many people came up to me and said that George had stopped one, I just wouldn't believe them.

'People imagine that we have endless conversations. We don't. The reason we've hardly ever had a cross word is that we confine our conversation to business. We have a professional relationship. If I was a window cleaner and not a trainer, G Duffield would hold the ladder and C Nutter could pass the bucket up.

'I firmly believe that all relationships are founded on one thing – respect, which once lost is not recoverable. Liking or loving doesn't come into it. I can only respect people who are good at what they do. George – like Colin – is an utter professional and, consequently, our professional relationship is founded on respect, which breeds confidence plus a million other things.

'George is the best stable jockey ever. He couldn't be better. He has all the attributes. He's honest, pleasant, cheerful: the lads and the owners like him; he never forgets to ring after a horse has run. He's never late, he never takes a day off: other people get flu or else their car won't start. He's always fit and feels well: he can drive a horse for one and a half miles and still never blow when he talks to you afterwards. George is like a greyhound in that they've both been stripped down by nature to just the working parts they need:

he's all wire and whipcord, as everyone saw when the TV cameras caught him stripped to the waist in the Longchamp changing room before the 2001 Arc. As Kevin Darley has said, "he has the body of a 20-year-old – there's not a picking on him." He polishes up well: he's always shaved, smart and on the ball.

'He's an excellent work-rider: the greatest slug ever born will get hold of its bit with George; he pulls a two-year-old together and gets it to use itself even when it's previously shown no aptitude. He always tries to do his level best whatever the race: he's just as keyed up at Carlisle as Royal Ascot – in fact he has never needed geeing up, if anything he needs settling down because he is always lit up. In fact, the best ride I ever saw him give a horse was on a next to useless three-year-old gelding called Pelion in a Catterick maiden in 1983 – he was so good I acquired the race video for him! He doesn't lose races he should have won: tactically he is better than he was – it's no good getting old if you don't get cunning.

'His greatest forte is that he imparts enthusiasm: you can't have a stable jockey moaning in the yard "Fancy having to go all the way up to Edinburgh to ride this fucking thing that's got no chance." Yes, George can be impatient on a horse: he's not a natural hold-up jockey, it's not in his nature – he wants to get on with it and fight them off, never faltering, daring them to pass. He's not blessed with the best of hands and security never was his salient quality if one whipped round. But his failings are amply compensated by the rest. He is still completely without fear – it's a great tribute to him that he's been the leading jockey at tracks like Edinburgh and Catterick that others hate because of the tight turns and the resultant falls – and he retains his innate ability to impart a sense of urgency into a horse: tomorrow bloody well won't do and today will! Nothing distracts George from getting to the winning post.

'I've said it before but, yes, I have looked at many another woman but I have never looked at another jockey. I suspect that

George rides far better for me than anyone else, and I would still not have any other stable jockey from the last 150 years ahead of him. If I have been good for him it is because I've known what he's like and have never pressurised him. Jockeys ride on confidence and if they have confidence in me that makes them better jockeys. George has never had to worry constantly about whether he will lose a ride. At Heath House, ALL the horses are ridden by G Duffield. He cannot be jocked off. If an owner doesn't want G Duffield, then the horse must leave. George is living proof that if you do something well enough for long enough even the blind will notice it. He is, and has been, an out-and-out professional, the ultimate professional, not a prima donna, so good that nobody noticed. How nobody realised his worth 20 years ago baffles me. Yet I'm very grateful they didn't.

'Perhaps George and I are out of our time. We don't show our emotions like so many people involved in sport today. I was brought up not to be a bad loser. It is often said "Show me a good loser and I'll show you a loser." But that is a nonsense. We all hate being beaten but I'd be horrified if I finished second in the Derby and anyone could tell from my demeanour. George and I are just as elated after a big win as Frankie Dettori when he does his flying dismount but, unlike him, we are not prone to outward displays of emotion.

'I'm very, very fond of George and I respect and admire him enormously.'

9

A TRUE PROFESSIONAL

I would not like to give the impression that my working relationship with Sir Mark Prescott has been one long misery dominated by
endless silences punctuated only by the sound of an occasional
grunt or monosyllabic comment, because nothing could be further
from the truth. Sir Mark is no sourpuss. As I think everyone in
racing appreciates, he is a storyteller of rib-tickling magnitude and
he has an infinite fund of these humorous anecdotes and tall tales
which he'll relate at the drop of a hat. Before you know it, he'll
have everyone in stitches or reduce them to tears. He is as acute an
observer of human behaviour as he is of equine behaviour which,
when allied to his tremendous memory and wonderful gifts of
expression, makes him a raconteur par excellence.

Sir Mark invariably features in most of these stories, though not
in any egocentric way. He is usually the victim of the piece or the
butt of the humour, and it is this one must bear in mind – along with
his inimitable delivery – whenever you read any of them in print.
Of course, they're even more hilarious if you're privileged enough

to hear the man himself retell them in person, and positively priceless if you happened to be present in the first place and can picture in your mind's eye the state of purple-faced apoplexy he was reduced to!

I've two particular favourites, both of them relating to work mornings at Heath House.

The first occurred during an irritating and frustrating period when the yard was plagued by coughing. You don't need to be Einstein to work out that morale was on the low side and Sir Mark's blood pressure on the high side. Anyway, the string is filing back into Heath House one morning, past Sir Mark anxiously waiting beside the gate to hear the latest bulletins from each rider.

The first horse and rider walk by.

'He coughed, Sir – three times.'

'Right.'

The next horse passes.

'Twice, Sir.'

'Right.'

Horse after horse goes past Sir Mark with the same sorry report from its partner. The very last rider in the line is a young girl.

'Well?' says an understandably exasperated Sir Mark.

No reply.

'How many times?' he barks.

Still no reply from the hapless girl who is now visibly nervous to the point of panic.

'Coughs!!' bellows the agitated trainer.

At that, the girl looks down at Sir Mark, puts her hand over her mouth, and ever so politely goes, 'Ahem! Ahem!'

However, the incident that sticks out in my mind as the most side-splitting happened one February in the days before Heath House had its covered ride and the string would still exercise on the heath itself. We were a bit short-staffed and Sir Mark was obliged to ride out on a racehorse instead of his hack. After he's legged everyone up, we pull out onto the heath and take a turn while he goes back to get his old horse. Well, even allowing for it being a bitterly cold morning, he's wearing far too much gear – sweaters, jackets, the lot – and, without anyone to leg him up, he's in all sorts of bother trying to haul himself up into the saddle as this old horse, who is mustard-keen to join his pals by now, begins to leap around.

No sooner has Sir Mark got in the saddle than there's an almighty clatter as another horse in the string rears and deposits its rider on the frosty ground before galloping off. Now this girl, Linda, was – how shall we say – a little on the plump side. There she was, flat on her back, motionless. Not a pretty sight. Sir Mark has to dismount to sort things out while someone retrieves the horse. Linda is revived and winched back up into the saddle. Not a good start.

Sir Mark's horse is well lit-up by all this activity going on around him and the instant Sir Mark clambers back aboard, the beast takes off up the sand canter like a steam train with Sir Mark hanging on for dear life, 'whoa-whoaing' at the top of his voice, and with his feet out of the irons looking for all the world like the ghost of Fred Archer. The sight and sound of this snorting monster flying past spooks Linda's mount, which with a fart and a buck, promptly deposits her on the deck for a second time. Once again the horse is retrieved. Once again Linda is winched up into the saddle. Once again Sir Mark, who has returned to the scene after eventually getting his horse under control, has been forced to clamber out of, and back into, the saddle. What with the multiple layers of clothing, it's fair to describe him as a trifle 'warm' in every sense of the word.

The string trots back down again and then turns to begin cantering up Warren Hill. All of a sudden Linda's off yet again, for the third time! The horse races up Warren Hill – followed at a respectable distance by the unfortunate girl who is huffing and puffing in pursuit and turning a violent shade of puce as a result. You had to give her credit. She must have run five furlongs up Warren Hill!

Linda is not the only person on Warren Hill who has turned a deep shade of purple and is giving off clouds of steam! Rivulets of sweat are streaming down Sir Mark's cheeks. All of us experienced Sir Mark-watchers recognise the symptoms. He is on the verge of meltdown.

'Now then, Linda, you can choose which one of these 20 fucking horses you ride, as long as you promise never to fucking fall off again! So which is it going to be? Which one do you want to fucking ride?'

Poor Linda is both breathless and thoughtless.

'Come on! Make up your fucking mind!'

Linda points to another horse – which just happens to be ridden by an equally fat girl!

The second fat girl slides off her horse and tries to give Linda a leg-up. The one fat girl heaving away, trying vainly to push and shove the other fat girl onto this poor horse. It's a farce and everyone is having immense difficulty keeping a straight face. As quick as Linda manages to get halfway up into the saddle, she only inadvertently boots the animal in the stomach, doesn't she, and away it goes with her virtually laying across its back!

Well, I'm in hysterics. Everyone's in hysterics. Except Sir Mark. He's had enough.

'You can fucking laugh!' he shouts across to me. 'You want to employ these fuckers! What do I fucking pay you? Four grand or something? You fucking get off and you fucking well leg her up!'

A story like that one endorses Sir Mark's assertion that fundamentally all horses are trying to kill themselves and all lads are aiding and abetting them! However, this amounts to a challenge which someone of Sir Mark's fertile mind finds irresistible. 'What I've tried to do,' he insists, 'is to make it impossible for the two of them to pull off their life's desire and kill one another simultaneously. I try to make it easy for the horse to do it right and hard for it to do it wrong, or so they frighten themselves. My approach is founded on trying to make a very tough regime more palatable to them. Nearly every horse at Heath House will go out twice a day – some on the walker and some will swim on top of normal exercise. I try to get them fitter without them realising it and, above all, I try not to lose a race through accidents in the yard.'

For example, because he maintained horses rush forward when they see anything narrow and straight, Sir Mark installed chicanes on the approaches to any potential accident black spot in Heath House and padded them with lengths of rubber piping so they wouldn't. He puts a lot of time and effort of this kind into discovering what horses want and what they don't want. He'll make everything he builds horse-friendly to such an extent that it becomes good to the horse's eye. He'll place a shrub here or plant a tree there.

His other great credo is they must be healthy. They must eat well, and they only eat well if they're healthy and happy. Then, if they're healthy, happy and eating, he can get stuck into them and get them superbly fit. If his eyes tell him they're not well, not lively enough, he'll wait and be patient. He's a firm believer that training is a test of character revolving around what doesn't go wrong as much as what goes right. A happy trainer, he reasons, is a bad trainer because he's not noticed what's going wrong. Not that he ever complains himself when things go pear-shaped.

'Some chap punching rivets in Dagenham would love to swap places with me,' he says, 'and I frequently think of him when things go wrong or I'm having to do something I'd rather not be doing. After all, when I go to meet my maker at the Pearly Gates and he asks what I did in life, I'll have to say "A racehorse trainer, sir. I spent my whole life trying to find a horse to run up a field faster than 20 others at Epsom on the first Wednesday in June in the

Derby." And he'll reply: "A what? I've got the likes of Mother Teresa in here! Don't waste my time. Go away!"'

Sir Mark would not want to waste any of God's time because he never wastes any of his own. He considers his role to be akin to that of a headmaster whose pupils happen to be racehorses – just as well as he dislikes children so much – and he must maximise their potential by finding the right opportunities for them. Although he likens his own institution to a comprehensive in comparison, say, to the universities presided over by a Henry Cecil or an Aidan O'Brien, he shares a similar attitude to his charges. He assembles the new intake each term before assessing and attempting to draw out their talent. They all receive the same treatment, they're all given the same opportunity to prove themselves and a career plan will be mapped out for each one based on its individual merits and requirements. To this end, he'll spend up to 14 hours a week with his head in the formbook and the programme book in search of the right opportunities – or as he is fond of saying, 'like WC Fields when asked why he was studying the bible – "Just looking for a loophole" – because most of mine are trained for opportunities not specific targets. With the moderate horse, I find what it can do and then get it doing it. I tend to keep these lesser lights simmering away, so I can bring them to the boil when the right race turns up. The programme for a really good horse almost picks itself.'

Sir Mark will plan these campaigns from the year before. In this respect he follows the advice Mr Waugh gave him: 'Most plans don't come off, but if you don't have a plan it cannot come off.' He approaches the task like any other academic exercise. When the Racing Calendar arrives at Heath House, Sir Mark can invariably place a horse's name alongside every race: the seller, the median auction, the 0-60 handicap, and so on. He finds it an enormous challenge to place cripples or quirky horses to win races, and when they do he derives as much satisfaction from that as winning a

Pattern race. He likes to feel that whenever he runs a horse, whatever the calibre of race, trainers of the other runners will be sufficiently frightened of his competitive reputation to look up its form. He may not be the champion trainer but, as he puts it, 'I'd like to be thought of like the movie actor Ernest Borgnine, who is perfectly capable of acting the star off the screen...everyone knows him but he never gets the starring role.' To run one in a conditions race, for instance, and find that it is not best-in or second best-in is regarded by Sir Mark as a cardinal sin; likewise, running one this week when it's better off at the weights next week. Geese most definitely must never be confused with swans, although he takes great pride in being able to distinguish the different types of goose at Heath House which are as numerous as the breeds of game fowl in his pens. He tries not to keep anything in the yard as a three-year-old that won't win. 'No one can help having bad two-year-olds,' he argues, 'but you shouldn't have bad three-year-olds – you should have got rid of them. You may lose the odd winner, and there'll always be the odd exception – the horse you couldn't assess properly due to injury or the horse that's bred to stay and may improve – but I find this to be the best way.'

Thanks to these tried and tested methods, season after season one in three Prescott runners returns to Heath House a winner – a strike rate few other trainers can match. Sir Mark must be doing something right.

No racecourse is ever out of bounds as far as Sir Mark is concerned and no destination too obscure or isolated if he discovers a 'loophole'. This explains how countless inmates of Heath House have been able to build up impressive win sequences and/or tallies irrespective of their innate ability.

During our early years together, for example, there were Mandalus and Marching On. Mandalus was a strong-looking brown colt, and a lovely mover, who after making his debut in the 1976

Woodcote Stakes went on to win 13 of his 28 races at around a mile during the ensuing four seasons before going to Ireland and, finally, a career as a stallion. Marching On was really nothing more than a sprint handicapper (he was rated 101 at best) but he was to win 13 in six seasons and also earn himself a place at stud thanks to finishing second in an Italian Group III.

Later on, Misty Halo set a postwar record for a mare (since beaten) by winning 21 of her 42 races between 1981-85 despite never being rated by Timeform higher than 93 – and every victory came in a non-handicap! That amounts to a masterclass in placement and planning. Another mare called Mrs Fisher was rated only 88 as a two-year-old but Sir Mark managed to win six races with her and get her placed in a Listed race before she retired at three. He got seven wins in a season out of other ordinary animals like Herradurra (rated 87 – and owned by Peter Savill!) from 11 starts in 1984 and Night-Shirt (rated 99) from 10 starts in 1990.

Although I partnered each of these at one time or another, Sir Mark's guiding principles decreed they'd appear in races confined to apprentices, amateurs and even ladies if the right opportunity arose. Mandalus twice won Ascot's valuable 'Diamond' race for lady riders in the hands of Elain Mellor and Misty Halo's successes included one in a trainers' invitation event at Catterick (when there was no prize money!) and two races for amateurs on the Isle of Man! No finer example of the old racing adage 'keep yourself in the best company and your horse in the worst.' And Sir Mark will never quit searching. When old Farmost got himself banned from running over here in 2000 after persistently refusing to enter the stalls, Sir Mark found a winning opportunity for him in a race at Tramore in Ireland that was started by flag.

Digging out opportunities at the unlikeliest of venues, for example, led us to harvest nine races at Ostend during the 1970s, which included the £3,000 Criterium de Vitesse de la Mer du Nord with Marching On in 1979 and a four-timer in 1976 with Ringed Aureole (Misty Halo's dam), Doublette, Damnation and Bustiffa, who collected the track's principal event, the two-and-a-half miles Prix Gladiateur d'Ostende worth £4,225 – very decent money in those days. Not that my riding style impressed the Belgians – the local press dubbed me 'Cowboy' Duffield!

Back home, Sir Mark's gameplan won me a different set of nicknames. According to *The Sporting Life,* I was 'MacDuff' and we were the 'Hammer of the Scots' and the 'Avengers of Bannockburn' as a result of our incessant expeditions north of the border. I'd take root in the north – where two-thirds of all Heath House runners earned their corn – for weeks at a time and got to know the Scottish tracks better than most. Edinburgh – now Musselburgh – is very sharp, they go very fast and they don't come back to you, whereas Ayr is a perfect galloping track; Hamilton resembles Ally Pally's 'frying pan' but you must be able to act downhill so that you're in touch three out. Yet nobody, it must be added, resented the presence of this Newmarket yard on what some might describe as 'pot-hunting' missions. After all is said and done, it was a level playing field because we were taking them on with the same standard of horse, animals bought for sums of money well within the price bracket of Northern trainers.

Sir Mark's eye for a 'loophole' and willingness to travel anywhere to capitalise upon it came to a glorious peak in the two-year-old career of Spindrifter, on whom I was fortunate enough to win 13 races in 1980. This equalled the 20th century record for wins in a season by a juvenile held by the filly Nagwa (1975), which was the best seasonal total by a horse of any age since the three-year-old gelding Hornet's Beauty collected 15 races in 1911. Spindrifter's tally also featured a winning sequence of ten not achieved by a two-year-old since the Gimcrack winner Polar Star won 12 out of 12 in 1906. And what about this for coincidence. Almost unbelievably, while Spindrifter was building this sequence, his dam, Late Spring, and Nagwa's dam, Tamarisk Way, were sharing the same field at the farm of his breeder Joe Crowley in County Kilkenny.

Foaled on 31 March, 1978, Spindrifter was a chestnut son of Sandford Lad, the champion sprinter of 1973, whom Ryan Price trained to win all bar the first of his eight races, which included the Nunthorpe and Prix de l'Abbaye. Sandford Lad never raced beyond five furlongs, while both Late Spring, her own dam and two of her three previous foals to win were also winning sprinters. By a strange twist of fate considering what was to befall Spindrifter, another of Late Spring's progeny called Lancerboss had been trained by Sir Mark until it broke a leg. Spindrifter cost 7,600 guineas as a foal before passing through the ring again as a yearling to fetch 10,000 guineas as a yearling. He was to race in the brown-and-white striped colours of Mr Grahame Waters, the owner of a caravan park in Clacton, one of the nicer people you could meet.

I liked Spindrifter from the outset, even before his first race. He was quite tall, around 16 hands, a bit on the leg but scopey. It goes almost without saying that Sir Mark chose to send him north, to Hamilton on 15 April, for his debut. He'd not quite come in his coat and was still rather immature but he was so far ahead of our other juveniles. Sir Mark told reporters after he'd won that 'if he did not win we would all be walking straight on to John O'Groats.' He made sufficiently hard work of beating a little colt called Boganach who managed to win one race from ten attempts that Lindsay Charnock yelled over to me: 'That won't win again!'

Spindrifter soon saw action again, at Pontefract, but Sir Mark put Colin Nutter on him to claim the 5lb in view of the fact that, as a winner, he had to give weight away. As it was, the gelding Horncastle, in receipt of 9lb, beat him a short head.

I was reunited with Spindrifter for a two-horse race at Redcar on 7 May, a facile victory which initiated his marvellous ten-race winning streak – my own streak on him, of course, amounted to 11 – that was not broken until he met a really top-class animal in Tina's Pet at Ripon on 26 August. After Redcar he added two more quick wins by the end of May at Pontefract and Catterick to start the tongues wagging – and, more importantly, Sir Mark's mind whirring. Nothing seemed to faze Spindrifter. He was an extremely placid individual who just slept, ate and raced. He had an iron constitution, wonderful powers of recovery and possessed the soundest of limbs. Sir Mark informed Mr Waters there were two options open to him. Go to Royal Ascot and win the Windsor Castle Stakes – whereupon Spindrifter would have to be sold because there was no future for him thereafter. Or he could miss Royal Ascot and mount an attack on Nagwa's record by racking up a sequence in small races all round the country. Mr Waters, bless his cotton socks, elected to have a crack at the latter. Accordingly, Sir Mark placed a bet at 500/1 that stood to net him £40,000 if Spindrifter could reach the magical total of 14.

Sir Mark really did burn the midnight oil on this occasion, scouring the programme book for tiny races which incurred no penalty. The fact that £2,695.80 was Spindrifter's most lucrative first prize and that five of his successes were worth less than £1,000 just demonstrates how Sir Mark left no stone unturned in the quest for that record.

Spindrifter won twice at Catterick in June and three times in July (Pontefract, Catterick, Hamilton) to get the racing press talking of 'Dynamic Drifter'. In actual fact, he was far from 'dynamic' as he rarely exerted himself and would beat a donkey as far as a good horse. I'd be chasing his ears off – and then he'd do it in three strides and that would be it. But the fact that there was always more in the locker allowed him to recover so quickly and be ready to race again in a matter of days – he was never off for more than three weeks. Sir Mark and me were forever hoping that each successive victory would frighten off the opposition next time, but, like when there's a crack gunfighter in town, there was always someone willing to take him on in an effort to make their name. They merely became further notches on Spindrifter's gun. He'd just play with them, treat them with utter contempt. I could ride him any way I wanted. Tactics were never a problem. I'd go on if the pace was slow, or sit in behind if it was fast. In point of fact, if he was in front, he'd actually wait for them to get to him – and then go again.

However, that ninth success, at Hamilton on 23 July, in which he beat one of Barry Hills's called Rosy Cottage (ridden by son Richard, claiming seven) by a length in concession of 20lb, did take a lot out of him. The filly had been five lengths clear at halfway, and after he showed signs of temporarily going over the top in winning his next race (at Thirsk on 2 August), Sir Mark decided to be slightly 'economical with the truth' and informed the press he'd got a bit of colic before giving him a short rest – forgoing an easy opportunity at Pontefract in the meantime.

This brief holiday worked wonders. Returning on 18 August, at Leicester, Spindrifter looked so hale and hearty he won the 'best turned-out' award prior to notching win number 11, each successive victory being recorded on the white T-shirt worn by his lad Steven Dodds by the appearance of an additional stripe in the style of Mr Waters's silks. However, eight days later we went to Ripon and caught a real Tartar in the shape of Tina's Pet, who wound up the season with a Timeform rating of 121 and eventually progressed to win twice in Pattern company. In receipt of 4lb, he brought the ten-race winning streak to an end by hammering us to the tune of eight lengths, breaking the track record in the process, thereby cruelly exposing Spindrifter's limitations at the highest level.

We began to rue the loss of that potentially soft race at Pontefract in early August when Spindrifter lost two of his next three outings and saw the season creeping into October. I felt the outside draw as much as the ability of the odds-on Piggott/Stoute animal Cavalry Twill (receiving 3lb) was responsible for our half-length defeat at Pontefract, but our conqueror at Newcastle on 7 October, Spindrifter's first crack at a mile which his pedigree suggested might not be in his favour and on unhelpful 'deadish' ground to boot, was another classy individual in Sula Bula who duly handed out a 2lb and four-length beating.

The ground was once again described as 'dead' at Catterick on 18 October but there was no Sula Bula or Sula Bula lookalike in the field for the Otley Stakes over seven furlongs, and the record-equalling victory was, in my view, his easiest of the 13. The clapping broke out with more than a furlong to run as we went on to defeat My Morton by two and a half lengths.

Of course, the papers were now full of Spindrifter stories, wondering where and when he'd make his first attempt at the outright record and whether he'd succeed. In one week alone Heath House was visited by seven different TV crews! Gilt-edged opportunities were now becoming non-existent and the race Sir Mark was obliged to select for the first attempt was the Carrs Stakes (worth less than £1,000, as usual!) up at Stockton, and back over five furlongs, nine days after Catterick. Unfortunately, we had to meet (at level weights) another very useful horse in Bill O'Gorman's Doc Marten, who had won the Clarence House Stakes at Ascot before finishing fourth in the Group II Flying Childers behind the outstanding filly Marwell.

We were denied by a head from taking sole possession of the record – and I take a lot of the blame. Even though he was coming back to five furlongs from seven and the ground was soft – and arguably this defeat still constituted his best performance of the season – I feel, looking back, he would have won had I'd ridden him more positively. As Spindrifter had run his last dozen races over longer trips, I let him find his feet through the first furlong and we were soon four lengths adrift and way out the back rounding the bend, which maybe cost us the race. I know Doc Marten was a decent opponent but once I got after Spindrifter – I'm almost ashamed to confess I struck him 18 times – he made up so much ground that we must have won had I taken closer order early on.

The quest went down to the wire, at Doncaster on the very last day of the season, Saturday 8 November. Not wishing to face either Sula Bula or Doc Marten, Sir Mark chose the Amoco Jockeys' Trophy Nursery instead of the Steel Plate Autumn Stakes (which Sula Bula won). We were more hopeful than confident. Spindrifter came out of the Stockton race with a swollen near-fore knee and was still intermittently lame, but in spite of this concern and despite carrying 9st 1lb and conceding 7-14lb to his 19 opponents in desperately heavy conditions, he was sent off 5/1 favourite. It proved a bridge too far. Spindrifter ran his solitary bad race of the 19, never travelling well and finishing 12th. 'It is better to have loved and lost...' Sir Mark told reporters, before adding with reference to one of the season's star juvenile performers, 'I wouldn't have swapped him for Shergar.'

Spindrifter's 13 victories had amassed the huge sum of – wait for it – £21,407.20!! Shergar's eventual Derby victory alone was worth over ten-times as much. Those wins came at six different tracks: Catterick (five), Pontefract (two – one of them subsequently renamed in his honour), Hamilton (two), Redcar (two) and Thirsk and Leicester (one apiece); at five furlongs (four), six furlongs (six) and seven furlongs (three); and on ground ranging from hard (once), firm (twice) and good-firm (three) to good (five) and dead (twice). *Pacemaker* magazine recognised Spindrifter's accomplishments by voting him a 'Special Award' in its seasonal roll of honour.

With Spindrifter having enjoyed such a flying start to his career, and with the record-chasing bit firmly between his own teeth, Sir

Mark viewed the 1981 season as merely the next step on the road to matching Le Garcon d'Or's 20th century all-aged career record of 34. After I'd ridden Spindrifter to be third in a valuable handicap at York on 14 May, Elain Mellor took over to win an amateur riders' race on him up at Hamilton the following month in preparation for his first main target of the year, the 'Diamond' race at Ascot on 25 July.

On Saturday, 11 July, a fortnight before Ascot, Spindrifter was about to set off up the Peat Moss gallop on Racecourse Side when his galloping companion, the five-year-old Carpet General, backed into him, lashed out and smashed his off-fore above the knee. Nothing could be done for him and he had to be put down on the spot. I was due to race at Chester that afternoon and was still in my room at the Grosvenor Hotel when Sir Mark phoned to give me the news. I was completely and utterly devastated. For the gods to treat a horse like Spindrifter in so cruel a fashion was so unfair. He didn't deserve a fate like that. Carpet General, incidentally, who had won the 1980 William Hill Gold Cup at Redcar before he came to us upon Tim Molony's retirement from training, failed to win a race for Heath House in six tries that season.

Before leaving the subject of Spindrifter it would be rather remiss of me if I did not champion his juvenile achievements in 1980 as exceeding Nagwa's in 1975. She never reeled off ten in a row – which no horse of any age has done since – and she needed 20 races to reach 13 whereas he got there in 17. Furthermore, it's fair to say Nagwa showed form far superior to Spindrifter – who was hammered when he met decent animals like Tina's Pet and Sula Bula – which actually made his victories all the harder to accumulate. For instance, Nagwa was rated 115 by Timeform, which is up to Pattern-winning standard, and received 8st 5lb in the Free Handicap, 12lb or 16lb respectively below the top juvenile, Wollow; Spindrifter, on the other hand, was rated only 102 and allocated 7st 11 lb, which placed him 32lb or 24lb respectively behind Storm Bird and nowhere near good enough to make a mark in Pattern-race company. As Tina's Pet and Sula Bula had demonstrated so crushingly, any good horses Spindrifter met had to have an off day if he was to get anywhere near beating them. Spindrifter also possessed the resilience to come back and win the following season as a three-year-old – something neither of the Bill O'Gorman pair of Provideo (rated 112 by Timeform in 1984) and Timeless Times (rated 99 in 1990) could manage once they had extended the 20th century record to 16 wins (equalling The Bard's all-time best of 1885).

Even with the passage of 20 years, Sir Mark's handling of Spindrifter remains right up there among his finest feats of training. He paid Spindrifter the following tribute: 'He made training as easy as kissing your hand. His achievement is that he had neither a zingy personality nor tons of ability but compensated for this with the most superb temperament and all the perseverance, toughness and courage in the world. He had all the rare qualities one would wish for in man or beast. I shall never have his like again.'

Sir Mark had a stone tablet in memory of Spindrifter added to the wall at Heath House on which are recorded the names of all the Classic winners and big-race winners that the yard has sent out since the Dawson days.

In my view, the legend at the bottom of the plaque might be applied to both the horse and his trainer: 'A True Professional.'

10

CHASING THE SUN

Before the advent of racing on the all-weather surfaces, I could invariably be found during the depths of the English winter – in company with a lot of British jockeys – chasing some income and some sun at one and the same time by plying my trade in warmer climes. This was especially so during the 1970s. Although I never returned to Jamaica after my third stint in 1972, I enjoyed – for want of a better word – two spells in India (1973-74 and 1974-75) and one in South Africa (1976-77). I can't say that either India or South Africa was a total success from the riding viewpoint or even a pleasurable experience as a whole, but they were experiences all the same. On the other hand, my trips to Trinidad, which commenced in the winter of 1979-80, proved extremely successful and very enjoyable.

India was a place I did not like. The job I took was for the owner LC Gupta, whose horses were based in Calcutta and trained by Bren Duffy. The Royal Calcutta Turf Club is one of India's four principal racing centres, the others being the Royal Western Turf

Club in Bombay, the Bangalore Turf Club and the Madras Racing Club. Owing to recent civil unrest in Calcutta, the horse population had declined to around 300, which was half that in Madras and Bombay, where the Indian Derby and Oaks are run. Loads of English jocks, like Eric Eldin, Bruce Raymond and Wally Swinburn (Walter's dad) rode out there before me, and the job came to me through Ernie Johnson, whom I'd been friends with for years. Ernie had been offered the job for the whole winter of 1973-74 but he didn't want to do the full period, preferring to come home at Christmas. He asked me if I'd go over and finish the stint for him when he came back to England. I agreed.

I flew out to Calcutta in November on my own. Our son Nicky had been born in January, so he and Gill stayed in England, back in Moulton. I was to live in the lap of luxury, first of all in the International Hotel, where the pilots and airline staff all seemed to stay, and then later on at the Grand, which is used by the England cricket team when it plays in Calcutta. Both hotels were faultless. But once you went outside it was a different proposition altogether. The contrast was amazing. Everywhere was filthy and the poverty was unbelievable. I just couldn't cope with it. And, of course, once you passed through the gates of the Royal Calcutta Turf Club, at The Maidan, it was like stepping back into another country where everything was clean and spotless, with bright, white buildings dazzling against the bright green grass.

The track I rode most of the time – right-handed and grass – was referred to as the 'monsoon track' and was laid out on the inside of the main grass track and raised several feet above it so that, when those monsoon rains fell, the water would drain away within half an hour or so. I managed to ride a few good winners, including the Calcutta Oaks on Goldfinder trained by Captain Fownes – which was particularly sweet because we beat Ernie aboard the favourite, Mr Gupta's Rose Blossom – and another valuable event on an animal called Midnight Cowboy (by the former smart English handicapper Young Lochinvar), probably the best horse I had anything to do with out there. He later went on to win one of the country's most prestigious races, the Indian Turf Invititation Cup, a race for four-year-olds which is hosted in turn by each of India's four major venues.

Ernie came home as planned at Christmas and my sense of isolation was made worse when I took a very bad fall. I'd ridden this colt work for Bren Duffy and it hadn't felt quite right to me. In quicker work the horse seemed to get the 'wobbles'. I told Bren, 'You do know this thing is going to collapse, don't you? You don't want to be running this.' He nodded, but wasn't taking a blind bit of notice of me because I soon saw it was entered up for the following Saturday. Lo and behold the horse wobbled again in its next piece of work! I jumped off it and said to Bren, 'I don't want to ride this on Saturday. It's going to break down and fall over!' Again he nodded. 'OK'.

Come Saturday, I look at the racecard and find my name next to this death-trap of an animal. So I go off in search of Bren Duffy. 'I said I didn't want to ride it, and you said you weren't going to run it!' Naturally, nothing can be done about it at this late stage. I have to go out and ride it.

The horse was a lovely, big, good-looking bay who had not run for some months. We were led into the stalls and as we're sat there I turned to the jockey in the next box and said: 'For your own sake, don't follow this horse. This horse is going to fall over. I'm not even going to give it a ride. I'll jump out, keep hold of its head and not even push it.'

Well, we hadn't gone 50 yards when this horse breaks its shoulder, collapses and slithers along the ground. I come off it, and before I know it, there I am sat up on my arse with my legs wide apart, sliding toward some concrete posts at the side of the track.

I'm thinking: 'Fucking hell! This is going to cut me clean in half!' Just as I'm about to hit this concrete upright groin first, I turn and it catches me across my calf and the edge of my shinbone instead.

That's the last thing I can remember until I woke up in the weighing room, or, as it seemed to me, cloud-cuckoo land since I was only semi conscious. There's no sign of Bren Duffy or the owners of the horse, who happened to be two stewards of the Turf Club. I'm whisked off to the private hospital that served the track and left in a big room on my own. I can barely walk. My calf muscle had taken the brunt of the collision and bled internally. I even had to drag myself across the floor, crawling, in order to reach the toilet on the other side of the room.

Eventually Bren Duffy appears and begins to grovel. 'I'd have put someone else on it, George, if I thought you'd meant it.' That was enough for me in this state. Light the blue touch paper! 'You didn't fucking care who you killed, then?' I shouted. 'I knew and you knew what would happen! And you're telling me you'd have sacrificed some poor fucker who didn't even know, someone who'd have been severe on it and caused even more of a problem! You didn't even have the decency to come and see me straight after the accident! Fuck off out of my sight!'

I was out for three weeks. There was to be an eerie postscript. I'd rung Ernie in England and told him to keep news of the incident from Gill, and when I eventually told her about it she said that she had actually dreamed I'd had a bad fall the very night it happened. The precise moment I fell halfway across the world in Calcutta, she'd been in bed dreaming about it back home in our bungalow in Moulton.

The following winter I went back to Calcutta to ride for LC Gupta once more, but this time I had Gill and Nick along with me. The riding wasn't too bad. I was associated with some half-decent horses. But the stay got off on the wrong foot because we were booked into a mediocre place that I refused to accept, and matters went rapidly downhill thereafter. Our accommodation was so, so dilapidated and the food was inedible. I'd been quite ill the previous year and had learned the hard way what to eat and what not to eat. It was finally agreed that we could either send out for food or go to a restaurant of our choosing. I tried to guide Gill through the food maze but, needless to say, something soon disagreed with her and she became extremely ill. It was coming out of every orifice, every day and all day, to such an extent that she became near enough bed-ridden toward the end. And though we were unaware of the fact, Gill was also pregnant with our second child (Nathalie was born in June), which obviously didn't help matters. I called in an English doctor and he told me to take her home. Mr Gupta was not amused. 'You can't leave,' he said. 'Mr Gupta,' I replied, 'my wife is more important than your job and I've been advised to go, so I'm leaving for England on Tuesday if I can get a flight.'

I managed to book the three of us onto a flight but Gupta wasn't done with. He set out to make life difficult. He knew all the right people and had connections in Customs. Everyone, including Gill and Nick, was ushered through onto the plane as per usual – except me! All my bags were kept behind and every one of them was tipped upside down and searched. There I am, trapped in Customs for what seems like an eternity and I'm starting to panic. But I couldn't afford to lose my temper or else I'd definitely be going nowhere. To my huge relief, they eventually allowed me through and I joined Gill and Nick on the plane. I took one last glance out of the window as we took off and thanked my lucky stars that I wasn't still down there on the ground. I couldn't wait to get home. I'd had enough of the place. I've never been back.

Having been west and east in search of sun and money, I suppose it was only fair to head south when the opportunity presented itself to spend three months in South Africa during the winter of 1976-77.

Brian Taylor was the contact on this occasion, but the trainer involved was a familiar face because James Goodman had once been pupil-assistant to Sir Mark Prescott at Heath House. James didn't last long! Tall, freckled and curly-haired, James was not the most industrious of assistants – he was forever wandering round Heath House with a transistor radio clamped to his ear – and was thus soon on a collision course with his boss. One day Sir Mark went to shake him after some indiscretion or another, but he was so much shorter than James that he was forced to abort the attempt and settled for whacking him instead!

James, who'd held a licence barely 18 months, was based in Johannesburg and for the first month, until Gill, Nick and Nathalie came out, I stayed with him in his flat. After Gill, Nick (now coming up four) and Nathalie (18 months) arrived, the three of us moved into a house complete with garden. Apartheid seemed to pass us by. We did have a black maid, but we saw nothing of the townships and the regime's restrictions or evidence of the hostility and animosity they created. South Africa struck me as a wonderful country, so that I could probably begin to understand why the whites and blacks were fighting over it.

Unfortunately, South Africa proved another salutary experience. James was very helpful and made us exceptionally welcome. He was in the minority. The warning signals were flashing from the outset when the local jockeys organised a petition citing numerous reasons why, in their opinion, I shouldn't be granted a licence. Now, very few British jockeys rode in South Africa outside of the big international race at Pietermaritzburg or the occasional invitational riders' competition, and I certainly wasn't expecting any favours out on the track, but this was something else altogether. That's not how we'd greeted Michael Roberts, their champion jockey, when he rode in the UK for the first time in 1978, for instance, or when America's Gary Stevens rode briefly for Sir Michael Stoute in

1999. In fact, these Jo'burg jockeys were no keener to welcome Michael Roberts onto their patch. Although Michael flew all over South Africa because he was so much in demand, he was essentially a Natal-based rider, and whenever he was due to come up to any of the four Johannesburg tracks – Turffontein, Germiston, Vaal and Newmarket – for a Cup race or a Guineas, you'd see the local boys huddling in a corner of the weighing room and hear them plotting what they were going to do to him in the race. I'd listen to all this and think to myself 'No wonder you can't get on with them if they're prepared to treat one of their own like that.'

The petition failed but the message was crystal clear. I might as well have had leprosy. I was snubbed at every meeting. I couldn't ever manage to communicate with them. The only South African jockey who'd talk to me was one up from the Cape, which ensured he was on the receiving end of the same frosty treatment as me. The trainers were little better. James's horses were not up to much so I tried to get as many outside rides as possible. I rode work for trainers and I'd say 'This'll win' and they'd say 'I'll get you the ride' – but come race-day some local jockey would be on board. 'The owner specifically wanted him', they'd tell me apologetically; yet when I'd ask the owner what had happened, he'd say 'The trainer wanted him.' Basically, they just wanted to pick my brains. This happened three times with one trainer in particular; when he asked me to ride work a fourth time I'm afraid I did nothing to further Anglo-South African relations because I told him to go forth and multiply.

This kind of attitude made me determined to ride a winner before my three months were up. Where it could possibly come from was another matter. Two months passed without the glimmer of a winner and available meetings – I only rode on the four Rand tracks – were becoming fewer and fewer. On 5 January, 1977, James had a four-year-old chestnut filly called Manterville (which he also owned) entered in a lowly D Division Handicap over 2000 metres (10 furlongs) at Newmarket. Not that I knew it at the time, but James fancied her chances and had approached James Maree, one of the local king-pins, with a view to him taking the mount. Maree declined, not surprisingly since he was also offered the ride on Blond Sky, a three-year-old that seemed sure to start a raging odds-on favourite.

Blond Sky (10/9 on) was drawn in the next stall to Manterville (a 20/1 shot at the off) and Maree leant across to enquire how I intended to ride my race. 'I'll drop her out,' I replied, 'she's no bloody good,' fully intending to do exactly the opposite. Once the gates opened, I went flat out and by the bottom bend had stolen ten lengths on the rest of the field. I kicked again after we'd straightened up and although Maree came at me on the favourite as anticipated and was chopping us down with every stride, Manterville lasted home by half a length.

Maree was none too happy – he did have a reputation for being a bit of a shrewd character who tended to 'organise' some of these races. I gather he now owns a nice spread near Johannesburg where he trains and runs a Jockey Club endorsed development programme for the 'disadvantaged'. Basically, he takes grooms, mostly blacks, and teaches them how to race-ride and filters them through the system as apprentices. Good for him.

So, much to my relief, and immense personal satisfaction, I salvaged a bit of professional pride before I left South Africa because to come away without one single winner would have been a nasty blow to my ego. I had made my mark. James Goodman later trained a horse called Duffield!

Riding in Trinidad proved an altogether more pleasurable experience. I've now ridden there during five separate winters to some degree or another and thoroughly enjoyed myself, both on and off the track. From 88 rides I've had 18 winners, including the Group

I Clico Stewards Cup on Sweet Tassa in 1992, the Group II St James Stakes on Fresh Prince in 1995 and a five-timer on Boxing Day 1994.

When I first visited the island in the 1979-80 season there were three racetracks: Queen's Park Savannah in the capital Port of Spain, Union Park at Marbella in the south, and the old Santa Rosa Park. I was based at Union Park to begin with, but by the time I returned for my third stint, in December 1994, Trinidad's racing administrators had decided to put all their eggs in one basket by centralising all racing at Santa Rosa. This was a sad occasion for the locals who mourned the passing of the Savannah, or the 'Big Yard' as they termed it, which had always acted as the mecca for horseracing in this part of the world. However, what with planning restrictions, its urban site couldn't accommodate the authority's ambitious plans for a 500-strong equine population and the laying of a 1700-metre left-handed dirt track on the outside of a 1500-metre turf track. Thus Santa Rosa, which is only 30 minutes out of Port of Spain and just five minutes from Piarco International airport, was refurbished at a cost of TT$25 million (£3 million) and reopened for racing in February 1994 a month after the 'Big Yard' closed its doors for the last time. Santa Rosa is a great track to ride and the racing is well controlled. Before the first race of the day, for example, every jockey must report to the clerk of the scales, sign against his name and select a numbered ball which, if it's drawn out of the hat, wins him the random dope test.

I'd been invited to Trinidad by a Chinese Trinidadian called Sunny Ackam, and after spending a few days in Miami with Bobby Hale (geared toward taking Gill and the kids to Disneyland), I reported for duty refreshed and eager to get on with the job. Unfortunately, this initial spell wasn't quite so successful as it should have been. Sunny's horses proved pretty slow but as they were mostly owned by his friends I was obliged to ride them instead of accepting the offers of better outside rides. I was in no position to complain because Sunny was picking up all the bills. As Trinidad only raced on Saturdays and public holidays, like Boxing Day and New Year's Day, I was never going to ride many winners and three was all I managed that first year.

I became pally with a trainer called Ian Gordon who used to drink as if it was going out of fashion! You'd never see Ian without his three bottles of beer – one in each pocket and one in his hand. He was a great guy and I loved him to death. Ian had no love for Bill Marshall, the former Whitsbury trainer now based in Barbados and who tended to rule the roost hereabouts. Ian Gordon was ecstatic when I chose to partner a two-year-old of his instead of the Marshall second string during an England v America v Barbados competition held that year in Barbados and proceeded to pip Bill's gamble of the race by a short head.

I must say, though, that the people of Trinidad were, and are, wonderful. People like Christian Maingott and his wife, whom we met through Ian Gordon, can't do enough for you, and in this regard are so unlike either the Jamaicans or the Bajans. I don't know whether this friendliness is because the Trinidadians are mostly of Asian origin or not, but their values and attitudes are completely different, say, to the Jamaicans who can be quite volatile. There was never anything vindictive or nasty about Trinidad, although we did have one narrow squeak.

We were staying one year in a hotel near the old Savannah and it was round about Carnival time. We were warned not to go 'downtown' because a few American tourists had been mugged and wallets and purses stolen. Tony Ives had been riding in Barbados, and he popped over, bringing his dad, John, with him. Foolishly, one day John and me decided to take a chance and go for a walk, accompanied by Gill, Nick and Nathalie. The first stretch, near the hotel, was uneventful but as we turned down toward Queen's Street and the hustle and bustle of the old town, I noticed this guy watching us. Then he began following us. If we stopped, he stopped. So I was positive he was following us. I told Gill and John and they said 'No. Don't be crazy! You're just imagining it.' I wasn't so sure. 'Let's see,' I said. 'Let's go into the next shop we come to and see what he does.'

We go into this bookshop, duck behind the bookshelves and wait to see what 'yer man' does. Lo and behold, his face pokes round the door. 'You're right, George,' John says, 'he's definitely following us. He's definitely up to no good.' Well, this guy is standing outside the doorway of the shop, trying to look all nonchalant but obviously waiting for us to emerge, so I just walk out and thump him straight in the guts. As if by magic a crowd suddenly gathered. I thought, 'What have I started here! We're going to be in serious trouble!', but luckily this mob quickly dispersed and the guy went his own way. I think the dig in the ribs frightened him more than his presence was frightening us.

My second spell in Trinidad came fully 12 years after the first, and then only as a bit of an afterthought. In 1992 the Trinidad and Tobago Turf Club invited me to ride at the Savannah, along with Julie Krone from the States and Sandy Hawley from Canada. But I'd had a long, busy season, what with User Friendly and chasing my first century of winners, and when the offer came I'd only just forfeited one week of the three-week holiday I'd booked in St Lucia owing to User Friendly's proposed participation in the Japan Cup. So I passed the invite over to Kevin Darley. Well, Kevin must have got lonely or something because he ended up asking for company and I eventually joined him.

I'm very glad I relented because the decision enabled me to win the big Group I 1200 metres (six furlongs) sprint, the Clico Stewards Cup, on the filly Sweet Tassa, owned by wealthy businessman Nasser Hamed and trained by leading Trinidadian handler Colt Durrant. This little bay by Forzando had been trained in Newmarket by Chris Wall but had never won a race in eight tries. We beat Julie Krone on Durrant's other runner by half a length. It certainly was a profitable stay. I also finished third on That Mass Dancer in the Group I Gold Cup (which I'd confidently expected to win) and went home having earned over TT$83,000 from my four victories and six places out of 20 rides. Even when I got off a favourite to let Kevin win a race I still beat him! No wonder we were upgraded to first class on the flight back to England!

The highlight of my third trip to Trinidad was the five-timer (from just the six rides) at Santa Rosa on Boxing Day, 1994. I'd already scored one West Indian five-timer back at Caymanas Park in 1969-70 but that quintet came from eight rides (the other three finished second!), and although the horses may mean nothing this side of the Atlantic the names Time For A Trick, So Melody, Key Witness, Windy Dancer and Star Recruit mean a lot to me. It was a fantastic day – I've never done better than five out of six – and it sparked an association with Nasser Hamed that brought me back for each of the next two winters.

Neither India nor South Africa nor Trinidad can lay claim to a place in the premier league of world racing nations. Of the major non-European countries, I have ridden in the United States, Japan and Hong Kong but never Australia. My American experience is limited to one mount at the Breeders' Cup – and that was hardly auspicious. Missed Flight hated firm ground, which was precisely what awaited him at Churchill Downs for the Mile in 1994 and running last of the 14 behind Frankie Dettori aboard Barathea was virtually assured from the moment we left the gate. They'd gone by the time he'd even thought about running. Mind you, Missed Flight's thoughts had been elsewhere throughout the whole week at Churchill Downs. Every single morning was the same. He'd turn very, very 'colty' with the lead ponies that are always employed on

American tracks and, to put it bluntly, wanted to shag everything in sight, which was not like him at all. As soon as he spotted a lead pony he'd get his cock out and start hollering! On the day itself, I declined a pony to the start to ensure he didn't disgrace himself on worldwide TV.

My taste of racing in Japan and Hong Kong is likewise minimal but was still enough to bequeath both an indelible and favourable impression. In late November 1992 I accompanied User Friendly to Fuchu, in Tokyo, for the Japan Cup. The set-up was fantastic – tunnels taking the horses along non-slip floors from the compound to the course with different exits for the different tracks – and the technology positively unreal. Promotion was first-rate and the money was phenomenally serious.

Back in the 1980s I had turned down a job riding for the Royal Hong Kong Jockey Club: the offer came at the wrong time in the sense that after riding moderate horses for so long some quality ones were at last starting to appear. Financially I'd have been far better off, but there you are. So, years later, in the Sprint at the high-profile invitation meeting at Sha Tin on 17 December 2000, Perryston View constituted my first and only Hong Kong experience. It was a perfect example of one of those fortuitous last-minute bookings that every now and again falls straight into your lap. I had won a race on Perryston View, a handicap at Doncaster toward the back-end of 1999 when he was trained by Peter Calver at Ripon, but once the horse had transferred to Jeremy Glover for the 2000 season after Peter's retirement, it was John Reid who partnered him to his most prestigious success in the Group II Temple Stakes at Sandown Park. Anyway, Kevin Darley was meant to be riding the eight-year-old in Hong Kong, because he was already out there for an international jockeys' competition, but, for whatever reason, he decided to come home. As Jeremy was mulling over who to approach, who does he bump into at a Hunt Ball but yours truly. I'd not been riding for two or three weeks, but I didn't need asking twice whether I fancied an all-expenses-paid trip to Hong Kong in the middle of the English winter! A few rides on the all-weather soon got me back in trim for the job, but the task was far beyond Perryston View's capabilities and he finished well behind the Australian sprinter Falvelon.

However, Hong Kong was tremendous and, when all is said and done, that's all a jockey can really expect when he goes chasing the sun.

11

LESTER TAKES A PUNCH

I absolutely adore being in the weighing room. Sir Mark Prescott thinks we jockeys behave like a bunch of silly schoolgirls at a hockey match. We probably do. But I love it all the same, I really do. Put me in an office and I'd be in prison.

I'm 55 and still doing all manner of stupid things. I've got the mentality of a kid which is probably one of the reasons I'm still riding today. I love messing around. Tony Clark and me are desperate. We love nothing better than making shit sandwiches for the kids – made of salt, pepper, cigarette butts – and derive great pleasure from feeding it to some poor unsuspecting soul.

Craig Williams, the little Aussie who rode over here for Mick Channon, was a particular target of mine. 'Skippy' used to love his sandwich and coke. I doctored a sandwich for him at Newmarket and stood back, waiting for him to take a bite. The minutes ticked by and he'd still not risen to the bait. I'm like a cat on hot bricks. Finally, he bites into this shit sandwich – and his expression doesn't change at all! He can't have any taste buds, is the only explanation

I could think of. Not even a blink. He has a second nibble. Then he slowly lifts the top slice of bread to examine the contents of the sandwich – before dropping it in horror! Another day at York, I put so much salt in his pint of coke that it fizzed and frothed like a bath of acid! He hid my underpants in return for that one!

Clarky and me are shameless. We'll cut the feet out of socks, tie knots in shirtsleeves, cut ties in half, put lead weights in bags, all kinds of puerile things. It's like being back at school, but that's why we're all jockeys, I suppose, because we're all kids at heart. Jockeys never grow up. Most people think of us as adult kids. We're small, fit and active. We're silly little schoolboys who actually do professional jobs. You can't believe how much fun we have in the weighing room and I love each and every minute of it!

Prankster in chief is Philip Robinson. One day at Yarmouth, Philip and me tried to superglue Michael Roberts to the floor. But we couldn't get him to stand long enough on the spot where we'd placed the glue, could we! Philip used to drive Michael Roberts demented at one stage. He'd put itching powder in his underpants or inside his shirt, cut his tie in half, pour water in his shoes. Philip was a complete bollocks. I'd have hit him but Michael Roberts is not the kind of guy to bear a grudge. He's full of fun himself and would enjoy a laugh and a joke with the best, but for some reason he brought out the worst in Robbo. He just loved annoying Michael and because he knew he was annoying Michael that only made him worse.

Robbo is a practical joker, full stop. A right pain in the arse. He once told us what he did to a Doug Missen, a bloke who was going out with his mother. Apparently Doug had a bad habit of nicking all the chocolate, so whenever Robbo fancied some it had all disappeared. Robbo is not one for any half measures. He drilled a hole in this chocolate bar, filled it with laxatives and neatly covered the hole back over with chocolate. Meanwhile, he covered the toilet seat with cling film and removed the bathroom light bulb.

Robbo's sitting there chatting to this guy, struggling to keep a straight face, as he waits for these laxatives to kick in after 20 minutes or so. Of course, he's given the guy way over the prescribed dosage. The rumbling eventually starts up like Mount Vesuvius. 'If you don't feel very well you'd better go to the toilet,' says Robbo reassuringly, 'you might mess your pants or something.' Off the guy rushes, followed at a discreet interval by Robbo who wants to overhear what happens. There's a gigantic 'sploosh' closely followed by a scream of 'Robbo, I'm going to fucking kill you!'

You'll no doubt be pleased to hear that occasionally the biter himself has been bitten. Sir Mark Prescott once rang Robbo to ask him about his views on field sports: he'd already rung me and the two Hills boys. Well, it was getting late when Sir Mark called and Robbo was in bed.

'Hello Philip, Sir Mark Prescott here.'

Robbo automatically thinks, 'No it isn't! It's fucking Duffield trying to wind me up!'

'Philip, I'm conducting a survey on field sports, and I know you do a bit of shooting and hunting. Could I have your views on the subject?'

'Well,' says Robbo, 'what I really like is being in the middle of a field with my missus, giving her a good shagging with a cow licking my arse!'

The phone goes dead.

Robbo dials my number. 'You fucking twat, fucking field sports!'

'What?'

'Fucking field sports, ringing me up at this time of night!'

'It wasn't me, it was Sir Mark. He's been ringing up everybody about it. Ring the Hills twins, they'll tell you.'

'Oh, bollocks! What am I gonna do?'

'Ring Sir Mark and apologise, he'll understand.'

'Not fucking likely!'

I don't think Robbo got a ride off Sir Mark for years after that little incident!

Someone else who can have us in stitches besides Robbo is Allan Mackay. One last day of the season at Doncaster, before all-weather racing kept us together during the winter, Allan Mackay decides to give us a memorable send-off. The final race on the card was a 20-runner one-and-quarter mile handicap, which started the far side of Rose Hill, where there are two or three smart-looking bungalows on the outside of the track. As we jump out of the stalls and go over the rise, we hear this 'Hey! Hey!' coming from near one of the gardens – and it's only Allan Mackay pretending to make love to this blow-up doll! How none of us didn't fall off, I'll never know because we're howling with laughter. Of course, we didn't see Allan for four months after that until the spring meeting. Everyone starts telling him how funny they thought it was, and he says: 'You're not going to believe this, but I got arrested!'

Lindsay Charnock, on the other hand, drove people crazy with his piss-taking instead of resorting to pranks or slapstick. Lindsay's preferred victim was Pat Eddery – no mean piss-taker himself – but his favourite pastime of all was to read out aloud the latest statistics in the paper to embarrass whoever was on the longest losing streak, usually some kid, though, top or bottom of the scale, it didn't matter to Lindsay. Then he'd wander over to his prey – whose confidence must be rock-bottom – and say: 'A hundred rides without a win, you know – could be 102 after today!' That's the last thing anyone wants to be reminded of. Then after the race Lindsay would go back and say: '101!' Mind you, if Lindsay ever went even ten or 12 without a win these kids would be on his back in the same vein!

Mark Birch was another great chum of mine. I often used to lodge with him, near Malton, when I was riding in the North in the old

LESTER TAKES A PUNCH

days. I'll never forget following him into the paddock at Redcar the day he had a big picture of Phil Bull pinned on his back in honour of being jocked-off one of Bull's horses. We were falling about laughing! He certainly got his own back on me when we stayed overnight at the four-star Gosforth Park Hotel in Newcastle. We bet each other who could race from our room down the corridor to the ice-making machine and back the fastest – with no clothes on! I got there first, so Birchy slams the lid down on my hand which enables him to beat me back to our door by a stride, just enough to get back inside and lock the door with me standing outside as stark bollock-naked as the day I was born. At that moment the lift doors opened to reveal two old ladies. With no place to hide, I held my hands in the appropriate position but couldn't think of anything better to say than 'Good evening, ladies.' They said 'Good evening' back and walked on – while all I could hear was Mark killing himself laughing on the other side of the door.

I could have killed Birchy myself one day at Redcar in 1978. I had the choice of two mounts in one of the track's big handicaps, the William Hill Gold Cup, and picked Ryan Price's Carriage Way, leaving Mark to ride Running Jump for Bill Watts. Mine was a lazy sod and Ryan Price left me in no doubt that I'd have to set about this horse to get the most out of him. So what does Birchy do in the race as I come to pass him and win the race? He deliberately knocks the whip out of my hands, doesn't he? My horse won't go without the whip and Birch's – which I could have ridden – gets back up and wins by a neck. I chased him halfway round the track after that escapade.

Although Pat Eddery has not changed from day one in spite of all his success, Willie Carson did undergo a change of character. I've known Willie since I arrived in Newmarket as a kid. The first time I met him was on Ely station when I was going home on holiday and he was travelling up to Lanark. I got on well with Willie. There were nights when I bathed his kids, Tony, Neil and Ross, and he held some serious card schools at his house in Newmarket involving me, Paul Tulk, Eric Eldin, Taffy Thomas and 'Kipper' Lynch. As he became more successful we drifted apart. Unlike Pat, he got to be hard to communicate with and you'd struggle to have a conversation with him in the weighing room. As jockeys go, you'd be hard-pressed to find one better. He developed into a helluva jockey, a serious jockey and one of the best, but as a human being he became prickly and, at times, very arrogant. Whether this change had anything to do with getting the job at Dick Hern's, I don't know. All I can say, is that I found Major Hern and John Dunlop – who Willie rode for a lot – two of the easiest men to ride for alongside Sir Mark Prescott. They were both gentlemen and a pleasure to ride for.

The weighing room acts as our sanctuary. We all feel safe in there and can be ourselves. Kieren Fallon, for example, has this dour image but he's far more himself in the weighing room where he feels more secure and he is perfectly adept at having a giggle. If we were to be honest with ourselves, everyone in the weighing room was shocked when he got the Henry Cecil job for 1997. Not that he wasn't capable of doing it, mind, just that he got it. We thought the job would go to Pat Eddery, who'd been riding quite a few of Henry's, like Bosra Sham and Lady Carla to win Classics during 1996. I suppose they wanted someone younger than Pat who could offer longevity. Kieren's exceptionally strong and horses do run for him, which is what being a jockey is all about – making horses run better for you than they do for someone else. Even so, none of us would have nominated Kieren. He was always a fiery so-and-so before the now infamous incident at Beverley in 1994 when he pulled Stuart Webster off his horse and then smacked him in the weighing room – punished by a six-month ban. This was a case of an ongoing feud coming to a head because there had been bad blood between them for some years. Kieren has learnt to control his wicked temper since getting the Cecil job and then the post with Sir Michael Stoute, but there were always plenty of people waiting in the wings equipped with knives to stab him in the back or with swords to cut him down to size. But he proved them all wrong. And, oh, was he Mrs Cecil's 'the man in the shower'? I honestly don't know!

I wasn't present at Beverley to see Kieren bloody Stuart Webster's nose but down the years I have enjoyed a ringside seat for the odd bout of fisticuffs in the weighing room. They are never that serious, merely spur-of-the-moment affairs, a quick slap or a punch. The first man I came across who wouldn't take any messing about was Eric Eldin. Regardless of who you were, he was a man to dish it out. But the real tough guy was Geoff Baxter.

Geoff was a decent jockey who had loads of success, firstly with Arthur Budgett on the likes of old Prominent, and later with Bruce Hobbs, for whom he won his Group I on Count Pahlen in the 1981 William Hill Futurity (the forerunner of the Racing Post Trophy) and he excelled on the Group-winning fillies Vielle and Acclimatise who both finished second in the Oaks: he also collected two Group sprints for Doug Marks on Singing Bede. But the one thing Geoff could really do was fight. He could handle himself, could Geoff. I saw him floor Colin Moss one day at Leicester, and watched him flatten an apprentice who was giving him plenty of mouth at Warwick. 'Do yourself a favour and shut up!' Geoff had warned him. When the kid took no notice, Geoff dragged him into the toilets and laid him out with one punch. 'Now fucking shut up!' he said. You did not fuck around with Geoff. If he hit you, you knew you'd been fucking hit! Geoff never backed down. It didn't matter who you were. Ask Lester. I was there the day Geoff poleaxed him.

The venue was Newmarket. As we were all cantering down to the start of this race, I could see Geoff's mount was giving him trouble as it came past me – fly-lepping and what-not – and so he tried to run it up behind Lester's horse to stop it. This animal clattered into the back of Lester's and, as Geoff goes by, Lester turns in the saddle and thumps him right in the chops. Had he realised the identity of his victim, Lester may have held his temper! As it was, you can imagine the force of the impact at that speed. Once the pair of them reached the gate there was a bit of a set-to. Lester jumped off and, foolishly perhaps, challenged Geoff to get down and sort it out there and then. Lester might have scaled a good 7lb heavier than Geoff at any weigh-in and possessed a longer reach, but there was only going to be one winner in this contest – and it wasn't going to require any decision from the judges! Geoff looked down at Lester and said ever so quietly: 'Not now. When we get back to the weighing room I'm going to fucking hammer you. Then we'll sort it out.'

True to his word, Geoff strode purposefully into the weighing room, put his saddle down, took off his colours, marched over to Lester – and wacked him, sitting Lester right on his arse. Lester went to get up and Geoff said: 'If you get up, I'll kill you! And if you want to go into the car park and finish it off, that's fine by me.' In his infinite wisdom, Lester declined Geoff's kind offer!

As Lester was a law unto himself, there was many an occasion when he stepped over the mark and might have got himself a right-hander off someone – me included. During a hot spell one summer I'd made things worse one afternoon at Newmarket's July Course by sweating to make a light ride – two or three pounds below my normal – and so I'd got myself a lovely iced glass of lime-and-lemonade that I could drink immediately afterwards to put back the liquid I'd lost through dehydration. Before I went out to ride, I placed this nectar under my seat. I came back to find the glass virtually empty, just a tiny drop in the bottom. 'Who's had my lime-and-lemonade?' I ask the valet. 'Dunno,' he replies. 'You must have seen who picked it up – you're in here all the time!' Still the valet shook his head. 'Come on,' I continued, 'who was it? Tell me!' Finally, he muttered: 'It was Lester.'

'Oi, you!' I shout at Lester, 'did you drink my lime-and-lemonade?'

'Nah, nah, not me.'

'Yes you did. The valet saw you drink it!'

'Nah, nah. It wasn't me.'

'All right, all right! I know it was you.'

I waited until Lester went out to ride. I knew he loved chocolate, especially Mars Bars, for the glucose and what-have-you. I felt in his jacket pockets and, sure enough, there's his Mars Bar. I thought, 'Right, you bastard!' I took the Mars Bar, ate two-thirds of it, wrapped up the rest and put it back in Lester's jacket. I couldn't wait to see him go for his own personal reviver at the end of the afternoon.

'Eh! What the hell's this! Who's eaten my Mars Bar?'

'Me – snap!'

'Eh, you little fucker!'

You may be surprised to learn that in spite of my temper I've neither given nor received a punch in the weighing room. The only person I can recall smacking – apart from Mr Savill – was a lad of Sir Mark's named, I think, Steven. He was yanking this filly's head around one morning, wouldn't leave her alone and was basically annoying her to death when it wasn't doing anything wrong. I said to him: 'Leave it alone, will you!' and he called back 'You can fuck off, you!' I couldn't believe my ears. 'What did you say?' So he shouts: 'Fuck off! Mind your own fucking business!' The red mists descended then. 'Right,' I said, 'when we get in you're going to get it. I'll clip your fucking earole for you!'

I put my horse in its box and ran to his box but he'd already got the tack off and was down in the saddle room. I walked in and smacked him right in the chops. Well, back in Osborne House, Mrs Jay spots his black eye and demands that he tells her where he's got it from, but he doesn't let on why he got it. She frogmarches him over to Sir Mark and says, 'Look what George has done to Steven.' Of course, Sir Mark wants to know why I hit this lad. 'Because I told him to fuck off, Sir.' And why did you tell George to fuck off? 'Because I was pulling this filly about and he told me to stop, Sir.' Sir Mark steps toward him and gives him another smack for having the brass neck to tell his stable jockey to 'fuck off' when he'd been caught pulling a horse about. So, young Steven got two smacks in one morning!

The only other occasion that might have resulted in a few blows being traded involved William Haggas, now a Derby-winning trainer, but for a time back in the early 1980s merely one in a succession of Sir Mark's pupil-assistants. Now, don't get me wrong, Mr Haggas was a good chap – and, boy, did he love to have a flutter on Heath House horses – but he was another little prankster. He called me over one morning in the yard, only to drench me with this water pistol he'd been hiding behind his back. 'Very funny, William,' I say. 'That's just about your level, that is.' Whereupon, I turned on my heel and strode away. Once William had disappeared to ride out, I sought out some of the lads and said to them: 'See that metal bath over there? Fill it up with cold water for when we get back. Haggas is going in there, make no mistake!' The bath was ready and waiting for us on our return, but as soon as I beckoned him over, Haggas, being Haggas, sussed something was afoot and made a run for it. I chased him across the paddock and eventually dived on him. The boys carried him to the bath and ceremonially dumped him fully clothed into the freezing water. 'That'll teach you to go round with your water pistol!'

Although I've met a few jockeys in my time with short tempers of champion proportions, I've never come across any champion drinkers. Most of us like a drink but mostly only in moderation. You

Mum and dad on their wedding day in 1946; mum's younger sister Margaret is in front

In the garden at Spa Fold: you wouldn't think this little angel would grow up with such an evil temper, would you?

No donkeys around on this occasion in Blackpool - just my cousin Lynn!

Penetentiary provides me with the sixth winner of my career in September 1967 at Folkestone

Jack Waugh: he turned the little boy into a man

Frankie Dettori isn't the only one who can look good in shades and swimming trunks: Dennis McKay, me and Stilly in Jamaica

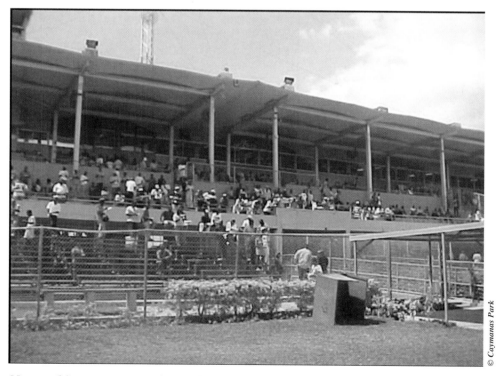

© Caymanas Park

No machine-gun towers in evidence but the wire-mesh fencing gives you some idea of how nasty things could turn at Caymanas Park

The start of a great day at Royal Ascot in 1970: Fluke scoots home in the Jersey Stakes

The completion of a memorable double as Calpurnius and me return after winning the Royal Hunt Cup

The head of a 'True Professional': Spindrifter

Sharing a quick word with Gavin Pritchard-Gordon (in Pamana hat) after Noalcoholic has provided each of us with our first Group I in the 1983 Sussex Stakes

© EMPICS

The 'Old Firm' in 1981

© George Selwyn

Steve Cauthen is a worried man as he senses me and Environment Friend coming to deprive him and Stagecraft of the 1991 Eclipse

It's just beginning to sink in that I've won my first Classic at the grand old age of 45!

User Friendly doubles-up in the St Leger – and gifts me the much-prized cap for the winning jockey (below)

© George Selwyn

© George Selwyn

Unblest wins the 1993 Champagne Stakes: our fortunes in the following year's Free Handicap were less pleasant and had unwelcome repercussions

© George Selwyn

The giant grey Hasten To Add does the business in the 1994 Ebor

© George Selwyn

© Pat Healy

The much-travelled Wizard King with me and Sir Mark after winning at Tipperary in 1997

© Sir Mark Prescott

Lily Augusta: I don't know whether to laugh or cry at the very sight of her!

Last Second unleashes that short, sharp burst of speed of hers to land the Nassau Stakes at Goodwood in 1996

© George Selwyn

© George Selwyn

Pivotal just manages to collar Eveningperformance right on the line in the 1996 Nunthorpe Stakes at York to give me and Sir Mark our first Group I in tandem

A fine shot of me and Pasternak going to post for the 1998 John Smith's Cup at York

© Martin Lynch

© Racing Post

Alborada and me in full flow during the closing stages of the 1999 Champion Stakes

A handshake says it all: a job well done

© Gerry Cranham

The clenched fist speaks volumes: after all I'd been through, I wanted this victory badly.

The whips are certainly flying as Giant's Causeway just edges out Kalanisi for the 2000 Eclipse Stakes: the public thought it was a great race between two brave horses but the stewards decided to give me and Pat Eddery a ten-day holiday apiece for 'excessive frequency'

Annie and me finally tie the knot on 18 December 1999

Shades of Osborne House in the old days: Gloria Charnock and Jack Berry are the villains making mischief with the cream at my 55th birthday party!

Group I George! Aristotle makes it Group Is on successive Saturdays by winning the 1999 Racing Post Trophy

A proud man: receiving one of my three 'Lesters'

The arch prankster of the weighing room – Philip Robinson

My children
Nathalie and Nick

Soaking up
some winter
sun in Tobago
with Annie
and A.J.

I don't look
so bad for
an old 'un!

It's a long way from Lime Pit Lane but I'm still never far from a horse

can't drink vast amounts and still perform on the racecourse. Nature dictates that people of our size and weight can't cope with much alcohol. It takes precious little to get us drunk. Speaking personally, I get giggly and silly when I'm drunk instead of getting all aggressive. Walter Swinburn had his much-publicised drinking 'problem', yet he wouldn't have been the biggest drinker in the weighing room. He was always sober and on the ball when he came to the races, that I do know; what he got up to elsewhere I don't know. But when you're constantly fighting nature like Walter and his great pal Steve Cauthen were, you're spending plenty of hours in saunas and missing out on many of life's little pleasures – like food! All that sweating dehydrates you so much that, for what you take off, you could drink a lake! You sweat off 2lb and promptly put back on 5lb through liquid. The temptation to compensate with perhaps a bottle of champagne can prove irresistible. Stevie Cauthen went through a phase of drinking champagne as if it was going out of fashion. Both Stevie and Walter liked London life, the parties and the champagne set, and they had to pay the price. But both of them were man enough to get out of that situation in the end.

And then there's Frankie! He's come a long way since his youthful indiscretion of being caught by the police in possession of a small quantity of cocaine back in 1993. Good God, he's a TV star! 'Top of the Pops', 'Parkinson', 'They Think It's All Over', 'TFI Friday' – thanks in no small measure to 'The Magnificent Seven' at Ascot in 1996 (which puts my 'Santa Rosa Five' right in the shade!), Frankie has managed to make that difficult step beyond the confines of his sport. Now he's got his own range of pizzas on the supermarket shelves!

I've a lot of time for Frankie. Every 20 years or so someone extra talented comes along. First it was Lester, then Pat and now Frankie. He's been so good for the sport, publicising it and putting it on the map far more than Lester, Willie, Pat or Steve Cauthen were able to do. We leave it to him to portray how we all feel when we've ridden big winners. Let him do the Angel Cordero flying dismount and be typically Italian and extrovert. That's fine by me, because he's doing it for all of us more reserved types. Sir Mark Prescott would turn upside down if he ever saw G Duffield execute a flying dismount!

Frankie rides very much in the American style that has taken hold over here thanks, in the main, to the influence of Stevie Cauthen. It took Stevie a couple of seasons to acclimatise and adjust to the different rhythm of our racing and the variety of our tracks, but he was clever enough and talented enough to make the transition smoothly and successfully. I loved watching him ride and marvelled at the way he was able to adapt without losing his basic American style. Put Stevie in front and he was deadly. He could pace a race to perfection – and that's the hardest race to win. You never quite know how they are going behind you and you mustn't go too fast or too slow. You must find the pace that suits you but nobody else and it's not so straightforward as it looks. Steve Cauthen was second to none in this aspect of race-riding. OK, he was riding some good horses for Henry Cecil and whoever, yet he still had to get it right when those gates opened. Henry Cecil's horses are always super-fit and can gallop, so the one thing you don't want to do with them is ponce about in midfield when there's no pace. You kick them out and gradually wind up the pace. No one has been more adept at that game in my time than Stevie.

I'm afraid no one can ever say G Duffield is a great stylist! I began in the era of people like Doug Smith, Jimmy Lindley and Eric Eldin who were coming to the end of careers which had commenced when riding styles were totally different to what they are today. Their way of riding, however, was bound to make a great impression on me because these men were the gods of race-riding and I was only a young kid trying to pick up the best bits of each of them – just like today's youngsters try to copy Frankie. No end of people tried to copy Lester, of course, and they all failed abysmally. Sandy Barclay, for instance, had been a terribly successful apprentice. The biggest mistake of his life was to try and emulate Lester. It ruined him and he gradually went downhill and disappeared into oblivion. He had a good job with Noel Murless; he should have stayed riding his way, taking pointers from every jock he rated. He wasted his talent trying to copy someone who was a supreme talent and completely on a different planet to the rest of us. You couldn't copy Lester. You just gazed at him in wonder.

No, when it comes to style I wouldn't be top of the class by a million miles. The main weapon in G Duffield's armoury is the ability to instil that all-important will-to-win in a horse because he has that insatiable will-to-win himself.

12

GETTING ON SOME GOOD HORSES

Apart from the virus-ravaged season of 1975 (when Heath House was reduced to nine winners and my own score to a meagre 26), Sir Mark and I ticked over quite nicely during the rest of the 1970s and early 1980s with just one major reservation: despite one or two decent animals like a Mandalus or a Spindrifter, in our first ten seasons together we never had a good animal to go to war with, one that could fight its corner in Pattern-race company. For ammunition of that calibre I had to look to Gavin Pritchard-Gordon.

Thanks to Gavin I won five Pattern races which included my very first Group I, the Sussex Stakes of 1983 aboard Noalcoholic, who has to be one of the best horses I've ever ridden. Even so, it was not Gavin who provided me with my initial Group winner. That distinction – bearing in mind the Pattern had not been introduced when I won the Duke of York and Jersey on Fluke in 1970 – fell to the Palace House trainer Bruce Hobbs, for whom I partnered the filly Stumped to win the Group III Child Stakes (now the Falmouth) at the Newmarket July Meeting of 1980. This was the only time I rode the three-year-old bay filly who was a granddaughter of Lucasland, an old acquaintance from Heath House. She had just run fourth to the Irish 1000 Guineas winner Cairn Rouge in the Coronation at Royal Ascot but got into the Child Stakes with only 7st 12lb – which is how I came in for the ride. This had all the appearance of a choice 'spare' and it proved just that as we held off the 1000 Guineas runner-up Our Home to win by three quarters of a length.

The Pattern-race success I enjoyed with Gavin was altogether more meaningful because he had actually taken out a second retainer on my services. The job offer came completely out of the blue. The intermediary was Brian Taylor, who had been stable jockey to Harvey Leader at Shalfleet where Gavin was assistant trainer. When Mr Leader retired in 1971, Gavin took over the yard until moving to Stanley House in the Bury Road – once the home of all those wonderful Lord Derby horses like Hyperion and Fairway – for the start of the 1977 season.

Gavin possessed no racing pedigree whatsoever. His father was a ship-broker and his mother was a barrister and, along with Michael Stoute, he was one of the short-listed also-rans in the now infamous round of 'dummy' commentaries at Newbury racecourse that secured the post of BBC Television Racing Correspondent for Julian Wilson. Gavin subsequently turned all his attentions to training, and after brief spells with Stuart Murless in Ireland and Peter Walwyn in Lambourn, he joined Mr Leader. Benefiting enormously from the legacy provided by Mr Leader's wealthy patrons, he got off to a cracking start by winning with five of his first seven runners in early 1972 to finish up with 22 winners, mostly ridden by Brian Taylor, Eric Eldin or David Maitland – although even Stilly partnered one!

It wasn't until the June of 1974 that eventually I got a chance from him and won a couple on the two-year-old colt Court Chad. Things began to click during ensuing seasons and our association gradually developed into a classic example of one of those situations where a jockey rides more and more of a trainer's horses to the point where he begins to ride work and a retainer makes sense. I consulted Sir Mark and he raised no objections.

Gavin was not at all the same sort of person as Sir Mark and we shared a different kind of relationship. He was an amusing guy, yes, but not nearly so strong a character as Sir Mark. Nor was Gavin as tough on his horses. At Heath House they are made proper fit; Gavin tended to work every horse over the same distance of six or seven furlongs, for instance, regardless of whether they were sprinters or stayers. Newmarket can be too easy for a horse, because with the exception of the Warren Hill canter, which is quite stiff, and Long Hill, which is on the collar towards the end, everywhere is so flat. Consequently, you must gallop them hard at Newmarket to get them fit. If I ever go to Lambourn, for example, they'll always tell me they don't want any of those 'Newmarket gallops' because everything is much stiffer there, all uphill on the collar, and the rider would risk bottoming the horse. On balance, things were not quite so businesslike at Stanley House as they were at Heath House. The atmosphere was more laid back. And I'd actually go into the house for some breakfast and a chat after riding out!

Gavin and I had teamed up to collect a few nice handicaps, notably Redcar's two principal handicaps (the Andy Capp in 1979 and Zetland Gold Cup in 1980) with Side Track before our first Pattern-race performers materialised in 1982 in the shape of the juvenile All Systems Go and the ex-French five-year-old Noalcoholic.

All Systems Go was a very strong, good-looking, well-balanced chestnut colt by the King's Stand and Nunthorpe-winning sprinter Bay Express from the family of Derby winner Crepello. He was a proper professional was All Systems Go, a jockey's dream: no quirks whatsoever with a good engine. He always worked well at home, usually with a decent, high-rated three-year-old through which we could readily gauge his ability. After running second to the future Irish 2000 Guineas winner Wassl on his York debut in June, All Systems Go won his maiden at Doncaster before returning to York in July and breaking the juvenile seven-furlong track record despite me easing down toward the finish. Gavin then sent him to Goodwood for the Lanson Champagne Stakes (subsequently elevated to Group III status) in which he received 6lb from the favourite, Guy Harwood's Lyphard's Special who had won all three of his starts thus far. All Systems Go showed what a competitor he was, for he really buckled down to the task and demonstrated just what a big heart he possessed. He had to be both tough and brave to get the verdict by a head over Lyphard's Special because it was hammer-and-tongs throughout the final furlong and I did not spare him one iota of assistance, I can assure you! In any good horse you need these qualities to go hand in hand with the ability.

Less than a fortnight after Goodwood, All Systems Go continued on his upward curve by achieving his Pattern victory in the now defunct Group III Seaton Delaval Stakes over seven furlongs at Newcastle in which he justified favouritism to beat Cause Celebre comfortably by half length, again easing down. Then we hit the buffers with him in a big way. Doncaster's Group II Laurent Perrier-sponsored Champagne Stakes was the next port of call, and here All Systems Go met the season's juvenile 'talking horse' Gorytus. Well, Gorytus may have been 'got at' when he later lost his invincible reputation in the Dewhurst and, for whatever reason, he never did scale the heights his early career had promised, but Dick Hern's horse proved this day that he certainly could walk-the-walk just as readily as he could talk-the-talk. Gorytus smashed the track record – while All Systems Go trailed in last of the five runners. He'd been noticeably on his toes both in the paddock and at the stalls, was beaten by halfway really, and I think the top and bottom of it was he'd gone over the top for the season.

Whenever you are associated with as decent a two-year-old as All Systems Go (who received 8st 10lb in the Free Handicap and a Timeform rating of 119), you're always looking forward to the following year's Classics. You hope your animal will strengthen-up and find a bit of improvement during the winter to narrow the gap between you and the top-rated juveniles, which in the case of All Systems Go was 11lb or so if he was to overhaul the likes of Diesis and Gorytus. Unfortunately for us, not only did such improvement fail to materialise but much of his juvenile sparkle also evaporated. He did run in the 2000 Guineas (only my sixth Classic ride in the 17 seasons since my first winner), which was won by Lomond, but we beat only three of the 16 runners, and he failed to win any of his nine races in 1983 before being sent to race in the United States.

At the same time as All Systems Go was tearing up the gallops with me as a juvenile in the early summer of 1982, Gavin and me were handed a real gift-wrapped surprise packet. I came in to ride work one morning and he said to me: 'Get on that one over there. It's here in quarantine for a month on its way from France to Australia to take up stud duties. It was only a handicapper in France, but let's see what it's like.' We took this horse, a bay son of the 1974 2000 Guineas winner Nonoalco, out onto the Limekilns – the best gallops in Newmarket – and worked him with a four-year-old colt called Buffavento, who was good enough subsequently to win a Group III in Germany. Buffavento was quickly made to look a selling plater. This bay horse made absolute mincemeat of him. He was no handicapper! His name was Noalcoholic.

Noalcoholic's American owner Bill Du Pont acceded to Gavin's plea to be allowed to run the horse and he went to Royal Ascot for the Group II Queen Anne Stakes on the opening day. Noalcoholic was a revelation. As there was no pace out of the gate, I let him stride on, sit quiet in front and see how things developed. The others, understandably, paid no attention to him. I've no doubt one or two of my rival jockeys had taken the trouble to look up Noalcoholic's French form. Olivier Douieb had trained him to win three out of three as a three-year-old but he was disappointing at four, winning only a small ten-furlong race at Deauville from eight attempts over the same kind of trip. Although he'd won his single race of 1982 prior to leaving France, this 33/1 'rag' who was running over his wrong distance and who was usually waited with to boot, was merely going to give them a lead to the two pole. They say 'knowledge is power' and I knew something different. I kept increasing and increasing the pace and one by one our rivals began to run up the distress flags until only Lester and the three-year-old Mr Fluorocarbon remained to be beaten off. Sadly, Lester got to me and won rather easily in the end by four lengths.

However, the Queen Anne confirmed our suspicions concerning the extent of Noalcoholic's ability. Whether it was the change of scenery and training routine or the complete turnaround in riding tactics that did the trick, no one can say for certain but who's worrying. In Newmarket, Noalcoholic proved a total gentleman at all times. He was clean-limbed and a proper athlete who wouldn't know how to do anything wrong. Of a morning his ears would be pricked in anticipation and he always worked nicely so we knew exactly where we were with him.

In addition, the front-running tactics that seemed to suit him also suited me. Because I'm a very aggressive sort of person I do like to take the bull by the horns in a race. Forcing tactics suit my personality. I'm not one of those jocks with the patience of a saint, like Scobie or Ray Cochrane, for example, who would sit and sit forever. I have executed those tactics, but that's not my forte. Once I'm in front I'm the hardest man in the world to pass because I hate being passed so much! Consequently, I try to make the horse's mind up for it, and I won't let it give in. I relish making the running, or taking it up a long way from home and positively daring anything to get by me. Noalcoholic was therefore a partner made in heaven as far as G Duffield was concerned.

The Van Geest Stakes (another race later elevated to Group III) at Newmarket the following week offered a tailor-made opportunity for Noalcoholic to open his English account and, even though it was over the even shorter trip of seven furlongs, they didn't see which way he went. We made all to beat Scarrowmanwick by a cosy two and a half lengths, which, to be fair, is what you'd expect of him after that Queen Anne performance. Both the obvious mid-summer targets for Noalcoholic, Goodwood's Sussex Stakes and Waterford Crystal Mile, were closed before he came to England, which meant, rather perversely, that he had to go back across the Channel for his next two races, the Prix Messidor at Maisons-Lafitte and the Prix Jacques le Marois at Deauville, both run over the metric mile.

The Group III Messidor was a carbon copy of the Queen Anne. The French jockeys thought they knew all about Noalcoholic, didn't bother to keep tabs on me and tumbled far too late that I was never going to stop. They were gob-smacked. 'He couldn't possibly win a race like this when he was in France,' Freddie Head said to me afterwards. The Messidor was notable for me also, since it was my very first victory in France. I'd enjoyed plenty of success at Ostend in the past but Belgium is the Nationwide Conference compared to France.

The Jacques le Marois proved a far sterner test. It lived up to its Group I status by attracting the winners of both the English and French 2000 Guineas (Zino and Melyno, respectively) whose subsequent clash in the Prix Jean Prat saw Melyno dismantle Chantilly's nine-furlong track record by fully two seconds. I can't say it was a surprise that the locals were not caught napping by my tactics on this occasion, but it was a surprise to see the race go to neither of the Guineas winners but the four-year-old The Wonder, who had not been able to make the first three in either the Lockinge or the Sussex. Noalcoholic (7/2 second favourite to Melyno) came in fifth, beaten just under six lengths, with the 5/2 favourite tailed off in some kind of distress.

Noalcoholic wasn't seen out again until the Queen Elizabeth II Stakes at Ascot in late September in which Willie Carson rode him to be second to the 50/1 so-called handicapper Buzzards Bay because I was claimed by Sir Mark to ride one for him (and win) up at Redcar. I was reunited with Noalcoholic for his last run of 1982, the Group II Bisquit Cognac Challenge Stakes over seven furlongs at the Newmarket Cesarewitch fixture in October, but although he secured his first English Pattern race he had to dig awfully deep to do so. On this occasion we were taken on for the lead and, indeed, headed by Motavato, a four-year-old trained by Barry Hills that had won the Group II Lockinge back in the spring. I'd got to him after four furlongs but getting past him took almost all the remaining three, and Noalcoholic was all-out to win by three quarters of length.

Since Timeform's *Racehorses of 1982* endorsed our high opinion of Noalcoholic by awarding him a rating of 122, we were mustard keen to keep hold of him for another season, or at least as much of it as possible. Mr Du Pont gave Gavin the go-ahead for 1983 and Noalcoholic reappeared in the mile conditions race at Doncaster in the first week of the new campaign, in which he finished a respectable two-and-a-half lengths second to Princes Gate.

The French jockeys might have been slow on the uptake in 1982 when Noalcoholic first returned to race at Maisons-Lafitte but when we returned for the Prix du Muguet at Longchamps we got totally mangled – and it was absolutely deliberate. I went to make the running and one of the others kicked like hell to get in front of me – and then it drops in and slows up the pace, allowing the rest to come up my outside and block me in. They made a proper job of it. I was bounced off the rails and done up like a kipper. They'd sorted out beforehand how to stop me dictating the pace and gone out of their way to execute the plan. I'd have needed to kill Noalcoholic to reach the front. I conceded defeat a long way out and didn't push him. It was a non-event.

The Lockinge (then a Group II not a Group I as it is now), on the other hand, went like a dream – more or less. We were drawn in the centre of the track and I was keen to get across to the far rail and, with the rail to help him, make the best of my way home from then on. If they caught me, so be it. Get across I did, but so quickly that the stipendiary steward on duty had a little word in my ear afterwards about it. One kick in the belly two out put us five lengths in the clear, stealing the race in effect, and we crossed the line still one and a half ahead of Valiyar. We were out cold toward the end, but so was everything else. 'A sterling performance from Noalcoholic and an inspired ride from George Duffield,' said *The Sporting Life*.

The Newbury ground had ridden very heavy and proved virtually impossible for a horse to come from behind as Valiyar had attempted. In the Queen Anne the ground was firm and although the weight differential remained the same 3lb we'd conceded in the Lockinge, Valiyar comprehensively turned the tables on us, beating Montekin by one and a half lengths with Noalcoholic a further six in arrears.

Noalcoholic's principal summer target was the Group I Sussex Stakes (worth £63,032 to the winner) at Goodwood on 27 July. Neither of his two races between Royal Ascot and Glorious Goodwood inspired the uncommitted. He ran pretty dismally in Ireland (without me) to finish third of five at Phoenix Park, before dropping back to six furlongs for the Group I July Cup in which he ran very creditably to finish less than four and a half lengths behind the champion sprinting filly Habibti in fifth place. That just showed how much pure speed Noalcoholic possessed if he could be in the firing line with Group I performers. None of this impressed the odds-layers at Goodwood where Noalcoholic was allowed to start at 18/1.

In 1983 the Sussex was the solitary Group I race over a mile in the country where the three-year-old Classic crop could take on its elders. Consequently, in addition to old adversary Montekin (whom Noalcoholic had already met five times during the season, with the score 3-2 in his favour), the 11-runner field contained both the first and second in the English 2000 Guineas (Lomond and Tolomeo) and the winner of the Irish equivalent (Wassl). Lomond was sent off favourite at 9/4. Only a trio of 33/1 no-hopers were considered to have a worse chance than Noalcoholic of upsetting the rising stars.

Gavin and I had obviously discussed the race in detail. Everyone accepted I'd go on. The problem, again, was my low draw. The mile at Goodwood is on a round course, not a straight one like Newbury, which, as the track turned right-handed, meant I was drawn well away from that vital running rail. They'd probably be perfectly content to let me come across, knowing I'd use up vital energy in the process, and then sit on my tail accepting a nice lead until picking me up in the straight. I knew I had to come up with something different or I'd play into their hands. Accordingly, I asked Gavin whether he'd mind if I stuck to my draw and refused to go over to the fence. That way I'd still be setting the pace that suited me but, and it was a big 'but', the rest of them wouldn't get a lead off me. 'Do what you think is right,' Gavin said to me.

So I jumped out and went dead straight, making no attempt to cross to the fence until approaching the turn, which comes just over three furlongs from the finish. My unexpected decision left everyone else pulling and tugging on the inside as they'd been deprived of a lead. I went as quick as they expected but not in the expected direction and this had the effect of completely unsettling the other jocks – who numbered Lester, Pat, Willie, Greville, Joe

Mercer and Steve Cauthen. I kicked hard off the bend and started down the hill holding a three-length advantage. It's testimony to Noalcoholic's class and ability that even when the remainder began to hit the gas once they realised the bird had flown the coop, he still had two and a half lengths left at the post. Further evidence came from the fact that he had now won the Lockinge (heavy) and Sussex (firm) on extremes of going, and had broken the Goodwood track record into the bargain. Once again, my riding drew some press plaudits: 'Duffield showed superb judgement of pace in his tactics of waiting in front,' observed Michael Seely in *The Times*.

Seventeen seasons after opening my account on Syllable in that lowly contest at Yarmouth I had won my first elite Group I race. Noalcoholic ran three more times but failed to register another victory. The Group I penalty proved his undoing thereafter, especially pitted against the up-and-coming generation. Despite Gavin confessing to the press that 'if it was up to me we would keep him until he is ten' this particular plea was more in hope than expectation and Noalcoholic duly took up those postponed stallion duties. However, his phoenix-like European career (he retired with a Timeform rating of 128, 2lb below the champion miler, the three-year-old filly Luth Enchantee who beat him four-and-three quarter lengths in receipt of 10lb in the Marois) ensured he found himself standing at the Side Hill Stud in Newmarket for a season before finally completing his delayed journey to darkest Australia.

Noalcoholic naturally signified the highpoint of the association between Gavin and myself. It gradually deteriorated into the same old story, owners wanting a different jockey for instance, and, whereas most people might only think something and not say it, if I'd something to say I'd say it. I wasn't best pleased at getting the 'jog' off some of these horses and told Gavin so. I remember Willie Carson riding this sprinter which I was informed wasn't going to run. Gavin couldn't even tell me himself: he got his assistant,

Mickey Greening, the former lightweight jockey, to give me some cock-and-bull story. Mickey was as embarrassed as hell having to spin this sob story. I went to Gavin and said, 'What are you, a man or a mouse? If you've got something to say to me, say it – don't get someone else to tell me. It's your job to tell me!' The horse got beat, and the next time it was due to run Gavin said I could ride it. 'Gavin,' I said, 'you can stick that horse up your fucking arse. I wouldn't ride that horse for £1 million!' – and walked away.

I've always been my own worst enemy and I'd pressed that old self-destruct button once again. The rot set in. Toward the end of 1986 Gavin announced to the press that he wasn't renewing my retainer for the following season. 'Would you like to know who wants to sack you?' he asked me. 'If you do, come up to the office on Sunday and I'll tell you.' So I drove up to Stanley House as arranged and went into the office. 'It would help to know the reasons,' I began, 'because apart from being a bad-tempered little fucker, I can't see what I've done wrong.' It turned out that his brother Giles was one of the main instigators. Giles reckoned I was 'no good on fillies' – which becomes a trifle ironic when you consider all my subsequent success on fillies such as User Friendly, Last Second, Red Camellia and Alborada. It's also amusing to note that I rode a filly for Giles Pritchard-Gordon at Lingfield years later, and won on it for him!

To be honest, it's never easy to keep two retainers happy and, to make matters even more complicated, I'd actually had a third retainer throughout this period from David Morley, a great friend of Sir Mark Prescott's from his days at Frank Cundell's, who was then training near Bury St Edmunds. I was always likely to struggle with a three-way retainer, and poor old David, who obviously bore the brunt of it, severed our association at the same time as Gavin.

However, no one could take away the satisfaction of winning five Pattern races for Gavin. Furthermore, hard on the heels of those three in 1982 and two in 1983, I maintained my hot streak by adding another couple in 1984. Much to my delight, one of them, at long last, was for Sir Mark.

Harlow was a big grey colt by Caro who came to Heath House from the United States in February 1984. He belonged to a Mr John Edward Anthony, who had made his money in the lumber business, and he had been in the care of Joe Cantey in New York, for whom he had won twice over six furlongs on the dirt at Meadowlands just before Christmas. Cantey reasoned this giant of a horse would best prosper on the galloping tracks and grass surface of Europe. In the States, even the sprints involved a turn.

Harlow was lame when he arrived! You soon appreciated why he'd been sent across the Atlantic. He must have been near 18 hh, far too big to race – and also train – on the tight American tracks where he'd get really fired up: he'd be a big old boy to argue with! Sir Mark started him off in Listed company, the Abernant over six furlongs at Newmarket's Craven meeting, to assess his capabilities. After being hampered leaving the stalls but running on to finish an honourable seventh of the 19, Harlow was stepped up to seven furlongs for his next outing on 28 April, the Holsten Pils Trophy Stakes at Leicester (now the Group III Leicestershire Stakes).

This was very nearly a disaster! I fell off him going down to the start, didn't I? As he was such a hard-puller, I lobbed him down solo, nice and quietly, alongside the far rail. Right by the junction with the round course there was a whopping great hole (apparently caused by a leaking water pipe) on the inside of the rail. Harlow spots this hole, ducks out and dumps me. Fortunately, he chose to hack quietly down to the seven furlong gate on the straight course rather than gallop headlong round the bend into the back straight and taking our winning chance along with him. Coming back was no problem. I let a 20/1 shot lead us to the one marker and then Harlow went by him as sweet as a nut to win by a length.

In stark contrast to the firm ground at Leicester, it was like a bog at Longchamp for the Group III Prix du Palais-Royal a month later. It made no difference to Harlow who won comfortably by one and a half lengths. Sir Mark displayed no emotion whatsoever at losing his Pattern-race virginity after holding on to it for 14 years! Harlow had achieved a lot in a short space of time but progressed no further. Three more runs – in France, Ireland and Germany – netted no victories but that afternoon at Longchamp was doubtless instrumental in securing him a stallion's berth in France.

My other Group III winner in 1984 was Long Pond in Epsom's Blue Riband Trial Stakes on 24 April. Long Pond was trained by Paul Kelleway, the former Gold Cup-winning jump jockey, who was, in the truest sense of the word, a 'character' and a laugh-a-minute to ride for. He used to say that had he not discovered horses he'd most likely have been a 'getaway driver for the Kray twins.' I once rode a 25/1 winner for him at Ripon and he won a suitcase-full of money on it. 'Do you know what I like about you, George?' he said to me holding this suitcase, 'You ride a fucking 25/1 shot as though it's fucking 5/4 on! I've won a right few quid here!' Though seldom having more than two-dozen horses in his yard and totalling just 26 wins in his best ever season, he comfortably lived up to his nickname of 'Pattern-race' Paul by collecting no fewer than 17 (including seven Group Is) in his 20-year training career. 'Some people think Goliath is too big to hit – I reckon he's too big to miss!' was the thinking behind his audacious tilts at the big races. 'Kelloggs' was also responsible for one of racing's finest quotes which, however many times you hear it, still brings a smile to your face: 'I'm usually first out on the gallops for first lot when 80 of Cumani's come over the hill, 90 of Gosden's over another and 100 of Cecil's over another. I know how General Custer felt!' So, even though he only ran seventh in the Dante at York, with a trainer like Paul, Long Pond was always going to take his chance in the Derby.

Hampered at halfway, he didn't disgrace himself in finishing seventh.

Before I could get used to the possibilities of becoming 'Pattern-race' George, my own little conveyor belt of Group wins ground to a halt. Five more seasons were to slip past before G Duffield struck again at Pattern-race level in 1990 courtesy of another 'spare', the John Gosden-trained three-year-old Maximilian in the Group III Ostermann-Pokal at Cologne in July. The following month I added the Group III Imry Solario Stakes at Sandown on Radwell, trained by James Fanshawe, a man I knew well.

James had only just taken out a licence to train at Pegasus Stables on Newmarket's Snailwell Road, having spent eight years learning the ropes with an acknowledged master in Michael Stoute. In spite of standing six-feet-two, he only weighed 11st dripping wet and had been a keen rider in point-to-points. Later on, he capitalised on his spindly physique via the self-deprecating advert of a skeleton adorned with his trademark horn-rimmed spectacles entitled 'Hungry for more Winners.' In fact, he used to ride a lot of Gill's pointers very successfully – and it was on one of them that he suffered the fall which broke his neck. For six weeks he was in traction and had a metal halo screwed to his head! 'I had visions,' he said, 'of becoming a lightning conductor and of my parents finding a pile of bones on a patch of scorched earth.'

I offered James my services as a way of saying thanks for the work he had put into Gill's pointers. I thought an 'old head' might prove helpful as he was finding his feet. I felt the experience of working with Sir Mark Prescott over the years might be of benefit to James. I wasn't trying to be greedy and nick rides. I told James I didn't expect anything from him. I just wanted to ride out and try to help him get started. If he wanted me to ride, so be it. At first James was reluctant to accept my offer, not because he didn't think I was up to riding his horses but because he wanted to start with a young team, both work riders and jockeys, nearer his own age. He was only 27 and wanted a young team around him. Walter Swinburn was his jockey of choice.

James wasn't alone in wanting Walter or maybe Stevie Cauthen to ride his horses, so it was only a matter of months before I got a call. Radwell had won both of his races prior to the Solario but his 12/1 outsider's tag at Sandown was an accurate reflection of their worth. He was a lazy so-and-so, however, and the combination of easier ground, a seventh furlong and a ferocious early gallop at Sandown possibly helped him get on terms with horses that might ordinarily prove his superior on most other occasions. Radwell possessed one trump card, though. He was tough. We were stone-cold last turning for home with three furlongs left to run, but once we met that Sandown hill he wore them all down to beat the favourite Alnaab by a length. The pack were beaten off by another six lengths. Radwell did win another race as a three-year-old but never featured prominently at the highest level. That three-from-three record as a juvenile was his particular high-watermark.

Radwell wasn't the only promising two-year-old colt in James's yard in 1990. I won races on two others and, arguably, might have added a second Group III on one of them. I'd partnered Sapieha to win a division of the Westley Maiden, invariably a tell-tale showcase for potentially decent three-year-olds at the Newmarket Cambridgeshire meeting. Next time out Sapieha won the Group III Horris Hill Stakes at Newbury – with Walter in the saddle while I ploughed an unfashionable furrow up at Pontefract. Bit of an omen, that. I'd also won the other division of the Westley for James on a grey colt called Environment Friend that belonged to owner-breeder Bill Gredley.

Bill Gredley had made a mountain of money as a property developer and loved to spend a lot of it on horses. Owning became breeding, and in the late 1970s he bought the Stetchworth Park estate near Newmarket. It was on a buying trip to Keeneland, Kentucky, in 1987, that Bill fortuitously acquired Environment Friend. Having bought nine of the ten mares he sought to come home with, he picked up Water Woo, the cheapest of the batch at $45,000, to make up the numbers. Water Woo's dam Waterloo had won the 1972 1000 Guineas for Bill Watts and she was in foal to Cozzene (another grey like Harlow by the French sire Caro), winner of the Breeders' Cup Mile. Her grey yearling colt came under the hammer at Tattersalls in 1989 but nobody wanted him at his reserve. Bill bought him in for 23,000 guineas and, as a kindly gesture, sent him to the young boyfriend (and future husband) of his part-time cook at Stetchworth, who was about to start up training. Thus were the cards dealt which resulted in Environment Friend becoming the very first horse promised to James Fanshawe.

I had partnered Environment Friend in both his races at two (he began with an unlucky sixth at Sandown after suffering interference) and it was obvious to me that although he lacked strength – he possessed the frame but not yet the body – he had a motor. My problem was staying on him. As Sapieha had signposted, Walter Swinburn could pick and choose (he rode Sapieha in his Guineas trial, the Greenham, and throughout the 1991 season), if not required by his boss Michael Stoute; and then there was Stevie Cauthen, a good friend of Bill Gredley's who actually lived in a cottage on the Stetchworth estate, if he was not required by his retainer, Sheikh Mohammed. The early weeks of the 1991 season were going to be very interesting – as they always tend to be – as the 'big boys' get on as many Classic prospects as they can to narrow down their options.

Steve had worked Environment Friend the previous back-end and pronounced him 'weak as spaghetti', so hopefully he might continue to be disinterested. However, even though I was the man who'd won on Environment Friend and was definitely available for the Guineas and Derby, I had nothing to do with the colt at the start of the new campaign. Once again G Duffield was out in the sticks (Carlisle on this occasion) for a couple of duff mounts when Walter took the ride on Environment Friend in Kempton's Easter Stakes. Although he was beginning to muscle-up, Environment Friend was a well beaten third behind Corrupt; and, with nothing better to ride, Walter rode him again in the Craven to finish a distant fifth. Not that I'd have partnered him anyway, because I was on the stable's first string, Radwell, who had that Group win under his belt. Radwell trailed in last of the eight runners!

Despite his mile-winning pedigree, it seemed apparent that Environment Friend lacked the necessary speed to excel at the distance. He missed the Guineas and went to York for the Group II Dante over ten and a half furlongs to see whether he had the makings of a Derby contender. This was where I re-entered calculations. Walter had to ride Habaayib for Mr Stoute and Steve was aboard Sheikh Mohammed's Hailsham. I got the nod. Lester made it a very fast gallop on the favourite Peter Davies, a pace Environment Friend couldn't go, and I was more than happy to hang at the back. Once into the straight we began to creep closer and closer to the leaders, until entering the final furlong we collared Hailsham and won going away by five lengths – thus reversing the Craven form by seven lengths at the longer distance

I couldn't get back into the weighing room quickly enough. The first person I wanted to see was Lester, to ask his opinion whether Environment Friend could win the Derby. The Dante had a reputation second to none as a Derby guide. Both Reference Point and Shahrastani had won it in recent years before going on to win the Derby and nothing had won the race by as much as five lengths in 14 years. And what Lester didn't know about winning the Derby wasn't worth knowing. So, it was a case of 'Lester, what do you think?' Lester said he was certainly good enough to be in it – no more than that! I don't think he could have been that impressed with Environment Friend because I don't think he even bothered to try and get the ride on him at Epsom! The *Racing Post* was more encouraging. 'Friend in the frame,' was its front page headline the day after the Dante.

Lester's dismissive attitude of Environment Friend's Epsom chances seemed franked when the horse worked very poorly the week before the Derby. The gallops were firming up – as was the going at Epsom. Perhaps he needed to get his toe in a bit more? On the other hand, Hailsham had boosted the Dante form in the meantime by winning the Italian Derby. Not that I cared unduly. This would only be my third ride in the Derby and I was prepared to make the most of it.

We were sent off sixth best at 11/1 in a field of 13, only to enjoy a distant view of Generous's backside as we crossed the line 40-odd lengths adrift with only two pacemakers behind us. He ran no sort of race. I was chasing him from the gate and never happy with him. He seemed as dead as a doornail, a dead horse, and I really wondered whether he'd been 'got at'. 'You'd have to be suspicious,' I replied to inquisitive reporters. Yet subsequent tests of his blood and for dope all found nothing.

This was one of those races you had to forget completely. It was a bitch that it just happened to be the Derby. The Irish Derby offered Environment Friend an obvious second bite at a Derby cherry, so you can imagine the looks on our faces when Bill told James and me of his intentions: he wanted to run Environment Friend in the Eclipse. 'Bloody hell, that's a bold move!' was my reaction. The ten furlongs might suit him better than one and a half miles and he was strengthening up with every passing week, but he would be taking on the best older horses after an appalling run in the Derby. Bill told us not to be so negative. Luckily for James and me, Bill was the one with the sense not us, thank God.

When you examined the opposition, to be honest, we didn't stand an earthly. The older generation provided a formidable trio. Steve rode the favourite, Stagecraft, who had recently won the Prince of Wales's Stakes at Royal Ascot; Pat was on the previous season's French Derby winner Sanglamore who had added the Prix d'Ispahan to his Group I tally a month earlier; and Ray Cochrane partnered the wonderful mare In The Groove, who had just added the Coronation Cup to the Irish 1000 Guineas, Juddmonte International and Champion Stakes she had won as a three-year-old. These were proven Group I performers. All these plus the Derby runner-up Marju, who already had two decisions over us. Environment Friend's starting price of 28/1 seemed an accurate reflection of his chances; only the pacemaker was at longer odds.

Two things contrived to work in our favour. The ground had turned good to soft and the early pace set by Green's Ferneley (with Walter obliged to do the honours, on behalf of Sanglamore, for once!) was taxing to the point of suicidal, just like the Dante. Moreover, my confidence was also high, because in the previous race I'd got the better of Pat to win the Listed sprint on Sir Mark's Case Law by a short head and then survive a stewards' enquiry. Unlike in the Derby, we were always travelling well in rear, and as I followed Steve through on the bend, Ray shouted across to me 'Go on, George! You'll win!' Steve kicked his horse past the pacemaker and I thought I'd have to settle for second, but then he faltered as we met the rising ground inside the two and I got upsides him. When Steve saw it was me and Environment Friend coming to beat him, a look of total bewilderment crossed his face, I can assure you. But beat him we did. Although Environment Friend faltered slightly, I sensed Stagecraft hadn't anything left. There was a head in it at the post with Sanglamore a full seven lengths further back in third spot. 'Not bad for an old 'un!' someone called out as the exhausted winner and his 44-year-old 'assistant' came back to unsaddle. Never had I heard a truer word. 'There's life in the old dog yet!', I shouted back.

The fact that 20 lengths covered the first six home categorically demonstrated how knackering a gallop the seventh horse had set. In that sense, the Eclipse unfolded as a carbon copy of the Dante. Had Walter gone too fast and tired too soon, left Stagecraft (trained by James's former boss, Michael Stoute) in front too long and played into the hands of a dour battling type like Environment Friend? Who cares? Certainly not me after drawing my biggest ever pay packet – seven and a half per cent of £147,825 – and only my second Group I in 25 years. The Jockey Club's middle-distance handicapper Anthony Arkwright reckoned Environment Friend had improved half a stone on his Dante form, though some were more instantly appreciative. 'Trainers agree Friend's victory was no fluke,' revealed J.A. McGrath in the *Daily Telegraph*. Let's face it, with us out of the way Stagecraft would have won by seven lengths and, as an acknowledged top horse, would have received every plaudit in the book.

I was on a roll! First of all, I added the Group III Gordon Stakes at Goodwood on James's Stylish Senor. In truth, this was as 'soft' a Group success as you could wish. There were only three runners and they were all 'monkeys'. It developed into one of those silly races where nothing wanted to win. Stylish Senor, for instance, had a fair bit of ability (both Walter and me had won on him) but you couldn't count on him to show it. He did his level best to give this one away. He looked like winning and then he stopped. Then he suddenly decides to go again and we get back up in the final furlong to deny Trebly by half a length. You couldn't call Stylish Senor a genuine Group horse by any stretch of the imagination.

Then, in late August, I won a second successive Solario Stakes, this year on a colt of Sir Mark's. Chicmond had been aimed at the Solario after recording a hat-trick of wins in low-key races at

Nottingham, Ayr and Catterick. Sir Mark being Sir Mark chose an embarrassingly easy opportunity on the all-weather at Southwell to get Chicmond spot-on for the Solario. From a maiden-at-closing on the all-weather to a Group III might have appeared over-ambitious to the bookmakers who allowed Chicmond to go off at a generous 16/1 but if they believed Southwell was Chicmond's proper habitat they didn't understand Sir Mark's mentality. Quite simply, if there's a race begging to be won Sir Mark just can't resist it. He knew he was pot-hunting on this occasion. Compared to his six Solario rivals, Chicmond had bags of experience – this was his sixth race – and the plan was to take up the running and make the race a severe test of character as well as ability: it was going to be one of those catch-me-if-you-can affairs.

Chicmond was a lazy bugger and needed maximum rousting but when they were thinking about getting on with the job in hand, he was already doing it. Three of them had a crack at him inside the final furlong but Chicmond held on by two necks from Seattle Rhyme (who went on to win the Group I Racing Post Trophy) and the odds-on favourite Artic Tracker. Both Sir Mark and I derive immense pleasure when the 'plan' comes off like that. Chicmond retired for the season with one defeat in six, but unfortunately he had trouble with his shins in 1992 and Sir Mark could never get him back on the track. It was a great shame.

I wish I could say that Environment Friend went on in 1991 to prove beyond a question of a doubt that he was an outstanding horse and that his Eclipse success was no 'fluke' but, hand on heart, I can't. That sunny afternoon at Sandown was his personal Everest. Never again did everything fall into place like it did that day. There was no pace in the Juddmonte International at York and it became a tactical sprint, which was no good for him, and virtually everything beat him, including Stagecraft; he ran much better in finishing a four-length second to the French Derby and future Arc winner Suave Dancer in the Irish Champion (beating Stagecraft on worse terms than in the Eclipse); but concluded his season by beating only two home out of 12 in the Champion Stakes at Newmarket (came back with a 'mucky' throat). That was him in a nutshell. One good run immediately followed by a stinker. He was so inconsistent, a real Jekyll and Hyde of a horse.

Environment Friend continued racing until he was seven (at times in combination with stallion duties – Bill always was one for those 'bold' ideas!), but he never won another race after the Eclipse and ceased to be my exclusive ride, although I did partner him to be third in the 1992 Champion Stakes which amounted to one of his better later efforts.

Nevertheless, boasting a Timeform rating of 128, he has to be in the top four horses I ever sat on. I shall always remember him with considerable affection, not only in his own right for those two gallant displays in 1991 but also for the absolutely crucial role he played in enabling me to realise a lifelong ambition during the following season that made 1992 the pinnacle of my entire career.

13

CLASSIC GLORY AT LAST

I have Michael Roberts to thank for my change of Classic fortune in 1992. It was a monumental season for Michael because he won the jockeys' title with 206 winners to become only the fifth man to record a double century, but it could so easily have been even more memorable for him had he not partnered a three-year-old filly for his long-time ally Alec Stewart in the Forte Airport Services Maiden Stakes over one and a quarter miles at Sandown on Friday, 24 April. Michael's loyalty to one of his greatest supporters meant he had to decline the offer from another, Clive Brittain, to ride an unraced filly belonging to Bill Gredley. Thanks to the Environment Friend connection, the mount was offered to me. So Michael Roberts rode Anghaam, whose solitary success was to be a lowly maiden, and I got to throw my leg across User Friendly who went on to provide me with the season of a lifetime.

You'd invariably find me riding at Thirsk, Catterick or Beverley when the Classics were being run. To be precise I had only partici-pated in 13 of the 75 Classics during my 25 seasons prior to 1992.

Even if you knock off the three years as an apprentice it was not much of a record. My first Classic ride proved all too typical. King of the Castle started at odds of 100/1 for the 1970 St Leger and came home last of nine to Nijinsky. I'd had three rides in the 2000 Guineas (66/1, 33/1 and 50/1), four in the 1000 Guineas (66/1, 50/1 and a pair of 200/1 rags), three in the Derby (150/1, 20/1 and Environment Friend at 11s), one in the Oaks at 100/1 and one more in the Leger (at 33/1) after King of the Castle. Ile de Nisky's fourth at 20s in Nashwan's Derby of 1989 was as close as I'd come (and that was seven and a half lengths back) to playing a part in a Classic finish.

Consequently, if there was an opportunity of riding winners elsewhere, the Classics could take care of themselves without the assistance of G Duffield. It's never been my policy to become disenchanted by missing the prestigious races or meetings for the less glamorous fixtures. Yes, we all want to ride in the Classics and the Group Is, but I've never seen the point of going to ride a 200/1 shot in the Derby if I can go to Beverley or Catterick for six good rides, because all the top men are at Epsom, and be in line for two or three winners. That 200/1 shot in the Derby isn't 200/1 for nothing: it's no good, it shouldn't be in the Derby, bar a miracle it can't possibly win. It's just there to make up the numbers and to get someone a mention. If I go to the lesser meeting and ride decent horses for 'fashionable' trainers deprived of their usual jockey, it puts me in for other rides for them in the future. On the whole, this policy has paid dividends, though some may argue it hasn't because I've not been at the top meetings to show my face. Then again, who sees you on a 200/1 shot trailing in at the back of the field?

User Friendly had been conceived with the Derby or Oaks in mind. The mating between Bill Gredley's staying mare Rostova, whom Steve Cauthen had piloted to victory in the 1985 Great Met over the Derby course and distance, and Steve's runaway Derby winner Slip Anchor of the same year (in whom Bill had a share) was planned as Steve and Bill tucked into dinner one evening with Rostova's trainer Clive Brittain and the wine began to flow. Slip Anchor was a remorseless galloper who made every yard in his Derby to spreadeagle the opposition and win by seven lengths. Rostova was way short of his class (Timeform rated her only 91 to Slip Anchor's 136) but she descended from one of the premier Classic bloodlines in the Stud Book, namely the Picture Play family of Mr Jim Joel. Close relatives of Rostova had won both Guineas (Royal Palace and Fairy Footsteps), the Derby (Royal Palace) and the St Leger (Light Cavalry), and her own grandam was a full sister to West Side Story who was beaten a nostril in the 1962 Oaks before winning the Yorkshire Oaks.

User Friendly may have had the pedigree to win the Oaks but when I first caught sight of her in the Sandown paddock she didn't remotely look the part. She was big, gangly and weak, lacking either strength or substance. She had been sent to the Sales but, like Environment Friend before her, she was returned to Stetchworth when failing to reach her 25,000 guineas reserve. Sandown was her first experience of a racecourse. The formbook entry for the race hit the nail right on the head: 'Opened 20/1, touched 33s; started slowly, headway from over two furlongs out, led approaching last, ran on well; distance two and a half lengths.' Anghaam and Michael Roberts were some 20 lengths behind us in tenth.

That could have been the beginning and end of my association with User Friendly. I'd won on her, but it was only a maiden and Michael Roberts seemed sure to get on her when she reappeared. But when the cards are falling for you anything is possible. Clive Brittain was eyeing the Cheshire Oaks for User Friendly's next outing and her Epsom prep. However, Michael Roberts had been riding work for Henry Cecil and he told Clive that the Chester race was also the target for Henry's Midnight Air, who had won the May

Hill Stakes and been first past the post in the Group I Fillies' Mile at Ascot as a juvenile. 'Don't take her on,' was his advice. 'Send User Friendly to Lingfield for its Oaks Trial three days later.' Clive took Michael's counsel, but unfortunately for Michael and very fortunately for me, Alec Stewart had one at Beverley that he wanted Michael to go up and ride. For once in my lifetime, it wouldn't be G Duffield languishing up in the North but M Roberts.

The Lingfield Oaks Trial was almost two furlongs further than User Friendly's Sandown maiden and the track is the same combination of bends and inclines that you encounter at Epsom. User Friendly proceeded to demonstrate that, gangly frame notwithstanding, such a course held no terrors for her and she showed how much the proper Oaks trip of one and a half miles would be up her street and how much she had come on from her debut by accomplishing her task with the minimum of fuss. We tracked Pat Eddery on Miss Plum until straightening up three out. Pat's filly rolled off the fence as she tired and we got a lovely run up the inner. It was merely a case of hands-and-heels after that and, with ears pricked, she easily accounted for the only one of our four rivals with anything left, Niodini, by two and a half lengths. Thirty minutes later Assessor won the Derby Trial in a time one and a half seconds slower than User Friendly had clocked. She was a racehorse, all right. We now knew that User Friendly could indeed justify those dinner plans of Bill and Steve.

Two events between Lingfield and Epsom convinced me not only could we win the Oaks but we would win the Oaks. On the Tuesday after our trial, York staged the Musidora Stakes, usually an even greater pointer to the Oaks in spite of being run over the shorter distance of one and a quarter miles. It was won by an unbeaten filly of Henry Cecil's called All At Sea. It was dreadfully slowly-run, and All At Sea, partnered by Pat, beat Walter Swinburn on Perfect Circle by a length in what amounted to a two-furlong sprint –

pursued by User Friendly's stablemate Armarama, whom we knew to be much her inferior. I watched the race on the weighing room's TV alongside John Lowe and I said to him 'I'll win the Oaks.' John replied: 'That's a bold statement.' These two fillies we'd just watched were meant to be the favourites. They looked non-stayers to me and I knew User Friendly could sustain a pace they'd find too hot to handle. No, if they were the best of the bunch, I'd nothing to fear. 'John,' I said, 'I'll beat both of those. I'm going to win the Oaks.'

It was very much out of character for me to say something like that. I'd rather undersell than oversell any of my mounts. On this occasion I was so bullish and cocksure about this filly's ability. She may not have looked a great mover – she tended to carry her head to one side, for instance – but she had an engine and could really gallop. Each time she worked she was upped in grade with a better class of horse and yet she was still up to beating them. She couldn't have been easy for Clive to train because she was a bit 'jointy' but there was no question that she was going from strength to strength. Clive continued to give her stiffer tasks, working her with animals officially rated 10lb her superior, with the same outcome. Finally, he staged a serious gallop over one and a quarter miles at level weights with Terimon and two lead horses.

Terimon was a six-year-old enitre who, after finishing second in Nashwan's Derby, had twice won the Group III Earl of Sefton over nine furlongs and under an inspired tactical ride from Michael Roberts had won the previous year's Group I Juddmonte International, in which me and Environment Friend trailed at the back. Terimon was a genuine yardstick of Pattern/Classic-race ability and one and a quarter miles was his distance. User Friendly stayed with him. She didn't work better than him, but she certainly worked as well as him. On the racecourse the three-years-older Terimon would have been giving her something like a stone in weight-for-age and sex. Terimon was also heading for Epsom to compete in the Coronation Cup which was two days before the Oaks. I couldn't wait to see how he fared. He finished third, just one and a half lengths behind the winner, Saddlers' Hall. That settled it. I was going to win the Oaks!

Bill, Clive and me discussed tactics. As it happened, nothing complicated struck us as necessary. It was all very simple and straightforward. We knew User Friendly (a very tempting 5/1 at the off) would handle the bends and undulations and we knew she'd get the trip. Whether All At Sea (favourite at 11/10) or Perfect Circle (second best at 9/2) would do likewise was highly debatable. We reckoned the Irish filly Fawaayid was bound to make it the good, testing gallop to suit User Friendly. If she did not go fast enough, we agreed I should go on and ensure the race developed into a searching examination of the two favourites' suspect stamina.

And that's exactly how the race panned out. We could not have stage-managed it better had we written the script ourselves – even the ground turned good to soft putting more of a premium on stamina – and with a field of only seven (the smallest in an Epsom Oaks since Pretty Polly beat three in 1904) it was extremely unlikely there would be any traffic problems to worry about. Christy Roche duly made the running on Fawaayid with me sitting second, and when she began to falter coming down Tattenham Hill I took over round the Corner, slid into the straight and then set sail thinking 'Pat'll have to go some to catch me because I'm not going to stop!' I momentarily caught sight of All At Sea's chestnut head at my quarters around the two pole, but it disappeared again in a matter of two or three strides leaving us all alone.

I knew then that I'd ridden my first Classic winner. None of the other five runners were capable of beating me. 'Fucking hell!' I was saying to myself, 'You've done it! At the grand old age of 45 you've actually ridden a Classic winner!' I was 20 feet in the air! On a different planet! I never thought I'd achieve a Classic victory in my wildest dreams. We went past the post three-and-a-half lengths to the good over the favourite; the rest were 20 lengths and more in arrears. All the other boys immediately congratulated me: 'Brilliant!'; 'Well done, George!'; 'Fantastic!' I leant over and kissed User Friendly's lass Wendy Meek as soon as she reached us, seconds before all the photographers began to gather round pleading for a 'Look-this-way-stick-your-thumb-up' picture opportunity.

Clive had won Classics before – Julio Mariner in the Leger, Pebbles and Mystiko in the Guineas – but this was a new experience for Bill as well as for me. It was an especially poignant moment for Bill because his wife Sara was seriously ill with the cancer that was soon to claim her life. The rest of the afternoon went by in a blur. I had one more mount at Epsom (finishing last!) before driving up to Leicester for a further three in the evening, but I'm ashamed to say I don't think I gave any of them much of a ride. It was so unprofessional of me. The day, however, had grown increasingly overwhelming and Leicester was a terrible anticlimax.

It was far too late for any celebrations by the time I got back to Cedar Cottage. A few glasses of champagne and it was straight to bed. The next thing I remember is waking up in the middle of the night sensing somebody crawling up the bed underneath the bedclothes! All of a sudden this head pops up between Gill and me – and it's only jockey Nigel Day! 'I fucking love you, you superstar!' he's saying, clearly having downed more than the odd shandy. 'I fucking love you, George!' I jumped out of bed like a startled rabbit. 'How the hell did you get in the house?' I asked him. 'Me, I get anywhere, me!' Only 'Nobby' Day could have pulled off a stunt like that! Apparently, the kids had let him in.

The following day, mind you, I did get seriously drunk. We held an impromptu party for close friends and some of the boys: Tebby,

Eric Apter, Colin Nutter and Sir Mark – 'See you won that race at Epsom, then' – who was nearly as pleased as me, his only regret (and mine) that this Classic had not been for Heath House. We drank so much champagne (me and Nobby polished off a magnum between us before anyone arrived!) that we had to send out to the pub for reinforcements.

Although Bill, entirely in character, contemplated taking on the colts in the Irish Derby, he eventually plumped for the more conventional and less arduous route for a three-year-old filly and supplemented User Friendly into the Irish Oaks. As none of her Epsom victims decided it was worth another crack at her, she started an 11/8 on favourite to become the first since Diminuendo in 1988 to record the Epsom-Curragh double. Aliysa and Jet Ski Lady had come unstuck in recent renewals and so, very nearly, did we.

User Friendly had suffered a couple of minor hiccups in the month following Epsom and she was only 85 per cent of the filly we saw in the Oaks. Heart and soul pulled her through in the Irish Oaks. Clive also ran Armarama in the race to make the running for us, but she never got to fulfil the role as the Irish filly Ivyanna, doing the job on behalf of Arrikala, quickly shot half-a-dozen lengths clear. In fact, when Philip Robinson attempted to pull out to challenge the leader rounding the bend, it was me who flattened him in my eagerness to reach the front.

From here on to the post, it was head down and push, push, push. Lady Luck was on our side. Arrikala was absolutely cantering on the rail but she had nowhere to go because we were directly in front of her and Market Booster, the Irish Guineas runner-up who was also cruising, had moved up on her outside. User Friendly had a tendency to lug left-handed. Had she done so this day, Arrikala would have been through and in the clear. As it was, User Friendly, bless her, ran as straight as an arrow and there was nothing Kevin

Manning on Arrikala could do about it. Furthermore, despite the apparent ease with which Market Booster was travelling, she could find little extra when Mick Kinane finally went for her. User Friendly, in contrast, responded gamely to everything I threw at her, and we held on by a neck to win our second Classic with the luckless Arrikala half-a-length further back.

Our Group I hat-trick was completed by the Yorkshire Oaks on the never to be forgotten day G Duffield very nearly met his maker in the skies above Lincolnshire when the light aircraft taking me to York was almost struck by an RAF jet fighter. On paper the Yorkshire Oaks looked a formality. The market went 8/1 (the Irish Oaks fourth Bineyah) bar User Friendly at 11/8 on in a field of eight. But nothing is ever a 'formality', as that plane ride had demonstrated earlier in the day. Looking back, I don't believe I was as focused as I would like to have been, even if I did have a perfectly understandable reason for being so.

Things began badly. There was a false start, and when we did get away properly User Friendly missed the jump, poodled out, and we were much further back than I'd wanted, with only three behind us. The sedate pace picked up noticeably at the three marker and, trapped on the fence, we were immediately in trouble. I had no option but to pull back, come five wide and try to launch a challenge down the centre of the track. This ground was the firmest she had been asked to run on and she wasn't liking it. This time she did lug to the left. Thankfully, she also showed how tough and gutsy she was. Slowly but surely we began to reel them in and although I was working overtime on the right rein to prevent her from interfering with the horses we were passing on our inside, we finally hit the front inside the final furlong to forge clear of Bineyah by two and a half lengths. I gather the Channel 4 commentator Graham Goode described User Friendly as 'The bravest of the fillies in training' as she passed the post, a verdict that was spot-on.

User Friendly's ultimate objective for the season was the Prix de l'Arc de Triomphe. But as both Bill and Clive were adamant she was superior to the Derby winner Dr Devious or any of the other Classic colts, the temptation to prove it in the St Leger became irresistible. The extended one-and-three quarter miles was never going to be a problem, and when Dr Devious opted for the Irish Champion Stakes as his Arc prep the colts heading for Doncaster looked pure second division. Apart from the discouraging statistic that Leger winners had a lousy record in the Arc, there was no logical reason why she shouldn't have a shot at raising her Classic total to three. Accordingly, seven days before the race, Bill dug into his wallet and stumped up the £25,000 necessary to supplement her. Then a problem did materialise. The ground began to dry up.

Cue Clive Brittain for any amount of kidology! Four times during the week Clive walked the track, on each occasion telling the press on his return that 'We don't want it this dry. I don't think we'll get away with it' in a thinly disguised attempt to persuade clerk of the course John Sanderson to water the track if he wanted to ensure his star attraction turned up on the Saturday. Clive even hinted at rerouting User Friendly to the Group I Prix Vermeille at Longchamp on the Sunday. But it was equally firm in Paris and, in any case, the Leger was the race we wanted. The bookmakers reacted by easing User Friendly's odds from 6/4 to 9/4 and at one point Bonny Scot (winner of the traditional Leger trial, York's Great Voltigeur) was promoted to favouritism in her presumed absence.

However, everyone knew User Friendly was the star of the show. Without her there'd be no spectacle. As the weather forecasters' promised drop of rain failed to arrive, Clive said he'd leave the decision until Saturday morning and risk being fined the £1,500 if he withdrew. Clive's 'pressure' worked. On Friday night, Sanderson ordered the taps to be switched on for seven hours (though denying it was purely for User Friendly's benefit), depositing a quarter of a million gallons on the track – the equivalent of one tenth of an inch of rainfall!

The going was still good to firm on the Saturday but the sting had been taken out of the ground and it was perfectly safe for her. The race, in all honesty, was tailor-made for her and couldn't have unfolded in a more copybook fashion. Lester took the field along at a decent clip on Mack the Knife with us contentedly lobbing in his shadow. One kick in the belly halfway up the straight and it was all over in a few strides. As we came out from behind the tiring leader, I glanced over my right shoulder to check where Bonny Scot was, and then checked left to make sure I was not going to edge across Mack the Knife. I need not have bothered. She murdered them. The margin of victory was three-and-a-half lengths without me being hard on her. 'Next stop Longchamp for Friendly,' prophesied the *Racing Post*.

Donning the famous Leger-winning jockey's cap after victory in our oldest Classic race which is run just 25 miles from my birthplace was the ultimate ambition fulfilled. I derived immense satisfaction from User Friendly's St Leger, but I can't say the feeling it gave me was quite so exquisite as the Oaks.

Although there were only three weeks between the Leger and the Arc, which is too close really, no second thoughts were entertained about having a tilt at the latter. No Leger winner had gone straight on to add the Arc. The great Triple Crown-winning Nijinsky had come second in 1970, while another Oaks-Leger heroine in Sun Princess ran second in 1983. Other than freshening her up, little was done with User Friendly in the interim, and I didn't even need to ride her. She'd had a long season but she had answered each and every call. A perfect six from six record including four Group Is and three Classics was something to be rightly proud of, and the £161,368 she won in the Leger (a far cry from that £2,469 maiden!) had raised her total earnings to over half a million – £523,905 to be precise. Victory in the Arc would see that figure doubled at a stroke.

In answer to our prayers, the heavens opened. And when it pours in Paris, Longchamp soon resembles a swamp. By race-day the penetrometer read 3.9, 'tres souple', very soft. As for race tactics and pre planning, there didn't seem to be much need. 'Do whatever you like,' Bill Gredley told me, 'but do not,' he emphasised, 'do not make the running.' Why Bill didn't want me to make the running, I don't know because he'd been happy for me to do so in the Oaks if circumstances demanded. Certainly, few Arc winners had made all apart from Lester on Alleged. Bill even considered supplementing Environment Friend into the race as a pacemaker but, on reflection, thought he was too good for such a task and, anyway, unlike the majority of French races, the Arc was invariably run at a fast gallop with or without pacemakers. But what if...

A cracking field of 18 lined up, 12 of whom were Group I winners. These included the Derby and Oaks winners from England, Ireland and France – Dr Devious, St Jovite, Polytain, Jolypha and ourselves. St Jovite had smashed the Epsom Derby winner by 12 lengths in a track record-time in the Irish Derby and then added the King George by six lengths before Dr Devious exacted revenge by a short head in the Irish Champion Stakes. The French Derby winner Polytain, by contrast, had added nothing to his reputation and ran very poorly in his Arc prep, but the French Oaks winner Jolypha had overcome traffic problems to win the Prix Vermeille User Friendly declined to contest. The principal French hope, however, was the four-year-old filly Magic Night, winner of the Prix Foy and second to Suave Dancer in the Arc 12 months ago. Few people gave much thought to the chances of the four-year-old colt Subotica, fourth in the Coronation Cup and twice behind Magic Night since winning the Prix Ganay in the spring. The biggest thing in Subotica's favour besides proven ability in the mud was the identity of his trainer, the 'Little Napoleon' of French racing, Andre

Fabre. Even among this galaxy of stars User Friendly was considered the brightest, and she was sent off the 7/2 favourite.

Unfortunately, the one thing this star-studded field lacked on the day was a pacemaker. Normally there'd be two or three of them. St Jovite had front-run to win his Derby and King George, but on this soft ground he could ill afford to use himself too early in the race. To complicate matters even more, he had been drawn on the wide outside which effectively prevented him from cutting across straight away to the rails because you must keep straight through the opening furlong in France. So, there was no guarantee he'd be of any assistance to us.

My worst fears were soon realised. There was no pace. I didn't need to see the electric sectional times they have in France to appreciate how slow we were travelling because I actually wound up fighting her and pulling her around in second or third as Sapience and St Jovite completed the first metric half mile in 56.1 seconds, some six seconds slower (which equates to about 30 lengths) than it should have been; a fraction slower even than the following year's race on heavier ground.

I'd love to have gone on. But my hands were tied. Had User Friendly been a Heath House animal, I'd not have been tied down so specifically to orders. Sir Mark would have tried to look for every contingency but if something unexpected materialised, the decisions would have been mine, and mine alone, to reach. I had explicit instructions. If I went on and got beat, I'm there to be slaughtered. If I do as I'm told and get beat, I can't be blamed. I knew it was the wrong thing to do but it was what Bill Gredley had wanted. I felt I had to abide by his wishes. Yet, here I was, riding a Leger filly coming back to one and a half miles in testing ground and I'm desperate to be testing the others and I can't! Many of them disliked this ground and would have been pushed to the limits of their stamina. I should have kicked her in the belly and gone on. I rue the day I didn't.

Although the tempo obviously increased eventually, that Arc – my Arc – was won and lost down the far side of the course. We went past St Jovite no problem as soon as we straightened up with two and a half furlongs to run but, in the process, gave a lovely lead to Subotica. From then on, it was hammer and tongs all the way to the line. One second we were in front, the next second he was. Less than 50 metres out I'm sure we got in front once again, but in the last couple of strides she faltered – racing so free in those critical early furlongs had left her without that vital bit of energy when she needed it most – and Subotica got there first by a neck. We ran the last half-mile in 51.8 seconds, over four seconds faster than the first. The final time was 13 seconds outside the record.

User Friendly had lost her unbeaten record. Yet she had done me proud. All the same, I was absolutely gutted. I'd probably never get another chance to win an Arc. All that kept running through my head was the thought that had I done what I felt was right, I might have won.

I kept these thoughts to myself in the heat of the post-race moment. When Channel 4's Brough Scott asked me about the importance of those pedestrian early furlongs, for once in my life I gave the diplomatic response: 'It didn't help with Christy Roche on St Jovite being drawn so wide. It took him such a long time to come by me and get in front of me. Sapience didn't jump as quick as Richard Quinn wanted, so it took him a while too, and I'm in front of those and they're chasing me up and getting me running free. I'm having to drag her back to get in behind them.'

After that, I didn't want to talk to anyone or discuss the race with anyone; on the way back to the airport, I was so annoyed and upset. What a fuck-up.

I felt no better the following morning having to read the headlines, 'Friendly fire foiled' in *The Sporting Life* and 'Oh so close!' in the *Racing Post*. Understandably, and in some ways justifiably, I came in for some criticism from certain sections of the press who questioned the wisdom of not forcing the pace. They had a point, as I well knew, but they weren't riding for Bill Gredley, a man who, once his mind is made up, means what he says. He'd never have forgiven me. Clive rallied to my defence. 'George has ridden her brilliantly all year and he rode a perfect race here,' he countered. 'If George had let her go and she'd been beaten, people would have come up with the argument that nobody makes the running in the Arc and would have asked why he hadn't held her up.'

If there is any moral to the story of User Friendly's Arc, it is this: the only time you get it right in a race is when you win.

The intention had always been for User Friendly to contest the Japan Cup in November, whatever the outcome of the Arc. Clive had won the race back in 1986 with Jupiter Island and knew what a massive production number the whole event was. The prize money was phenomenal: the equivalent of £920,813 for winning and going down to £92,000 for fifth. Nevertheless, I don't really believe the Japan Cup is the right kind of race for a European three-year-old campaigned in the Classics like User Friendly, who'd contested – and won – three Classics plus enduring a gruelling race on very soft ground in the Prix de l'Arc de Triomphe only a few weeks before-hand. But when the prize money involves that many noughts, the invitation takes some refusing!

The Arc had bottomed her and she ought not have run in Japan. This was patently obvious before we flew out. The Japanese actually came over to Newmarket to film her working and she couldn't get by her galloping companion, which was a horse you wouldn't normally canter her with let alone work. 'I think she's gone,' I told Clive. Even so, she was made favourite for the race and still ran pretty well in it: on ground like a motorway she faded in the straight and finished just out of the money in sixth behind the home-trained Tokai Teio.

Much to my delight, User Friendly was kept in training for a four-year-old campaign aimed at the King George and another Arc, but she was never the same filly at four as she was at three. I saw nothing of her in the spring, when there'd been contrasting reports of her wellbeing. In fact, I didn't see her or sit on her until being reunited in the paddock prior to the Coronation Cup. 'How is she?' Bill Gredley asked me. 'I don't know – I've not ridden her,' I replied. 'Why?' goes Bill, incredulously. 'I've not been asked.'

Whatever problems User Friendly may have had during the off-season (Clive did have the virus in his yard for a time), she certainly had no fire in her belly this day. The field swung wide, right over to the stands side, coming into the straight and, once I put her under pressure, she began to hang left in her usual style, down the camber, conceding valuable ground and impetus. She finished fourth to Opera House – and even trailed Environment Friend by five lengths. This was not the User Friendly I knew.

After Epsom, I did ride her a couple of mornings and she seemed to be picking up. User Friendly's cause at Epsom had not been helped by her tongue getting over the bit, so Clive decided to fit a 'cheeker', a V-shaped piece of rubber fitted on to the top of the bridle to keep the bit up in her mouth, to make her run straighter. Some consideration was given to running in the Eclipse, but the shorter trip and the fact that Sandown was right-handed saw the notion discounted and she was sent to France for the Group I Grand Prix de Saint-Cloud. Saint-Cloud is all left-hand bends like Lingfield and Epsom, so we knew she'd come round them like a greyhound. On this occasion I went out to do battle in France armed with the permission that, if nothing was prepared to set a decent gallop, I could take the bull by the horns and attempt to run them into the ground. I did – and we did. We landed an on-course gamble from 9/2 to 2.4/1 in beating Apple Tree by one and a half lengths:

in the Coronation Cup he'd been nearly five and a half lengths ahead of us. 'Friendly floors French,' declared *The Sporting Life*'s front page. 'Brittain's brave filly blazes the trail to set up King George showdown.'

For the first time in public, in response to post-race press queries regarding my new tactics at Saint-Cloud, I referred to the fact that I'd been told 'not to make it' in the Arc – which made Bill's comments in a subsequent interview all the more interesting reading. 'The great thing about having an experienced jockey such as George is that you can leave it to him,' he was quoted as saying. 'You can make suggestions, but the day you tell a top jockey what to do, either you should be riding the horse yourself or you have got the wrong jockey.' No comment!

In this kind of form, I was confident User Friendly could turn the tables on Opera House (who only beat Apple Tree by a head in the Coronation Cup) in the King George, and when Clive told me he was sure she'd improved 7lb from Saint-Cloud, I had no reason to think victory was out of the question despite the participation of current Derby winners Commander in Chief (English and Irish) and White Muzzle (Italian). A fair amount of rain falling 24 hours before the race did us no harm, either. But, in the race itself, I could never manage to sit secure on an uncontested lead. The rest were right behind me, hustling her up all the way, and we were quickly gobbled up by Opera House and Commander in Chief after we'd rounded the bend, to eventually finish fourth some dozen lengths adrift. She blew an awful lot afterwards (and was found to have an abscess in her mouth), a sign which Clive took to mean she had gone too fast in front due to the attentions of the others.

By this stage, Bill had sold a half-share in User Friendly to the American businessman Gary Tanaka and she only raced twice more in Europe, and on neither occasion did we see anything approaching her best form. After hanging all the way down the straight in the Yorkshire Oaks, she was only third to another four-year-old Only Royale (who had never won a Pattern race before); and in the Arc (which was again run on soft ground to suit) we were drawn nearest the rail and virtually put through it by Willie Carson on Armiger within 30 seconds of leaving the gate, which put paid to any chance we may have had of gaining compensation for the previous year. We beat one home.

That was the last I saw of User Friendly. After the possibility of the Breeders' Cup was shelved (for which I'd have been replaced by an American jockey in any case), Mr Tanaka acquired Bill's 50 per cent and she was sent to be trained by Rodney Rash in California. Racing in the States wouldn't have suited her style of racing. All she managed to win before being finally retired in early 1995 was one little allowance race at Del Mar. The whole experience demeaned her. It was a crying shame her career finished on such a low note, which, I feel, was the price she paid for the Arc and the Japan Cup.

She was so brave and possessed so much class. Timeform rated her 128 as a three-year-old, one pound higher than Dr Devious, which, with the added bonus of the 3lb fillies' allowance, supports my contention that she could have won the Derby. That rating of 128 suggests, according to Timeform, she was on a par with Environment Friend and Noalcoholic and 4lb inferior to Giant's Causeway among the best horses I've been associated with. I beg to differ. She won me five Group Is inside twelve months where it had previously taken me 25 years to win two. She had fulfilled a lifelong ambition of mine and more than anything else had helped make 1992 the season of a lifetime as far as I was concerned. To me she was THE best.

14

JOURNEYMAN BLUES

When you've had your snout buried in life's tastier troughs you most definitely do not relish swiftly returning it to the burger bar. Even best bitter tastes awfully flat after champagne. Yet beer was what I was going to have to get used to. Sir Mark Prescott's exploits with Spindrifter, for example, only gained him three new orders at the end of the season. In similar vein, winning two Classics and four Group Is in 1992 seemed to have no impact at all on my profile – I continued to be so much in demand when the Classics came around that I didn't ride in another one for eight seasons! Those American Blues singers would have a load of raw material for a song if they ever get around to writing one about that world-weary breed of jockey who glories in the description of 'journeyman'.

If you are a journeyman jockey you live as much on the roads as the racetrack. It's the one aspect of being a jockey that really depresses me. It's all very well and good being described in the racing headlines as a 'Motorway Marvel' or the 'King of the Road', and to read that 'Duffield dashes are paying off', but I was clocking up to 60,000 miles a year on the roads and was beating up and down the A1 so often it got to the stage where it was so depressing I actually detested getting into the car. I don't like to think just how many hours I've wasted in traffic jams, for instance, or the number of near misses I've had in traffic.

It doesn't matter where you go in the country, the traffic has become increasingly horrendous and gets worse every year. In the early years, I used to be forever driving up the A1 in the company of Graham Sexton and Peter Madden; we'd often meet up with some of the Northern boys at Scotch Corner and get a lift with them for the last two and a half hours if it was Musselburgh or Hamilton so we could get a kip, but the whole drive would take six hours. Most journeys are a chore and take hours longer than they should, or you expect. You have to give yourself so much spare time, especially with the London meetings. Now I'm based in Yorkshire, there are days when it takes seven hours to get back up here from Sandown Park, for example, instead of four to five – and that's a bloody long time to be vegetating in the back of a car. From here to Sir Mark's takes three hours (from Cedar Cottage, of course, it used to be a ten-minute doddle!). In order to ride work at ten to seven twice a week, I'll be up at three and be on the road by 3.45. You feel you're the only man on the planet apart from the birds. I'll pick up my current driver, Les Robson (the latest in a long line!), at Leeming Bar and I'll drive the first leg to the other side of Doncaster, where he'll take over, allowing me to snatch some sleep. We jockeys are all trying to cut corners and take in two meetings during the height of the season but I have tried to get out of that mentality and just do one meeting a day if at all possible. Ironically, it's quicker coming home after evening racing because at least the traffic has eased off. But there are still days when I could be out of the house at 3.45 and not back until midnight.

In these circumstances a decent car is an essential part of the job.

My first car, the precious Vauxhall Viva with the twin aerials, lasted less than a season after Eric Eldin drove it far too fast one day and the engine blew up! After that came a Ford Corsair and then the MGB Sports; since then I've been through Mercs, BMWs, a Toyota Supra Sport, Audis and now I've a Peugeot 607 – in its first five months it's clocked up 48,000 miles.

Most jockeys, believe it or not, are good drivers because we are used to thinking quicker than most people. Through race-riding, our reactions and thought patterns are much faster than the majority of people on the roads. We are used to making decisions in seconds.

We tend to drive like we ride! A 'ton' is an automatic ban, so although there may be odd occasions when you're forced to drive that fast to make up for lost time in a traffic jam, you avoid reaching those speeds. But there are some of us who would give you a fright. Clarky loves fast cars, for instance. He used to own a Ford fitted with a microchip, a modified engine, that enabled it to really fly! My Toyota Supra could also motor. It had a cruise control facility on it: you flicked the switch to knock it off and touched the brake to return to normal mode. This almost proved the undoing of Gary Carter one day. Gary was at the wheel – while I was sleeping – on a trip up the A1 when this artic pulls out into the fast lane. Gary goes to brake to cancel the cruise control and nothing happens – so he flicks the switch and for some reason the car surges forward and rams into the back of the lorry. The car just ran away of its own accord. The artic didn't even realise it had been struck and carried on regardless but it put the wind up us.

My first bump was in the old Ford Corsair, on the way to Goodwood with Stilly. We were following Taffy Thomas's Jag and approached a set of traffic lights. Jockeys never stop on amber! Well, this guy known as 'Big Wal' was driving Taffy's Jag and for some unknown reason he broke the unwritten rule and stopped on amber when yours truly, coming along behind him, was sure he'd drive on. My Corsair smashed straight into him, and was put completely out of action. Taffy Thomas gets out and calls me all the names under the sun – but he still gave us a lift to Goodwood.

Run-ins with the police are an occupational hazard. I've been stopped loads of times and always seem to have an average of nine points on my licence. Recently I was pulled over doing 108/109 on the way back from York one night, which meant an automatic ban. Luckily for me, when I got out my licence the copper looks at it in the headlights and says 'Are you George Duffield the jockey?' His partner in the police car, however, was clearly intent on 'doing' me. 'Do you know how fast you were going?' he says. 'Do you know how lucky you are that my friend likes you? I'm going to give you an on-the-spot fine on this occasion.' He didn't have to keep telling me how lucky I was – only the previous week I'd been collared in the same going to Southwell!

Of course, you can always reduce the hassle involved in covering two meetings in a day by the use of a light aircraft, but in the aftermath of the tragedy involving Frankie Dettori and Ray Cochrane in the summer of 2000 which killed their pilot, Patrick Mackey, we've all become understandably reluctant to resort to a plane unless we're really left with no choice in the matter. Nor is it as cheap as it was in the 1980s and early 1990s.

I know for a fact that I've had at least four decidedly dodgy incidents in the air. The first one was during take-off on the Rowley Mile when oil started gushing out of one of the engines. The pilot couldn't see it because he was looking straight ahead for take-off, but fortunately we passengers did and alerted him before we left the ground. On another occasion an engine packed up and the pilot, Neil Forman, had to bring it down and make an emergency landing at Lincoln with only one engine. This is a serious feat, as the plane was pulling to one side all the time and Neil had to fight it all the way down.

Another fraught landing was at Newmarket in a plane with Sir Mark and, I think, Jimmy Quinn. This plane had two tanks of fuel: when one runs dry the pilot flicks to the other. As we were coming in to land, we hear this ominous 'pht, pht, pht' as the tank it's on runs out. The result is that the plane begins to descend cock-eyed before the pilot can switch to the second tank. He has to abort the landing, and pulls out left-handed over the Devil's Dyke – just like Frankie's plane did – before dropping down through the running rails onto the Rowley Mile somewhere near the one and a quarter mile start.

The incident that made the front pages of the national dailies was the one on Wednesday, 19 August 1992, when Lester, Philip Robinson, Michael Hills and me were flying up to York in a twin-engined six-seater Piper PA34 and got 'buzzed' 4,500 feet over Lincolnshire by a Tornado jet fighter from RAF Coningsby. Philip was sat in the front with the pilot, Dave Smith, a former RAF pilot himself, when he spots a couple of jets in the middle distance. 'Don't they always fly in groups of three or four' he's thinking to himself, when another one comes right up in front of us, so close that Philip swears he saw the whites of the pilot's eyes. The downdraught flipped us over sideways, flinging us out of our seats toward the roof of the aircraft. I'd been asleep and woke up with Lester's head in my lap! Dave is yelling 'Mayday! Mayday!' into his radio and I'm thinking 'Fuck! It's a long way down there. We're going to die!' No one said a word apart from Dave. We just looked at each other. Somehow Dave got us back on an even keel and made an emergency landing at RAF Waddington.

The pilot of the jet fighter had already radioed in to say he had taken out a light aircraft and presumed its occupants must all be dead. All I could think of as the aircraft was sat on the runway being checked over, was that I'd got to reach York to ride User Friendly in the Yorkshire Oaks and there was no way we could get there in time by road. I'd no regard for my safety or anyone else's. Even though we were surrounded by fire crews and safety teams I just wanted to get back in the air.

Fortunately, Dave received the 'all-clear' and we continued the journey to land safely at Rufforth, just outside York, and we arrived on course in plenty of time for the first race. It was only then that I began to realise how lucky we'd been, although it was still hard to take it all in. I'm afraid I didn't give my first mount much of a ride but User Friendly won her Group I so everything panned out OK in the end.

Then the relief set in. I was sat in my usual corner of the York weighing room and Lester sidles over, and in his customary drawl, says: 'You know how lucky we are don't you? We should be dead.' During our return flight, Lester and I shared a bottle of champagne, as much to forget where we were and what we were doing as in celebration of my Group I victory on User Friendly. A subsequent inquiry by the Joint Airmiss Working Group declared that we had been ten feet from death that morning. The report laid the blame at the feet of air traffic controllers for 'poor judgement' in allowing the Tornado 'to climb into confliction with the PA34' and stated that had the fighter pilot not spotted us in the nick of time and rolled his plane to the left there would have been a collision with catastrophic results.

I escaped from that near disaster with bruised ribs. I've not always got away scot-free on the racetrack – that horror fall in Calcutta instantly springs to mind – but apart from the damage incurred in the fall at Bath and the head butt from Lily Augusta at Carlisle, I've been pretty lucky with injuries on home territory. I did break a toe when my horse reared in the stalls at Musselburgh in 1984, and ten years later damaged my ribs just before I was due to ride Hasten To Add at Royal Ascot. Beyond that, the only two major mishaps I can recall were stupid and bizarre in equal measure since they were both of my own making.

Thanks to the Duffield temper I managed to break the index finger of my left hand in June 1999 – which might have had calamitous repercussions because I was due to be riding Alborada in the Eclipse the following Saturday. It occurred as I was taking a three-year-old filly of Sean Woods's called Tomoe Gozen down to the gate on Newmarket's July Course. This filly could pull a bit and she bolted with me after the saddle slipped up her neck. I managed to pull her up but had to jump off. She then persisted in trying to jump all over me as I attempted to lead her toward the stalls, finally hitting me with her head. Bingo! I'm having none of that. I had my stick in my left hand and went to jab this thing on the nose with the handle but, as I did so, she opened her mouth like an alligator causing the handle to go right inside. The outcome was my fingers collided with her teeth!

The doc reckoned I'd be off for six weeks! With the Eclipse only seven days away that was not the news I wanted to hear. I went over to Carlisle to see Hugh Barber, so famous for putting jump jockeys back together again in double-quick time. 'Well, I can speed things up with a screw through the finger and hopefully you'll make the Eclipse,' he said upon examining the X-rays, 'but I can't guarantee it. It's up to you. How much do you want to ride?' I was desperate to ride! Fortunately for me, Alborada saved my bacon because she could not run in the Eclipse.

I was off for ten days and pushed my luck by returning too soon. I rode a double for Sir Mark at Southwell but I was like a man with one arm. I couldn't pull my whip through, and the finger was so weak that the lad had to pull the saddle of one of the horses for me in the winner's enclosure. Apparently, I'd not only reopened the wound, causing it to bleed, but also pulled the two bones apart again. I had to give it best and after riding Pasternak in the John Smith's it took another 12 days (which included a helpful six-day suspension) to get it sorted properly.

The second accident occurred, would you believe, in a football match! I was playing in goal for the Southern Jockeys XI versus the Northern Jockeys XI on 24 October 1986 at the Doncaster Rovers ground, opposite the racecourse. Now, it would give totally the wrong impression to term this a football match. It was a war. I don't really know why we bothered having a ball on the pitch because it was a free-for-all. Pat Eddery walked off! 'I've got to ride Dancing Brave in the Breeders' Cup next week,' he said. 'You lot are fucking mad!'

The match was supposed to be for charity but it descended into nothing more than a vendetta! It was survival of the fittest! And I only lasted 15 minutes! This ball came over into the penalty area along the ground and I went out to collect it. It was a 50-50 ball, so I decided to dive on it – just as Lindsay Charnock and Nicky Connorton came charging in for it. One of them must have kicked me in the face, because I was laid out unconscious for five minutes. I woke up – like a good goalie, still holding the ball! – with a fractured cheekbone. Off I went to Doncaster Royal Infirmary for an operation. That was the end of my season – leaving me six short of my maiden century. Adding further insult to injury was the fact that the match had been brought forward from its original post-season date after the organisers discovered Doncaster Rovers had a home fixture on that day!

'Agony of Duffield the Nearly Man' was how *The Sporting Life* reported my misfortune. This was the fourth season I'd become stuck in the 'nervous nineties' when seeking to record my first century: 1981 (94 – earning me fifth place in the table behind Lester, my highest ever position), 1982 (92) and 1983 (98) being the others. When you're a journeyman jockey who is never going to be champion (although I did lead the table in 1993 until almost the end of May!) or pick up mounts in Classics or Pattern races left, right and centre, this type of milestone assumes even greater significance. I'd already passed one notable landmark by riding my 1000th winner in Britain when Gavin Hunter's three-year-old filly Color Blind won her maiden at Warwick on 8 April 1985, and although a century had never been a specific target of mine, I was determined to get there having come so close so often. It was all about pressure and how you handle it. It's the same in any sport as the pressure on you increases, and I don't kid myself. As demonstrated by that unreasonably harsh ride I gave Reem at Folkestone, which annoyed Sir Mark, I didn't handle it particularly well. I tried too hard and did things I shouldn't.

What a relief when I eventually reached the magical figure for the first time, at Chepstow on 20 October 1992. The occasion was made doubly pleasurable because my partner in the Spinney Stakes was the old gelding Two Left Feet, trained by Sir Mark. I dedicated my 100th winner to the miners, men of my own ilk, who had been experiencing a hard time. I completed the season on 108 (38 of them for Sir Mark) for fifth place in the list behind Michael Roberts; the following year I increased my score to 116 (a record 40 for Sir Mark) for another fifth place behind Pat Eddery. Besides being the highest total in my career, this second century had additional kudos since it made me only the 21st jockey to have scored a ton at least twice since World War II. To win a Classic, ride 100 winners and ride in a hurdle race had become my three riding ambitions and they'd all materialised in the same 1992 season – the last two on the same day when I'd also participated in the Flat Jockeys versus Jump Jockeys race over hurdles.

Being regarded as a 'Northern' jockey is on a par with being labelled a 'journeyman'. Neither description is especially desirable or carries sufficient respect. The North-South Divide is a strong term but, in my opinion, you can ride lots of winners in the North and still not get noticed. If you rode the same amount of winners in the South you'd get greater recognition because the Southern tracks receive more media coverage. You'd have to flick through the pages to find mention of G Duffield riding a double at Hamilton but there'll be pages devoted to the man who has ridden two at Ascot or been beaten on an odds-on favourite at Sandown. I know Kevin Darley became champion jockey in 2000 and he is a Northern jockey, but to win the title Kevin had to spend plenty of time in the South – and if he'd been Southern-based I'm sure he would have received greater recognition. Even good Northern jockeys can find the going hard in the South once they move away from an area where they command lots of rides and the pick of any decent horses that come up from the South. Even someone as good as Eddie Hide struggled in the South when he took the job with Sir Gordon Richards for a year or two. You need a top yard like Stoute or Cecil behind you, as Kieren had, in order to make the break through.

I know for a fact that a jockey will get more coverage riding 60 winners in the South than riding 60 in the North – because I came into that category season after season. Nobody really noticed. It didn't pull any strings with anybody. I was merely regarded as someone who spent most of his time riding in the North riding plenty of winners, but winners of no consequence. They were of consequence to me because I was still doing the same job, albeit on lesser horses, to achieve the same objective – winning races. I never moaned about it. I wasn't riding the quality horses or riding in the quality races, but that's life. Just get on with the job and one day it might happen.

Fashion is a funny thing. You're either fashionable or you're not. I've never been fashionable. I've been capable, never fashionable. Yet given the chance, I've usually come up with the goods. In this respect a jockey's agent is a crucial factor. If you're not that fashionable, your agent has to be able to sell you and be completely on the ball so that he knows what's going on and where horses are going. I've had a few good ones and one, Peter Harris, who left a lot to be desired and I had to sack him. My current agent, Keith Bradley, is second to none, absolutely brilliant. Shippy Ellis did a good job for me for a long time, but gradually I began to wonder whether I was getting value for money. I was just not getting the outside rides like I had used to. Keith managed to re-establish all the links with trainers that had seemingly disappeared.

I think being fashionable means riding regularly in the high-profile races, the Classics and Group Is, being seen on the BBC or Channel 4. The right people need to be watching at the right time. You hear it all the time: 'He's a big-race jockey' or 'He's cool on the big occasion'. And in some respects they're right. But if you're never given the opportunity to prove yourself, you never will. There's plenty of jocks in the weighing room who are quite capable of winning the Guineas, Derby or Leger if they're on the right horse. But fashion dictates that they'll never get that opportunity.

Unfortunately, I've always ridden for a trainer who only occasionally has a horse in those kind of races. Sir Mark has never had a runner in a British Classic, for instance, and from this standpoint Sir Mark himself argues that he may well have held me back. But I don't regret one day of trekking to Hamilton or Musselburgh because our association has been so good, so honest, and Sir Mark has always backed me to the hilt whenever I've made a bollocks of something. It never helps to be hidden away at Carlisle doing the same job you could be doing at Ascot but that was my job as first jockey to Sir Mark Prescott. I'd sooner ride winners at Thirsk than a 200/1 shot in the Guineas. I didn't care where I was as long as I was winning races.

You see the same distinction among trainers, those who are fashionable and those who are not. Many of the 'lesser' trainers I've come across on the circuit in 30-odd years are just as good as lots of the high-profile guys, but they're saddled with different images. Bryan McMahon, a nifty trainer with two-year-olds; Reg

Hollinshead and Reg Akehurst were the 'handicap kings', they were the kiddies for laying one out. David Chapman bought cast-offs and turned them into money-spinners. He'd buy horses with proven ability that had lost their way. It was a case of reviving their enthusiasm, which is a knack, a talent. These weren't bad horses, they just needed to regain their enthusiasm. Dandy Nicholls, who used to ride a lot for David Chapman, obviously acquired the knack because he's now doing exactly the same but on a slightly larger scale. These two wouldn't train them much at home, they'd run them and then turn them out to give the horse a totally fresh outlook on life. Paul Felgate is another unsung trainer who works wonders with unpromising material. Yet when he had decent material he also showed he knew what to do with it. I rode Gemini Fire and Shuttlecock Corner, who were both Group-winning juveniles back in the 1980s and should have been his stepping stone to better things, but his main owner, David Abell, removed all his horses and that was that. Ironically, despite a lot of money and effort with trainers like Mark Johnston, Mr Abell has never owned a Group winner since Gemini Fire and Shuttlecock Corner.

Although the question of being 'fashionable' doesn't get up my nose, the subject of stewarding certainly does. Racing today seems to revolve around the application of Rules rather than the application of common sense. We're tied to all these Rules and Regulations, and if something doesn't quite fit, they'll invent a new rule so it does. Each year we get a new rule on this or the other because the old one didn't work properly. The rule-makers are constantly at work making new ones to compensate for their failure.

When I started there were no such things as 'guidelines' on the use of the whip, for example. Of course, there was minmal camera patrol, no pictures in betting shops either, so you had to offend the naked eye to attract censure but unless you went completely over the top nothing was ever said about use of the whip. Crucially, in those days the stewards seemed to be blessed with a far deeper knowledge of racing and you couldn't help but respect them. You knew they knew what was going on, and a tap on your shoulder followed by a word in your ear was normally all that was required. 'Be careful. You know what you did!' On occasions, they only had to look at you and the point was made! Today, we have people doing a professional job adjudicating on the Flat, like Phil Tuck, Paul Barton and Robert Earnshaw, who were jump jockeys – but there's a world of difference between the two spheres.

The Jockey Club has dug a hole so deep for itself regarding the use of the whip that it's difficult to climb out of it. Once you've given in to a minority of people who, however well-meaning, know nothing about horseracing and race-riding, there's no coming back. All the jockeys have bent over backwards to adapt their styles and use of the whip to appease the 'do-gooders'. Yet to the people who matter far more – the punters in the stands and in the betting shops – we can't hit a horse hard enough or often enough. You put your stick down and they think you're not trying hard enough on their behalf. But the more the animal welfare people, or even racing people like Peter O'Sullevan and John Oaksey (who has argued that 'the best and most effective deterrent of all would be to disqualify horses on which the whip has been misused'), talk and write about the subject the less likely it'll go away and leave us jockeys to get on with our jobs. To be honest, I'd have no whip rule at all and leave it to common sense. Let's not make a big issue out of it. They even make an announcement on the track these days when someone gets a suspension. If you say nothing about it, it'll go away.

Surely it wouldn't be too difficult to treat each case on its individual merits? Take the instance of Giant's Causeway in the 2000 Eclipse. I received a ten-day ban for 'excessive use of the whip' (as did Pat Eddery on the runner-up Kalanisi) after winning the race by a head. People often ask me whether jockeys have to use a whip? This race and this result is their answer. You only get what you ask for. Once you stopped asking a horse like Giant's Causeway for effort he stopped. When I put my stick down, that's when Pat passed me. As soon as I picked it up again, Giant's Causeway went on again and won. When Mick Kinane dropped a rein on him in the Breeders' Cup Classic at the end of the year, the horse again thought he'd done enough – with the result that he lost the race by a neck. Some horses are like big, sloppy kids who need a kick up the backside to make them get on with it. Those you know will stop if you hit them, you don't hit. Just look what Giant's Causeway and Kalanisi achieved after that Eclipse. Their Sandown experience didn't deter them. They went on to greater heights, especially Kalanisi who definitely improved. After Giant's Causeway beat him once more by a head in the Juddmonte International (gaining Pat another two days for 'excessive use'), he added the Champion Stakes and Breeders' Cup Turf.

We jockeys do not go out to punish horses. They are our livelihood. We love horses. We don't want to beat them to death. Horses have a far higher pain threshold than humans. I've seen horses stand there with a broken leg having a pick of grass. Would you stand there eating a biscuit if your leg was broken? We'd all love to win 'hands-and-heels', looking pretty, but lots of horses don't respond to that. The racehorse has the odd tough day in its life, that's all. I tell you, there are loads of humans who'd love to be as well fed, bedded and groomed as a racehorse. And there are far worse things than hitting a horse.

Dropping your hands on one, for a start! Now that is a cardinal sin. I've been done twice for it and on both instances it was John Lowe who came and got me, once for second at Ripon and he actually stole a race from me at Catterick when I was riding a two-year-old for Jack Berry. I just put my hands up straight away. 'Surrender!' They fined me half the maximum for my honesty! The worse part was having to phone Jack and tell him. However, neither case was as bad as Darryll Holland on Island House in a Listed race at Chester in 2001, or Tony Culhane at Pontefract earlier this year, or Willie Carson when he dropped his hands in both the 1993 Cheshire Oaks on Bashayer and on that odds-on shot at Lingfield three years later. 'Oooh dear!' we go in the weighing room, 'That's naughty!' whenever something that blatant comes up. Top spot, though, must go to Seb Sanders, who was caught napping aboard one of 'Nasty Nev' Callaghan's at Lingfield in 1995. I shudder to think what colour the air was on that occasion! Ah well, there but for the grace of God...

Putting all these stewards' enquiries into perspective is the fact that once upon a time they were only called for interference. I received my first ban for putting Willie Carson over the fence at Doncaster in a three-horse race! He had all the racetrack to pass me on and he decided to come up my inner. I ask you! He clipped my heels and shot through the rail. I still won the race but duly lost it in the stewards' room and got four days.

The technical revolution has made race-riding much tighter. You can't get away with some of the things you did in the 1960s and 1970s. Then there'd only be one camera, so if you got someone at the right place at the right time, you could inflict no end of damage. And the stipendiary stewards are not so lenient nowadays. I don't think the changes are necessarily for the better. They're starting to take a lot of the fun out of racing. There are too many Rules and Regulations, too many camera angles. Pretty soon the authorities will have us racing in lanes up the track. They are creating too many issues that shouldn't be issues.

The biggest something-out-of-nothing I've ever been involved in was the case of the so-called 'Haydock 21' in 1996. This 'cause celebre' sums up everything I've been saying about the inadequacy of modern stewarding. What a song-and-dance they made of it. The whole affair was a fiasco from beginning to end and far more was made of it than should have been.

The conditions at Haydock on 16 October were desperate, terribly wet as it often can be at the track, and before racing started the clerk of the course, Philip Arkwright, warned us that a part of the course was unfit and had been dolled off. After the first race was completed four or five jockeys were muttering that they didn't want to ride. I'd not ridden in the first, but in spite of all the toing-and-froing and all the chit-chat going on, I'd got my helmet on and had weighed out ready to ride in the second by the time Paul Barton, the stipe on duty, came in and asked whether we wanted to ride. He stated at the subsequent Portman Square enquiry that no one wanted to ride – and that's what he conveyed to the stewards, who were ultimately left with no option but to abandon the meeting.

I'll state here and now that was untrue – and I told them so at the subsequent Portman Square enquiry. Paul Barton asked me if I was prepared to ride and I told him that I, for one, was happy to ride. He also stated the door of the jockeys' room at Haydock was locked while we discussed what we were going to do. It wasn't anything of the kind. There was no jockeys' 'pow-wow' behind closed doors as some wanted to make out. The clerk of the scales had shut it, not us.

At no stage of the proceedings had I any intention of getting embroiled in the discussions which followed that first race and which eventually led to the abandonment. I'd been there before. I'd been part of deputations that walked tracks in the past and had done my bit to try and persuade people to ride. It's not worth the aggravation. The day I had that bad crash at Bath, I was one of the idiots mad-keen to ride in the fog on slippery ground because I was on a 'cert'; and then there was an evening meeting at Beverley in 1989 that was delayed because heavy rain on firm ground had rendered the bend unsafe – 11 jocks refused to ride in the second race (being fined between £250 and £750 for their defiance), Walter Swinburn and Steve Cauthen disagreeing with the remainder of the inspection party, which included Sir Mark, that it was safe to continue.

There'll always be a fuss between those who do want to race and those who don't want to race. At Beverley, for instance, I'd told Sir Mark 'For you, I'll ride' because he'd always stood by me when I needed support and I felt it was only right and proper to return the compliment. At Haydock it was Frankie Dettori ('Who is riding, the stewards or us? We are not paid to kill ourselves.') and Walter Swinburn (actually with no ride in the second) who voiced their misgivings the loudest, and the younger element followed their lead, 'like sheep' according to one of my colleagues. A few trainers were much more scathing: Mick Easterby (true to form!) called us 'overpaid and windy'; Alan Bailey chipped in with 'It's a case of the well-off jockeys wanting to get home early again. I'd ban those responsible for a year – they're a bunch of misfits; windy, gutless and overpaid.'

Once the course had been inspected by a group comprising the clerk of the course, four stewards and a delegation of eight senior jockeys and been passed 'fit' for racing to go ahead, what Paul Barton ought to have done was say to Frankie, Walter or anyone else who didn't fancy it, 'If you don't want to ride, tell your trainer and have the horse withdrawn.' But he panicked because two high-profile jockeys were involved.

The communication thereafter was a shambles. The stewards' decision that it was safe to proceed with the second race, for example, was announced over the public address system before any of us jockeys were informed. That, as much as anything, caused us to dig our collective heels in. None of the 21 due to ride in the second race left the weighing room and the stewards were obliged to abandon the meeting. We had to stick together – we always do – but Mark Birch, Gary Bardwell, Jimmy Quinn, Dean McKeown, Roddy Lappin, young Darren Moffatt (who actually rode work on the track after the abandonment) and myself were quite happy to go out and ride in that second race. North-South divide at work again? Could be.

Although, as ever, common sense was sorely lacking in the first instance, thankfully some common sense prevailed in the end. After a hearing that lasted 17 hours spread over two days we were all exonerated of charges of 'bringing racing into disrepute', although Frankie was found to be in breach of a Rule (143) because he'd weighed out for the second race but subsequently showed he had no intention of riding in it by changing into his street clothes. The fact that Frankie was not even fined for this offence demonstrates what a farce the whole thing had degenerated into.

When jockeys make a 'horlicks' of something we have to pay the price. A suspension stops us earning. If a clerk of the course makes a poor decision about calling off or continuing a meeting when he shouldn't have, or a stipe reaches a bad decision, they always seem to escape punishment. Neither Paul Barton nor the other stipe on duty at Haydock, William Nunneley, came out of this mess smelling of roses. They were found to have erred in the advice given to the Haydock stewards, who were also found to be negligent themselves in not informing the jockeys that the meeting was to proceed before informing the general public. Yet only the jockeys were charged with anything, and any disciplinary action taken against Messrs Barton and Nunneley was dealt with 'in-house'. One rule for us and one rule for them? How fair is that? Everyone was to blame on the day, not just the jockeys. Everyone got it wrong. It was a cock-up that never wants to happen again.

The loss of income resulting from the decision of some panel of stewards hits a journeyman jockey harder than his high-profile colleagues, who are quite capable of recouping the lost earnings with one big win. No easier for the journeyman jockey to bear, is getting 'jocked off'. He quickly becomes accustomed to being 'jocked off'. It's part and parcel of his status within the game. You get something ready for its target race, prepping it round some smaller track in an egg-and-spoon race for instance, and you may even be assured you'll keep the ride, but when the day that counts duly arrives, you get the 'jog.' My position on Heath House horses was, and is, pretty sacrosanct – although I must confess to not being happy at being replaced on Wizard King for the Hong Kong International Bowl of 1997 by Wendyll Woods (who had won on him in the past) on the grounds of 'local knowledge.' That still rankles. I had been jocked-off other people's horses in the past by the likes of Lester and Pat a few times. I didn't like it but I accepted it when those two were involved. Getting the push from James Fanshawe's Unblest in the 2000 Guineas of 1994 to make way for Cash Asmussen was a different kettle of fish. I was livid and, probably unwisely, I gave my views on the matter to the press.

Unblest was a sturdy, bay son of Alzao with whom I'd always been impressed, and after he'd won three of his four starts as a juvenile, topped by the Group II Laurent-Perrier Champagne Stakes at Doncaster, I foolishly allowed my hopes of a third English Classic to rise prematurely. Unblest won his maiden at Nottingham from one or two fancied horses boasting decent form who were made to look very ordinary. Another facile success at Doncaster prefaced his first attempt in Pattern company, the Group II Gimcrack at York's August Festival. Turtle Island (already a Group I winner in Ireland and to win the following year's Irish Guineas) beat us a head at the business end of a real ding-dong battle through the final furlong – with the future winner of the English Guineas, Mister Baileys, well beaten-off.

Unblest was living up to all our expectations. The step up to seven furlongs in the Champagne Stakes would be right up his street and, having ridden him twice a week between York and Doncaster, I knew he was well up to the task in hand. However, although only three others went to post, Unblest started at a tasty price of 3/1 because all the money (£65,000 in big bets) was for the unbeaten

State Performer, who had won the Chesham at Royal Ascot. John Reid must have been counting his percentage as he cruised to the front on State Performer one and a half furlongs out, and might be forgiven for so doing had it not been for the fact that me and Unblest were right on his heels travelling just as cosily. We went past State Performer 50 yards from the post and won by threequarters of a length. 'Unblest puts Guineas case' headlined the *Racing Post* as Unblest was elevated to second favourite for the Classic behind State Performer's stablemate Colonel Collins. 'George gave him a super ride,' said Unblest's owner, Lord Vestey. Although a temperature was to rule Unblest out of his Group I target, the Dewhurst, he went into winter quarters full of potential and I could afford to dream of further Classic glory.

Then it all went pear-shaped. Unblest had been working well prior to his first run, which was to be the Free Handicap over seven furlongs at the Craven Meeting, a race Mystiko had taken en route to his Guineas victory three years previously. It proved to be one of those silly, fiddly-arsed races with no pace and when there's no pace you always get hard-luck stories. They chose to race up the centre of the track and I was drawn in the middle, which ensured I was racing in a pocket, tracking the leaders with horses on either side of me. I'd nowhere to go. No doors to open. I had to sit and sit; sit and suffer. They only really picked up the pace in the final three furlongs and when the gaps eventually came, it was very, very late in the race. My options were twofold. Either be exceptionally hard on him and try to reach the leaders, maybe winning but maybe getting beat a head or neck: whatever eventuality, he'd have a tough race and the Guineas – the one that matters – is only a fortnight away. Or, I could accept that I was shut-in, and look after him – in traditional Heath House fashion – for another day.

I chose the latter option. Some people were always going to find this explanation unacceptable. It was far simpler just to think I'd ridden like a prat. I knew Unblest should have won the Free Handicap. He was definitely the best horse in the race. But I was thinking of the Guineas not the Free Handicap. As soon as I came back in, I knew neither Lord Vestey nor his new racing manager, John Warren, shared my views. The look in their eyes instantly told me no way was G Duffield going to ride this horse again. They didn't have to say anything, and all I could do was apologise and say I was thinking about the Guineas. My words seemed to cut no ice. I knew I was history. I told Gill that night 'That's the last I'll see of that horse.' I went to bed with the words ringing round my head of that poem which goes something like:

> There are some that ride like sailors do,
> With arms and legs and teeth;
> Some ride on the horse's neck,
> And others underneath.
> But of all the greatest sportsmen,
> And those to beat the band,
> You'll find them in the crowd
> That ride their races in the stand.

A day or two later, I was at Catterick when James Fanshawe rang to give me the news that Cash Asmussen was going to replace me in the Guineas. It was a big, big blow and I told James so. He said he had fought my corner as best he could. I told him I was disappointed after putting so much work into this horse, in addition to others in the yard since he'd commenced training. (I'd partnered a quarter of his winners.) But, in James's defence, he was under a lot of pressure for a young man. He hadn't yet acquired the strength of profile to be as dominant with his owners as some trainers would be in these delicate circumstances. The owners do pay the bills. They call the shots. It was the beginning of the end for our association. I've ridden very seldom for James since 1994.

After I'd received the order of the boot, journalist Tom O'Ryan rang me and asked whether I wanted to put into writing my thoughts on the situation. Perhaps unwisely, I gave him his story. 'A dream becomes a nightmare,' was the headline to the piece which appeared on Guineas day, 'George Duffield feels a deep sense of injustice after losing the Guineas ride on Unblest.' The interview went on to quote me as saying: 'It's like a severe kick in the balls. For years I've struggled to get to the top and ride some decent horses. I've had disappointments all through my career, and I've always tried to pick myself up and get on with it. But this has knocked me back a long way. I've put a year's work into the horse and helped bring him to this stage. I've looked after him and have always put a lot of thought into him, and his future. Then something like this happens and you start to think "Is it worth it?" I'd be lying if I said I wanted the horse to win. I wouldn't wish the horse any harm but deep down I wouldn't want him to win. It's the way I feel. I can't help feeling any other way.'

That final sentiment was not guaranteed to win friends and influence people. It did not read well in the cold light of day. A jockey is meant to say something along the lines of 'I'm very disappointed but I hope the horse wins for his own sake.' Sir Mark was quick to point this out to me after we came in off the gallops that Saturday morning, on one of the few occasions he has deliberately drawn me aside. 'Remember Richard Quinn,' is all he said, in reference to the dignified silence Richard adopted after losing the ride on Generous who went on to win the Derby, Irish Derby and King George under Alan Munro in 1991. Sir Mark, of course, was quite correct. But my heart is forever worn on my sleeve – to good and bad effect, I'm afraid. And this may not have been one of my finest hours.

I had instructed Shippy Ellis, my agent at the time, to get me as far away from Newmarket as possible when Unblest contested the

Guineas. Consequently, while the colt I'd helped bring to Classic standard was finishing 15th of 23 to Mister Baileys, I was up at Thirsk riding a double. Unblest later won a Group race in France (his only win in seven starts as a three-year-old) before taking up stallion duties in Ireland at the end of the season.

When something like the loss of the Unblest ride happens to a journeyman jockey he mustn't allow himself to become bogged down. You must snap out of it straight away. If you decide you've done nothing wrong, you must just keep doing what you think is right. In this respect, being jocked-off is no different than fighting your way through the kind of long losing streak that now and again afflicts every jockey. Try extra hard not to worry because if you do, you start to think about the things you shouldn't be doing – and the net result is you wind up only making things worse. The Oxley job taught me that lesson. Stay focused and wait until you turn the corner.

Around my 'corner', waiting to lend a helping hand yet again, was the ever supportive figure of Sir Mark Prescott.

15

THE SWEET LIFE

As the 1990s wore on Sir Mark gradually began acquiring a better class of horse. Twenty-one of the 24 Group races Sir Mark won in the 31-year life of the Pattern up to the end of 2001 arrived from 1994 onwards, and I was on 17 of them. Prior to 1994 we had amassed just two, Harlow's Palais Royal in 1984 and Chicmond's Solario in 1991, both at Group III level. As I also rode a further six for other trainers post 1994, this gave me a total of 23 Pattern-race winners in eight seasons. The fact that it had taken me 23 seasons to accumulate my first 20 goes to show what a purple patch me and Sir Mark had entered. After Last Second, Wizard King, Pivotal, Brave Act and Red Camellia had collected seven Pattern races between them in 1996 a genuinely gobsmacked Sir Mark told the press: 'I don't feel that I'm on the same planet – I normally manage one of these every two years or so!'

The explanation for this long awaited upsurge in the fortunes of Heath House is not hard to fathom. Sir Mark began to receive better quality stock. One vital source was the Cheveley Park Stud. The principal recipient of its choicely bred products had tended to be Michael Stoute, or possibly Luca Cumani, but in the shape of Pivotal and Red Camellia, Cheveley Park provided Sir Mark with two outstanding prospects in 1995 and 1996. Further strokes of good fortune manifested themselves in the acquisition of two animals owned by wealthy Arab patrons that between them would win eight Pattern races, namely Wizard King and Last Second.

Although Wizard King was already in the yard, running and winning for two seasons, it was the emergence of the filly Last Second in 1995 that Sir Mark considers to have been the real turning point. He paid IR120,000 guineas for her at the Goffs Irish National Yearling Sale of 1994, the top price paid for any offspring of Alzao that particular year, on behalf of the Saudi Prince Faisal Salman, the brother of Fahd and Ahmed, the respective owners of the Derby winners Generous and Oath. The filly got her name from the 'last second' arrival at Goffs of Prince Faisal and his subsequent intervention in the bidding: he'd set a limit which could not be topped unless he saw the filly personally, and he'd endured a delayed journey. Last Second inherited her grey coat from her dam Alruccaba, whose other produce had played, and would play again, significant roles in my story. One of her earlier foals was Arrikala, who had given me and User Friendly such a fright in the Irish Oaks, and another was Alouette, who would later become the dam of Alborada, our dual Champion Stakes winner. Miss Kirsten Rausing bred and owned the whole family. Hence the importance of Last Second. I think it's fair to say that without our success with her in 1995-96, the arrival of her close relative Alborada at Heath House would have been far less likely.

Colin Nutter made me aware of Last Second's ability before I'd even sat on her. Colin is an excellent judge of a two-year-old and he rated her from the word go. You wouldn't have thought she was any good to look at her, though. She was leggy and very frail, very delicate in appearance, like a piece of porcelain – she looked as if she might snap at any time. She looked a real little lady, in stark contrast to Alborada later on. Of course, races are not won on looks. Sir Mark soon discovered Last Second possessed a trump card in a telling, but short, burst of speed. Even so, riding Last Second was going to be a piece of cake compared to training her. She was a poor 'doer' and was not particularly tough physically or mentally – certainly not in comparison to her 'niece' Alborada.

Last Second won her maiden first time up at Redcar in September with Kevin Darley aboard, while I sat on the sidelines with a ban, after which Sir Mark had no hesitation in dropping her straight into Group III class for her next outing, the CL Weld Park Stakes at the Curragh a month later. From a maiden to a Group III is a fair step but Last Second accomplished the feat thanks to a phenomenal burst of speed. 'You'll look brilliant or be crucified! Be brave!,' warned Sir Mark, as he legged me up. Michael Kinane, riding the other co-favourite Super Gift (winner of her previous two starts), was in front of me approaching the final furlong, and he cunningly showed me a gap between him and Christy Roche's mount Ribot's Secret before instantly closing it when he sensed me going for it. Left shut-in on the rails, I had to pull Last Second out and round in order to get any kind of run. Boy, did she fly. We caught Super Gift in the dying strides to win by a head. 'George, you and I are too old to be as brave as that!' was my greeting from Sir Mark after that one.

Given her delicate constitution there was never any likelihood of Last Second being prepared for a crack at the Guineas ('Too many horses are ruined at the altar of the Guineas' is a verse from the gospel according to Sir Mark). Either the Pretty Polly Stakes over one and a quarter miles at the Curragh or the Coronation Stakes over the round mile at Royal Ascot were designated as her debut options. Prince Faisal opted for the Coronation. The field was headed by the first and second in the French Guineas, Ta Rib and

Shake the Yoke, plus the runner-up in the Irish equivalent, Dance Design. Shake the Yoke was deemed unlucky in her Guineas and was made even-money favourite to take revenge on Ta Rib and the rest of us. Last Second could be backed at 33/1 on the morning of the race. She started at 12s!

Prince Faisal's hope was to get her Group I-placed. But how to do it? If I tried to put her in the race to win it, the chances were she'd fade right away in the closing stages. But, if I held her up and used her burst late – because it would last barely a furlong, no more – I'd probably pinch a place. I only had the one chance. I could only use it once. I couldn't use it up before I really needed it. I could pull her out at the one pole and then run on past those horses who are tiring, having tried to win the race, when I'm probably not entitled to be there. Nine times out of ten this strategy works. Greville Starkey was a past master at it. And you may even fluke a win.

I agreed with Sir Mark's opinion and we then agreed tactics. Nevertheless, we both knew that holding one up in this cold, calculated manner was not my preferred style of riding. 'So, that's four valium for Prince Faisal and three for you, just to keep your nerve,' he quipped, before sending me out to ride her as if she was not 'off'. The ploy very nearly worked to perfection, because Last Second finished with such a flourish that Shake The Yoke only just had too many guns for us, her advantage reduced to a neck at the line.

The gentlemen of the press were quick to criticise the ride I'd given Last Second. Why had I left it so late? They were not privy to our plan, of course, but I was surprised by their reaction all the same. Perhaps some of them were speaking through their pockets as a glut of money on course had been responsible for slashing Last Second's odds down from 33s to 12s. I could have understood it had she been a 5/4 shot but when they were writing up their tips in the morning none of them gave her a chance, so why should I come in for grief after getting her so close to an even-money favourite? She'd actually run the race of her life to get within a neck of Shake the Yoke.

Last Second's acceleration was as potent over six, seven, eight or ten furlongs. The distance of the race made no difference. This she amply demonstrated in each of her next two races, the Nassau at Goodwood and the Sun Chariot at Newmarket, both of them Group II. I couldn't have written each race down better on a piece of paper. We got a nice lead to the furlong marker – and then I let her loose.

That was the end of Last Second for 1996 but it was decided to keep her in training with the view, in particular, of trying to win the Coronation Cup with her. How a filly will winter is always a concern, and for one of Last Second's fragility even more so. Sadly, she failed to come up to scratch as a four-year-old, not reaching the frame in either of her two runs, the Prix Ganay and the Nassau. Last Second may not have given Sir Mark his first Group I success but she certainly verged on Group I class.

Wizard King could not have been more different than Last Second if he'd tried. This son of the 1989 Irish 2000 Guineas winner Shaadi was one of that breed of racehorse, very much in the mould of Spindrifter, who was mentally as tough as old boots, and because he had the right mind he became better and better with age. He campaigned six seasons and retired at the age of seven having won 18 of his 41 races, five of them Group IIIs at the ages of five and six.

Wizard King was nothing special to begin with. He was tall and lengthy, a scopey sort but not much of a mover in his slower paces, and he didn't run as well as he worked. It took him five tries before winning a seven-furlong nursery at Brighton with Gary Bardwell riding at a ridiculous 7st 7lb. The following season he added the Britannia Handicap (confined to three-year-olds) at Royal Ascot with John Lowe riding at 7st 7lb. I gave him his last 'blow' – a spin for two furlongs up Warren Hill, letting him go as fast he wanted without any pushing – and I'd no hesitation in telling John I couldn't see the horse getting beat at Ascot as I couldn't remember one 'breezing' so well as this. Wizard King turned this prestigious handicap into a procession, winning by three and a half lengths. By the time he and I lined up for the even more valuable Tote Festival Handicap back at Ascot in September, Wizard King had risen over two stone in the handicap, from a mark of 60 to 92, allowing me to ride him at 8st 7lb. Once again he experienced no trouble whatsoever in putting four lengths between himself and 24 tip-top handicappers – this time of all ages. Sir Mark reckoned he was 'the most improved handicapper I've ever handled.' He had to be a Group III horse, particularly as there were relatively few of them around at his specialised distance of seven furlongs.

By the same token, there were not that many Group III races around at seven furlongs for Wizard King to run in! Accordingly, Wizard King was sent to Dubai during the winter of 1994-95. Fortunately for us, he didn't thrive out there and he was back at Heath House for the 1995 season. I missed the single Group III he managed to win in England (the 1997 Beeswing at Newcastle because of suspension) but Ireland had a trio of them, and as their going tended to be easier and he was 7-10lb better on a softer surface, Wizard King was always popping over to the Curragh for the Boland Stakes, to Leopardstown for the Ballycorus and to Tipperary for the Concorde Stakes. I missed his 1997 victory in the Boland because I'd contracted measles! But I was in the saddle for the 1997 Ballycorus and the Concorde double of 1996/97. He also won Listed races at Fairyhouse, Leopardstown and the Curragh, in the first of which he was partnered by Michael Kinane – and therein lies a tale.

You could ride Wizard King any way you liked, from the front or from behind – with but one exception. You couldn't sit upsides another horse in front. Then, he'd wear himself out. Michael Kinane knew all about Wizard King's idiosyncrasy and had won on him from the front, which was Wizard King's preferred style of running. In the 1997 Ballycorus Michael was booked by Mark Tompkins to partner what we believed to be Wizard King's principal opponent, Cool Edge, whom we'd beaten in the previous year's Concorde by making all. There is always a risk of being 'typecast' when you are constantly running into the same horses time after time. A change of tactics was called for.

As we sat waiting at Stansted for our morning flight out to Ireland, Sir Mark turned to me and said: 'At this very moment, Mr Kinane will be on the phone to Mr Tompkins in Newmarket saying: "I've ridden that old Wizard King, and the one thing he can't do is race upsides. So what I'll do, is let my horse come out of the stalls slowly – if this meets with your approval – and let Wizard King make the running for a furlong before joining him and sitting upsides. He won't be able to drop in behind us and he'll hate us racing upsides." In that case, George, you yank Wizard King back on his arse as soon as the stalls open; Mr Kinane will have to jump, because he's expecting to follow Wizard King whom he thinks will be making the running – and he won't be able to pull his horse back. You can then sit last on Wizard King and come sweeping by in the straight. Does that make sense?'

When Sir Mark Prescott has thought out a race as carefully as that, the answer to that last question may safely be described as a foregone conclusion! His plan worked like the proverbial charm. We whizzed by Cool Edge in the straight to win by four lengths. They thought they knew Wizard King's style of racing, but we'd taken them to the cleaners. As Michael brought Cool Edge past Sir Mark on the way in, he just looked down from the saddle, smiled and said: 'I should have known you'd do that!'

The Cheveley Park horses arrived at Heath House thanks to the bonny little chestnut sprinter Case Law. He had a heart bigger than himself, did Case Law, and Sir Mark sold him to Cheveley Park who kindly left him in the yard till the end of his racing career. The net result was the arrival of some Cheveley Park yearlings. One of the early intake was the filly Red Azalea who won a couple of races in 1994 and 1995. The following year we received her half-sister Red Camellia, by the Cheveley Park stallion Polar Falcon who'd won the Lockinge and Ladbroke Sprint Cup in 1991. The sisters were from a family famous for producing performers as diverse as the champion sprinter Owington, Irish Leger winner Ibn Bey, the Yorkshire Oaks winner Roseate Tern and that wonderful gelding Teleprompter who won a Queen Elizabeth II Stakes and the Arlington Million in Chicago. Red Camellia certainly didn't resemble Teleprompter! She was long and a bit lean but with lovely manners – 95 per cent of the good horses tend to be easy to deal with – and although she possessed a lot of natural speed, that pedigree of hers suggested she might even develop into a ten-furlong horse.

Red Camellia was started off in customary Heath House fashion – in a little maiden over six furlongs up at Carlisle in June. She struggled to beat a filly of Red Hollinshead's called Danehill Princess that never managed to win a race all year despite 16 attempts. Red Camellia ran very green. I knew she'd improve for the experience – our juveniles always do come on for a run – and said so afterwards, but when she vindicated my opinion in a seven-furlong Listed race at Sandown next time up, Richard Quinn was in the saddle because I was suspended. Not only did Red Camellia beat the Cecil hot-pot Yashmak (later second in the Group I Prix Marcel Boussac) by two lengths, she also lowered the juvenile track record. It's amazing how much they improve mentally (more than physically) from that first race once the penny drops.

How much Red Camellia had improved since Carlisle was to be

investigated by running her in the Prestige Stakes, a Group III over seven furlongs at Goodwood on 25 August. She'd made every yard at Sandown, and Sir Mark's orders for this Group race were simplicity itself: 'Go out in front and rattle every bone in their bodies!' I did my level best to oblige, and when I stole a peep entering the final furlong there was nothing but daylight behind us. Even after easing her, the winning margin was six lengths. The papers went wild: 'Camellia's the cream', 'Camellia on the climb' and 'Camellia is red-hot property!' being typical examples of the headline-writer's art. She was now second favourite for the 1997 1000 Guineas. Six days later, Brave Act, a tough-as-teak colt by Persian Bold, repelled every boarder by making all to win us our second Group III Solario round Sandown Park. What a week!

The logical progression for a filly of Red Camellia's class was elevation to Group I company and she was stepped up a furlong to contest the Fillies' Mile at Ascot. Despite her exploits, she did not start as favourite. That honour going to the Cecil representative Sleepytime, who had won her only race at Sandown. We set out to repeat the tactics that proved so successful at Sandown and Goodwood but Red Camellia faded in the straight, changing her legs and edging left, and finished only fourth behind the Cecil second string, Reams of Verse. I felt she didn't quite get home – that is until I heard she'd fractured her off-fore knee. In that context being beaten around one and a half lengths by the future Oaks winner (Reams of Verse) and a short head by the future 1000 Guineas winner (Sleepytime) seemed a bloody good performance. Timeform rated her at 116, equal best of her sex alongside fellow Cheveley Park product Dazzle, trained by Michael Stoute.

The subsequent operation to repair her knee ensured she bypassed the English Guineas in favour of the French equivalent on softer ground a week later. I sat and sat in front until picking her up at the top of the stretch but she just began to falter inside the final 200 metres and we were caught and passed by Always Loyal and Seebe, who beat us by a head and threequarters of a length. This was no mean effort, considering what Red Camellia had been through, and augured well for the rest of the season. Sadly, because of her knee, Sir Mark couldn't risk training her until the rains returned, and she saw a racecourse just once more, and that after nearly five months on the sidelines. Fourth of six in the Group III Supreme Stakes was a low note on which to bow out, because if you ask Sir Mark Prescott about Red Camellia he'll tell you she was the best horse he's ever had. Better than Last Second, better than Alborada, and better even than the other Cheveley Park horse who eventually broke Sir Mark's Group I duck during Red Camellia's juvenile season of 1996.

The horse who was to end Sir Mark's agonising 26-year wait was Pivotal. Although Pivotal was a strong, angular sort who looked as if he might be a sprinter, his pedigree suggested he might need further. Another product of Polar Falcon, he was out of a mare by Environment Friend's sire Cozzene, whose immediate antecedents all prospered at a mile or more. Sir Mark's plan, I think, was to work upwards in distance but in the event he found himself doing the reverse when Pivotal turned three. Last Second's presence in the yard at the same time proved crucial. Over five furlongs she was no match for Pivotal on the gallops; at seven, a distance Pivotal's pedigree suggested would suit him better, he could not beat the filly. This informative yardstick convinced Sir Mark shorter trips would be his forte, pedigree or not.

The first sighting I had of Pivotal was on Racecourse Side one morning. 'Get on that chestnut two-year-old over there,' Sir Mark said. 'He's not done much. You lead, and Colin will sit second, and he'll then come and join you. When you meet the rising ground, give him a squeeze.' I did as I was told, and Pivotal quickened up so well for a horse who was really still just a great big slob. 'What's this horse done?' I asked Colin. 'Nothing, George, he's done nothing. That's the first proper piece of work he's done.' I took a sharp intake of breath. 'Colin, this is a bloody good horse!'

Colin rode him on his debut at Newbury in mid-October because I was at Nottingham, and he finished a running-on ninth of 20 – a typical Heath House introduction. Eleven days later I rode him up at Newcastle in a pretty hot six-furlong maiden. Willie Carson was on one of Sheikh Hamdan's for John Dunlop and Frankie partnered a John Gosden animal that they thought was definitely Group class. My orders were not to be too hard on Pivotal. Well, we tracked these other two until inside the final furlong, I switched him out, and that was that: two and a half lengths, easy as winking. Sir Mark gave him one more race, at Folkestone on the very last day of the season, back at five furlongs, and Pivotal hacked up – which still failed to stop him knocking 0.3 seconds off the all-aged track record with a time of 58.5.

As you can imagine, the one horse I'm desperate to sit on in the spring of 1996 is Pivotal. My first morning in the yard, I hurry over to his box – number 15 in the big yard, I think – to see how he's developed over the winter. I'm mortified! There he is shuffling across the box like a cripple. I walked him out but he could hardly put his feet on the floor. Sir Mark's stood outside the box and I say to him 'He's a bit lame, has he just been shod?' It transpired that Peter the blacksmith had cut his feet back so much, he'd lamed him. Pivotal was so sore, it knocked him back weeks. His shoes had to come off to let his feet grow again. The best horse in the yard and he's lame the first occasion I try to get on him!

Sir Mark had told journalists that he thought Pivotal 'not quite good enough' for Group competition. Royal Ascot was to be his first port of call, and he was entered in virtually everything from the King's Stand at five, the Cork and Orrery at six and the Jersey at seven furlongs among the Pattern races, to the six-furlong Wokingham and the five-furlong Palan Handicap confined to three-year-olds on the Saturday's Heath meeting. At home, Pivotal was now working like a real star, giving silly weights – 10 or 12lb plus a heavy lad, so he was working worse off than his rating would suggest – to inferior horses on the gallops and beating them. Over five furlongs, for instance, he was five lengths superior to Last Second – though, as I've said, the outcome would be reversed if they worked over seven. The deciding factor in Pivotal's Ascot destination was Cheveley Park's desire to create another stallion prospect to follow in the hoof prints of his own sire Polar Falcon. So, the Group II King's Stand it was.

I consider Pivotal's Ascot victory to have been one of Sir Mark's greatest pieces of training. To win a Group II at Royal Ascot with a horse having its seasonal debut, and against older horses, is a feat that takes some topping. Of our 16 opponents, the one I felt we had to beat was Jack Berry's four-year-old colt Mind Games, who had won the Norfolk Stakes on the track as a juvenile and had recently won the Group II Temple Stakes at Sandown to stake his claim for the sprint crown of 1996. We were drawn on opposite sides of the track, Pivotal toward the stands side which all week had seemed to hold the advantage.

Mind Games was a renowned trapper. Up to halfway, I'd been content to have a lead but when I looked across for him the first time, he was already skipping away up the far rail. I thought I'd never pull him back. It was all hands to the pumps. Pivotal really began to motor and ate into Mind Games's lead. I sneaked one further look across at Mind Games as we approached the line but it was impossible to judge whether we'd got to him or not as the Ascot track is so wide. The verdict, in fact, was as much as half a length in our favour.

'I'm playing at being a proper trainer now,' joked Sir Mark with reporters. 'I'm very relieved but I must say I'm rather concerned about the rise of such indiscipline among my owners! I was tempted to run Pivotal in the Wokingham but Cheveley Park is obviously keen to promote its stallion and they intimated they would rather he ran in the King's Stand if I thought he could win it or run respectably. Had Pivotal been owned by 'the boys', they would have missed Ascot with him, waited for the three-year-old handicap at York, had their brains on him, and given the bookies a hiding!' Bearing in mind Pivotal's starting price was 13/2 compared to a morning line of 12/1, it's safe to assume that some of 'the boys' still donned their betting boots.

The July Cup beckoned – but still Sir Mark's first Group I was not forthcoming. I think Ascot took the edge off Pivotal, it was his first race of the season after all. Pivotal ran flat at Newmarket. You could say we ran to form with Mind Games – beating him a head – in finishing sixth to the French sprinter Anabaa but this was over six furlongs, which probably did neither of us any favours, and on this occasion we had the worst of the draw. This was not the real Pivotal.

The real Pivotal, however, did show up at York for the Nunthorpe, the five-furlong sprint championship of Europe, on 22 August. 'Two men with one wish' declared the *Racing Post's* preview in reference to the continuing quest of both Sir Mark and Jack Berry for that elusive first Group I success. 'Even our worst enemies can say we've waited long enough!' said Sir Mark; 'If anybody beats me I hope it's Sir Mark,' responded Jack. The following morning's banner headline across the front page confirmed one man had finally been put out of his agony: 'Prescott does it!'

Mind Games was made favourite to beat us for the first time in three encounters but he could find nothing extra when push came to shove. Henry Candy's five-year-old mare Eveningperformance, on the other hand, was another notoriously fast starter who tended to run out of steam in the final 100 yards and it was my plan to get a lead off her up to that point – but this day she kept on going! She must still have been four lengths clear entering the last furlong. I had to pull out all the stops to reach her, and the post flashed past us at one and the same time. I had my head down, looking at the brown line of grass as well as the winning post out of the corner of my eye. I'd no idea whether we'd won, and neither did Sir Mark or Henry Candy. In truth, we'd have happily settled for a dead-heat. The photo took 15 minutes to interpret. My heart was pounding! 'First' – said the announcer over the tannoy, before pausing for customary dramatic effect – 'number four!' We had made it by a whisker.

Both Sir Mark and I were engulfed with back-slapping well-wishers and ushered before the Channel 4 cameras for the obligatory interview. Sir Mark's upper lip remained as stiff as ever. 'I said I wouldn't cry and I won't. I may do for Mr Waugh, to whom I shall be eternally grateful, but I won't cry for my first Group I winner.' He was content to praise the bravery of the horse, thank all the Heath House staff and revel in our lengthy partnership. 'Hurry up, George,' he called over to where I was being grilled by reporters, 'you've been talking so long you must have said something stupid by now! When a jockey starts to talk, just allow your mind to wander!'

Pivotal's sixth race was his last. Cheveley Park had achieved its aim – or, should I say, Sir Mark Prescott had achieved it for them. They had 40 mares lined up ready for Pivotal at six grand a time. He might have run in the Abbaye, but he wasn't a soft-ground horse who'd relish Longchamp in October. It made sound financial sense to retire him, although I'm confident he would have made more hay in 1997 because all the top sprinters retired with him.

Sir Mark pretty much succeeded in keeping his emotions securely under wraps at York – though I suspect many an experienced Prescott watcher might echo Brough Scott's observation in the *Racing Post* that 'he was so proud you could feel it glowing from his feet.' Yet, I'd not bet against the mask dropping later that evening when Sir Mark took the telephone call from Mr Waugh offering his congratulations. 'It's nice to think a little bit of knowledge might linger on in those that follow you,' Mr Waugh told him. 'Makes it all worthwhile, you know. Well done to you both.'

If Sir Mark's eyes were not brimming with tears upon hearing those words from the man he respected above all others, I'd be amazed. I know I'd have been reaching for the handkerchief.

16

WHEN THE MONEY'S DOWN

If winning Pattern races was a strange sensation for me and Sir Mark, winning big handicaps was most certainly not. The very appearance of a Heath House representative in the list of entries for the Cambridgeshire or Cesarewitch, for example, would be enough to send the bookmakers immediately scurrying for cover. Imagining some 'Prescottian' plot, they'd take no chances and would promptly install our horse at some ludicrously short price in the ante post betting. Then again, one could sympathise. There is no one better at laying one out than Sir Mark Prescott and, when the money's down, I like to think there's no one better at booting them past the post than G Duffield.

Nothing sinister or underhand is resorted to during the waging of this eternal holy war against the bookmakers. In this day and age, the technology is so good you couldn't, for instance, deliberately 'pull' a horse, if you wound up in a position to win but the money wasn't down, in order to save him for another day. Today, they've got cameras coming out of your arse, with so many different views and angles – front, back, side – that it's near enough impossible. We're so overrun with cameras today, they can see you picking your nose. Years ago, yes, you could get away with making sure you got the result you wanted. I'm sure it was being done when I started back in the 60s and 70s. That's why all those horses were able to end up winning the big betting mediums, handicaps like the Royal Hunt Cup and the Wokingham at Royal Ascot, the Stewards' Cup at Goodwood, York's Ebor, Doncaster's Portland and, of course, Newmarket's 'autumn double' of the Cambridgeshire and Cesarewitch, with only seven stone on their backs. They only won when it really mattered, when the big money was riding.

In reality, there are only two things the trainer can do, and both ploys are easily spotted by the truly attentive punter. The trainer either runs the horse over its wrong trip or runs it at below peak fitness – occasionally both. In the paddock, the jockey will not have much trouble deciphering what's afoot from a piece of 'trainer-speak' that roughly goes: 'I don't want this horse knocked around today. If you can win without beating it up, fine, but this is not actually D-Day for this one. I don't want it to have a hard race.'

You see, there's no law insisting a horse must be jumping out of its skin before it's allowed to race. There's no law saying you have to run a horse in a certain race. There's no law that states you can't run a horse over its wrong trip. The trainer commits all these 'mistakes' to get it beat. All he has to say is that he made an error: he thought the horse might benefit, for example, from a drop/step-up in distance. It's up to the punter to spot what's going on when he looks down the list of runners. It also helps to go racing, so you can look at the horses in the paddock and judge for yourself whether your fancy is fit or not. Some look fit, perhaps, but aren't fit because they carry lots of condition. Watch a horse like this in the race, see how it runs and draw your own conclusions as to whether it was truly match-fit or was being laid out for something else in the weeks to come. A working knowledge of how certain trainers and jockeys operate is essential.

When Pat Eddery or Kieren Fallon takes over on something that has been ridden three or four times out the back by some lesser light, you know this is meant to be the day because the trainer is not going to put up either of those and tell him to look after the horse.

It's not a science, just being aware of what you should be looking for. If the horse's intended long-term target can be concealed, all well and good, but this is seldom possible with the high-profile handicaps nowadays, and certainly not easy if the trainer's name happens to be Sir Mark Prescott – or in days gone by, Reg Akehurst.

Reg was the acknowledged 'Handicap King.' Reg's owners included several wealthy men, such as Stewart Aitken, who loved to take on the bookies and Reg saw it as his job to set up the gamble without transgressing any rules. In return, the bookmakers were the first to admit they treated Reg's runners with exaggerated respect when framing their prices. Reg frequently took other trainers' cast-offs, would run these horses round the gaff tracks, get them on the right mark for the targeted handicap and then, usually with the assistance of Richard Quinn, wallop, in they'd go! Collect the money! Gone!

Just look at these examples from the 1990s alone. Sarawat started at 14/1 for the Ebor and netted Stewart Aitkin £250,000 after being available at 40s ante post; Urgent Request reputedly won Aitken half a million when he took the Northern Dancer Handicap at Epsom by seven lengths, starting at 8/1 having been on offer at 14s in the morning; Sharp Prospect was backed down from 16s to 8/1 second favourite for the 1995 Spring Mile and duly obliged by three lengths; Red Robbo was a 33/1 shot for the 1997 Royal Hunt Cup when the betting shops opened, but he attracted a welter of money, started at 16s and landed his only success of the season. The list of Reg Akehurst 'coups' is virtually endless. Reg was the kiddie, all right. How the bookies must have cheered when Reg retired at the end of 1997!

Personally, I've never been approached for 'assistance' by either gamblers or bookmakers. Of course, I've ridden for a few owners who happened to be choice gamblers. One of the heaviest punters must have been Walter Grubmuller, the owner of Missed Flight, who'd made his pile from a fruit-machines empire back in his native Austria. Walter won half million pounds in one six-month period – on horses, golf, football. I know this for a fact because he showed me the bookmaker's cheque. I rode Missed Flight to win at Redcar in late 1993 when Walter had plenty of dough on him. I nearly gave him a heart attack, as we were last for most of the race! The following spring, we were confident of winning the Lincoln with the horse, despite his top weight. That objective wasn't achieved, as we finished third and got disqualified for coming off a straight line. I got three days and Walter blew all his each-way bets. But we got the money back in the Newbury Spring Cup a few weeks later! That was the last Missed Flight saw of handicaps – and, consequently, gambling as the be-all and end-all. He had proved himself up to Group class, especially when the ground had plenty of give in it. During the ensuing 18 months we won a pair of Group IIs, the Prix du Rond-Point and the Sandown Mile, plus the Group III Prix de Meautry at Deauville.

During my years as an apprentice, my allowance ensured I was utilised on a number of occasions to secure a nice 'touch' by some trainer or another, in the manner of Messrs Todd, Mitchell and Ormston described earlier. These were little fish, however; sweet – as they say – but little fish all the same. The big fish were landed courtesy of Sir Mark Prescott.

Although we had won a Zetland Gold Cup in 1986 with Forward Rally, the first major gamble landed was with Quinlan Terry in the 1988 Cambridgeshire. As early in the year as February – when Quinlan Terry had only run the once – the decision was taken to aim him at the Cambridgeshire on 1 October, and as soon as the weights were published and Sir Mark saw Quinlan Terry was allotted 7st 13lb, he availed himself of the 40/1 on offer. This was an extraordinarily significant pointer to anyone privy to Sir Mark's betting policy. Contrary to any public perception, Sir Mark seldom bets. He'll always answer any press inquiry concerning his betting habits with something along the lines of 'I don't believe there's a bookmaker anywhere in the world who could tell you that I've had a bet', but he's not averse to seizing the opportunity when it arises. By and large, he'll restrict himself to the days when one of ours has suddenly come good and the odds on offer do not reflect such insider knowledge. In other words, there's no plot involved and, equally as important, the price on the day is not being spoiled for the owner. Sir Mark appreciates that no owner must be allowed to feel that he, the trainer, has pinched the price or in any way influenced it. However, each season you can be sure two or three of ours will successfully carry Prescott money.

Quinlan Terry was a big horse by Welsh Pageant. Lord Fairhaven (the senior steward!) bred him and gave him to his wife as a birthday present. He was named after the famous architect who had recently been hired to undertake some work at the Fairhavens' Anglesey Abbey home. The Cambridgeshire is a race which is usually won by a horse that hasn't been overdone or hasn't been at it a long time. Quinlan Terry had run just seven times, winning an apprentice maiden at Hamilton in May and an Epsom handicap in June. After a short break at the Fairhavens' stud, we brought him back for the Courage Handicap over one-and-a-quarter miles at Newbury on 17 September. Ile de Chypre, a good horse later to win the Group I Juddmonte International, gave us 12lb and beat us three lengths. The 5lb penalty the winner incurred for this Newbury success would prove crucial to the outcome of the Cambridgeshire a fortnight later.

The nine furlongs at Newmarket is a one-off. It's a long straight grind, worth ten furlongs on any other track. You need a ten-furlong horse like Quinlan Terry, with a high cruising speed, a real grinder to see it out effectively. As always with these big races, we went into it well planned. You don't get many opportunities like this. You can't go into them half-cocked. We have a firm idea of what we're going to do and at what stage in the race we're going to do it. If it goes wrong, tough! I improvise! You always want your mount to be away and running into the Dip, kicking from the top of the hill, two furlongs out. You mustn't go into the Dip at half-pace. You need full momentum to carry you out and up the final incline to the post.

Fortunately, I'd not had to worry about making the 7-13 as the weights rose 6lb. Weight is a huge factor for most jockeys. All the wasting can drive you mad if you let it. I try not to miss out on one proper feed a day so I'm not picking at things all the while. If you don't eat seriously at least once a day you only have to put yourself on one of those diets you never keep.

Ile de Chypre and Quinlan Terry (an 11/1 shot at the off) were drawn on opposite sides of the track in a 29-runner field, which is always liable to make judging a finish next to impossible. I could see Ile de Chypre leading the far side as I commenced my run to lead our group going into the Dip as planned. After that, it was ride for dear life and hope we were in front. We won by a neck. That 5lb penalty had made all the difference. Had we won at Newbury and been penalised, we'd not have won the Cambridgeshire – and Sir Mark's money would have gone down the plughole!

The attention paid to Prescott runners in this calibre of handicap ensures that our candidates tend to be run sparingly prior to their target races. That way, the handicapper can't keep putting them up and some of their ability remains concealed. Both Hasten To Add and Pasternak are prime examples of how Sir Mark handles this kind of situation.

Quinlan Terry was a big horse but Hasten To Add was bigger than him, closer to that other grey giant we had by Cozzene, Harlow. He was a gentle giant, though, very well balanced for his size. He didn't know how to misbehave, he'd just stroll around on the Heath, and would never exert himself any more than he had to. In his races, he travelled so well and was so easy to push with that great long length of neck, you could really get behind him.

Hasten To Add's owner was in the same larger than life category. Josephine Abercrombie, of Pin Oak Stud, near Versailles in Virginia, had had five husbands, had owned the Houston Aeros ice hockey team and had managed world-ranked prizefighters such as heavyweights Frank Tate, Carl 'The Truth' Williams and Tony Tucker, plus featherweight Steve Cruz – the man who took away Barry McGuigan's title in the heat and humidity of Las Vegas. Boxing promoter Bob Arum dubbed Josephine Abercrombie 'the most dangerous woman in the world.'

Hasten To Add was far too gross to run as a two-year-old in 1992, but he won his maiden over one and a half miles on the sand at Southwell by eight lengths the following June en route to his first target, the Batleys Cash & Carry Handicap at York in September. Shortly before this race he was 'tried' over one and a half miles on the Limekilns with the six-year-old Witness Box and the year younger Mashaallah, two animals trained by John Gosden (who also had some of Mrs Abercrombie's horses). The previous year I'd won the Northumberland Plate on Witness Box carrying 9st 9lb, and he'd been short-headed in both the Goodwood and Doncaster Cups; for his part, Mashaallah registered a hat-trick of Group Is in 1992, including the Irish St Leger. These were no gallop fodder. Hasten To Add beat them by five lengths.

It was clearly safe for Heath House to don its betting boots. Hasten To Add was backed on course from 6/1 to 11/4 and won as a good thing should. The next target was the Cesarewitch, for which he had received 7st 8lb; he was instantly promoted to favourite at 12/1 in the ante post lists. How irresistible a price this was can be gauged by the fact that Sir Mark – a man who had not, and still has not, run a horse in an English Classic, considered supplementing Hasten To Add for the St Leger.

On the day, the market went 12/1 bar Hasten To Add at 3/1 (carrying 8st 1lb including me thanks to a weight-rise) in a field of 31. Our only concern was the two and a quarter miles. Would he get the trip? We went clear three furlongs out. Up in the grandstand, Sir Mark was thinking to himself 'Ladbrokes, Hills and Coral, you've been got at last!' as we lobbed along toward the 'Bushes'. Then all of a sudden the petrol ran out and we fell away to finish fourth. The gamble had been foiled. Sometimes it happens that way. In 1989 it happened twice in one week at Goodwood when Plain Fact got beat a short head in the Stewards' Cup and Serious Trouble was beaten the same distance in the Schweppes Golden Mile. 'It's a bit like being in a car crash,' a shattered Sir Mark muttered afterwards. 'You don't know if you're unlucky to have been involved or lucky to have survived.'

As the cat was obviously out of the bag as far as Hasten To Add was concerned, his schedule for 1994 numbered just three races: the Bessborough Stakes at Royal Ascot, the Northumberland Plate and the Ebor Handicap. The season had not started well for Heath House or me. A virus closed us down for 51 days between mid April and early June during which time not a single horse was allowed out of the gates. Then there was the Unblest business. It was proving to be one thing after another, one of those patches where you have to keep your head down and trust you'll come out the other side. I'd ridden barely a dozen winners as Royal Ascot approached, some 40 fewer than the previous year. To cap it all, I bruised some ribs in a fall at Doncaster, and was forced to watch as Richard Quinn substituted for me in the Bessborough and was beaten a neck into second place. I was back for the Northumberland Plate and the stable had begun to reel off winners, but still lurking in the back of my mind was Hasten To Add's ability to stay extreme distances. The Bessborough was one and a half miles; the Plate was back up to two miles. When I went to win the race he hung fire with me, and we got caught right on the line by Quick Ransom. 'He'll be the death of me,' gasped Sir Mark, 'The Cesarewitch, the Bessborough and now here!'

At Ascot, Hasten To Add had beaten Quick Ransom by 25 lengths. Whether or not this dramatic turnaround had anything to do with it or not I don't know, but my riding came in for some criticism and suggestions were aired in the press that perhaps Hasten To Add had suffered from not having Richard Quinn aboard. That was below the belt, an injustice. Apart from anything else, the Plate was half a mile further, for God's sake! 'The best way to answer those snide criticisms,' Sir Mark reassured me, 'is to win the Ebor.' To do so, he reckoned Hasten To Add would need to run 3lb better than ever before because the handicapper had continued to put him up after every race. Sooner or later Hasten To Add was bound to hit a brick wall and be incapable of further improvement. Could he deliver a bit more in the Ebor? The public made him a 13/2 favourite to pull it off. The 15/2 second favourite was Admiral's Well – trained by Reg Akehurst and ridden by Richard Quinn!

Our success in the Ebor was thus made all the sweeter because the fast-finishing horse we did deny on this occasion was the selfsame Richard Quinn-partnered Admiral's Well. Tactics were changed for the Ebor. I kept Hasten To Add handy rather than leading but, in the absence of any appreciable pace, I had no alternative but to launch him on a long run for home once we straightened up. Even at the conclusion of this one-and-three quarter miles he was beginning to tie up as Admiral's Well got to within half a length of us at the line.

Even though Hasten To Add had completed his planned campaign he was started once more, in a valuable one and a half-mile handicap at the Ascot Festival in September, before Mrs Abercrombie withdrew all her horses from Europe, including Hasten To Add. Her reasons, I believe, were nothing to do with racing: tax restrictions or something of that nature was what I heard lay behind the decision. Hasten To Add won in Toronto for trainer Jim Day before joining the string of Bill Mott, the trainer of Cigar.

Pasternak's success in the 1997 Tote Cambridgeshire was described by the sponsor's PR man Rob Hartnett as 'far and away the biggest handicap gamble of the season', taking £5 million in total off the bookmakers, and was celebrated as such on the front page of the *Racing Post*: 'Pasternak lands gamble of the season.' His victory in the one-and-a-quarter mile John Smith's Magnet Cup at York some three months earlier was no less a punter's benefit: 'Mystery Plunge' and 'Pasternak fools 'em' were two of the headlines after we'd cleaned up on this occasion.

Pasternak was no 'mystery' to Heath House or the infamous 'boys' who owned him, Graham Moore, Wally Sturt, Neil Greig and Graham Rock – in whose colours he ran. We all knew how good Pasternak was from home gallops. The workhorses he galloped with and the weights carried told Sir Mark precisely what rating Pasternak was capable of winning off. All that had to be done was keep this knowledge from prying eyes – especially the handicapper's. Accordingly, there was never any intention of running Pasternak in more than the two races in 1997. As a galloping one and a quarter-mile horse with a turn of foot, he was perfect for the Cambridgeshire – obviously one of the prime betting mediums of the season – and for his mid-season target there was nowhere better to get a lot of money on at the track than York – where Pasternak already had a course and distance win – on Magnet Cup day. Furthermore, the two races were worth over £110,000 in prize money alone.

It wasn't until the autumn of his three-year-old career in 1996 that

Pasternak began to fulfil the promise he'd shown in three runs as a juvenile over seven furlongs. His mother, Princess Pati, was an Irish Oaks winner and he wanted further. He won his maiden at Bath and a decent one and a quarter-mile handicap at York in October off a mark of 80. The handicapper upped his rating to 85. Neither he nor the public would see Pasternak again until he returned to York on 12 July 1997.

Drying ground was our only real concern and it wasn't until Sir Mark was driving back from Wolverhampton on the Friday afternoon (he was stuck in a traffic jam at the time) that he rang Graham Rock to confirm it was OK for Pasternak to take his chance the next day. Pasternak had been 8/1 at the beginning of the week: when the prices went up on course for Saturday's Magnet Cup he was 3/1!

My personal dilemma was the draw: 1 of 21. The assumption was that I'd drop back out of the gate, pick them up in the straight and use his turn of foot. The reality proved different. This was one of my improvisation jobs. The pace was not quick and, consequently, I had trouble holding him behind the leaders – he was a big, strong, free-running horse – and we were clipping heels for a time. The lack of pace naturally caused some bunching and, with two furlongs to run when the sprint was already being cranked up, we had very little room in which to manoeuvre. Luckily the two in front of me rolled apart and I was able to shoot Pasternak through the gap and win pretty comfortably. 'The trainer might not know what he's doing,' Sir Mark told reporters, 'but the jockey certainly does.'

Pasternak went up a further 6lb for this win, which put him on 9st 1lb in the Cambridgeshire. Once again, Sir Mark expressed some fears about the good to firm ground (he even left Pasternak in a handicap at Wolverhampton on the same day) before casually informing Graham Rock on the Friday morning (having walked the course) 'I think I'll run that horse of yours tomorrow.' Rock, who sadly died from cancer in 2001, was as shrewd and astute a racing man as they come. Former Timeform employee, racing tipster in the old *Sporting Chronicle,* stipendiary steward in Hong Kong, founding editor of the *Racing Post* and the agent who took Michael Roberts to the jockeys' championship – and backed him to do so at odds of 100/1 – he needed no second bidding. He stood to collect a great deal from the bookies as he doubled the Cambridgeshire with the Magnet Cup. Within two minutes Rock was on the phone, grabbing some of the 100/8. Twenty-four hours later, *Racing Post* readers were greeted by huge headlines saying 'Why you must back Pasternak' and 'Pasternak plunge – bookies running scared.' Any punters still in need of the hint seized it with a relish. The best-priced morning line odds of 11s lasted all of 15 minutes and had shrunk to 9/2 on course and 4/1 at the off.

Sir Mark had a second runner in the race, Cheveley Park's Rudimental on 8st 4lb. In their last gallop, with Heath House's trusty workhorse Farmost, Pasternak beat Rudimental threequarters of a length at their Cambridgeshire weights. Sir Mark had lunch with Cheveley's owners, Mr and Mrs Thompson, on Cambridgeshire day and when they asked him where Rudimental was likely to finish he replied 'threequarters of a length behind Pasternak – that's all I can tell you.'

And that's precisely how they finished – in first and second! I'd been forced to the front sooner than I wanted. There was the traditional massive field (36) which split into two groups, and the far side began to get away from us on the stands side. It was a case of having to go whether I liked it or not. But this left Pasternak in front too long and Johnny Lowe brought Rudimental out of the pack to gradually whittle away our advantage. Up in the grandstand, Sir Mark felt a hand on his shoulder and turned to see Graham Rock. 'I do hope you're not going to fuck this up, old man,' he said with a wry smile!

No chance of that! The Heath House gallop was reproduced to the ounce. Pasternak held on by, you've guessed it, three quarters of a length. 'A masterpiece in every sense,' wrote Brough Scott in the *Racing Post*. 'The combined age of my jockeys was 98, but the old boys still know how to ride them!' joked Sir Mark. 'Pasternak is not an easy horse, so I thought he ought to run only in the big ones!'

Pasternak never won another race in two more seasons. He had gone up a stone since his Magnet Cup when he tried for a repeat in 1998 but he was to be confronted by an incarnation of himself the previous year in the improving Henry Cecil three-year-old Porto Foricos, rated 10lb inferior but receiving 21lb, and was beaten half a length. The handicapper had finally got his measure.

It didn't take long for Heath House to find a replacement. 'Has Sir Mark found another Pasternak?' asked the *Racing Post* on the morning of the 2001 John Smith's Cup, as the Magnet Cup was now titled. The horse in question was Foreign Affairs.

Foreign Affairs (bred by Kirsten Rausing) started life on the all-weather at Wolverhampton, winning the second of his two races there as a juvenile. He looked way above that standard and began 2001 running second off an official mark of 85 to the filly Lailani in a ten-furlong Epsom Handicap on Oaks day. This was Lailani's fourth win in a row and she was giving him 7lb. Any disappointment we felt at this reverse was dispelled when she proceeded to win the Irish Oaks next time up; later on she added two more races at the highest level, the Nassau Stakes and the Flower Bowl International at Belmont Park in New York.

Foreign Affairs quickly picked up the winning thread at Salisbury and Goodwood within a few days of Epsom (capitalising on the same handicap mark), before heading up to York for the John Smith's, which had always been the intention. Four days before-hand, Alphaeus, Foreign Affairs's galloping companion, won at Newmarket. Once again, we knew the score. From being available at 9/1, Foreign Affairs's odds were increasingly cut until he wound up a 5/2 favourite going into the gate.

It could all have ended so easily in tears. 'You'd like to think he is a horse capable of doing a bit of damage in a race like this,' I had warned the press. After the race I was telling them how 'Plan A and Plan B went out the window as soon as the stalls opened.' Basically, the 'plan' had been to sit third or fourth, but we missed the kick entirely. Kevin Darley's filly reared in the stalls, upsetting a few of those already in, and it seemed an age before the handlers sorted out the rest of us. We went in second last, with a blindfold. I pulled off the blind expecting the starter to let the field go, but something else was messing about by now and the starter held us again. When he did release us, Foreign Affairs just ambled out as if next week would do!

This tardiness proved a blessing in disguise. So many jocks wanted to be sitting in the first half dozen that they were going hell for leather up front, knocking spots off each other along the inside rail. Heath House telepathy was in full cry. Up in the grandstand, Sir Mark was praying I'd not choose to stay on the inner. I obviously heard him. With only three horses behind me, I decided to give the inside route a wide berth because if I went up there I'd never get out again. Instead, I drifted to the outside, got myself a lead that towed me toward the front, and kicked on from two and a half out. Foreign Affairs unleashed a very impressive burst of speed to win easy. You couldn't believe the number of hard-luck stories from the guys on the inside. Even if luck had been on my side, this victory had to go down as another triumph of improvisation.

Foreign Affairs was raised 8lb to 105 after York, which put him in the Ebor with 8st 8lb. Even though his ability to be as effective over the four-furlong longer trip had to be largely taken on sufferance, Foreign Affairs was the Prescott representative in another big handicap and nobody, punters or bookies, were about to take any chances. He started 6/1 favourite. He looked like landing the spoils, too, leading into the final quarter mile until a fellow three-year-old in the shape of Aidan O'Brien's Mediterranean (receiving 4lb from us) came past to beat us by half a length.

Foreign Affairs had demonstrated, like Hasten To Add and Pasternak before him, how progressive he was. Sir Mark once more mulled over the possibility of a late entry into the St Leger – before choosing to go for broke in a major way by lashing out the best part of £39,000 to supplement him into the Prix de l'Arc de Triomphe. Although Foreign Affairs didn't recoup the outlay, he didn't disgrace himself. I tracked Sakhee through most of the race, but couldn't live with him once let him loose in the straight. We finished a respectable tenth of the 17 runners and, with a Timeform rating of 117, Foreign Affairs must be regarded as one of the better animals I've ridden.

That Ebor of 2001 is a perfect illustration of a gamble that was foiled. We felt that if Foreign Affairs stayed the one-and-three quarter miles he would win. Mr O'Brien obviously had similar confidence in his horse's ability: in fact, Mediterranean did go on to contest the St Leger, unfortunately breaking down in the race. That's the way it goes. Some you win, some you lose. For instance, as the 2001 season drew to a close, Heath House reckoned it had the handicap certainty of all time.

It seemed only an act of God or a broken leg could stop our three-year-old filly Alleluia winning the Cesarewitch. She was a smallish half sister (by French Derby winner Caerleon) to Last Second that Miss Rausing owned in partnership with Mrs Sonia Rogers, of the Airlie Stud in County Dublin. Alleluia began the season on a lowly rating of 66 and only started to prosper in mid-summer when raced over two miles, winning handicaps at Folkestone and Thirsk. Sir Mark made the Cesarewitch entry and Alleluia was allotted 7st 9lb off her current handicap mark of 86. In the interim, seeking some 'black type' to boost her credentials as a broodmare for her co-owners, Sir Mark ran her in the Doncaster Cup, a Group II race that frequently cuts up to a small field. That it didn't do so in 2001 made no difference because Alleluia, in the hands of young Jamie Mackay (son of Allan 'Blow-Up Doll' Mackay) as she only carried 7st 11lb, showed plenty of improvement to win by threequarters of a length. Her rating was promptly jacked up a further 26lb to 112.

Even with her 7lb penalty for this Group success, Alleluia had the Tote Cesarewitch at her mercy since she was still 19lb well-in – 'The handicap blot of the year,' according to the sponsor. But handicaps don't read as purple on a broodmare's CV as a Group race, and Alleluia was also entered for the Jockey Club Cup on the same day as the Cesarewitch. 'Her owners have opposing views about which race to go for,' Sir Mark revealed to the media. 'They are both very strong-minded – and I've refereed enough boxing matches to know you never get between fighters until they've fought each other to a standstill!' I've always found Miss Rausing a very pleasant person, very intelligent, and I've no doubt she'd be more than a match for Sir Mark. There would be a lot of mutual respect between the pair, which makes it easier for compromises to be reached.

Alleluia went for the Cesarewitch, for which she was dispatched as the 7/2 favourite in a field of 31. Her penalty allowed me to ride at 8st 2lb. She was a bit keen early on but we came there cantering two out, and I thought, 'Here we go!' Then she faltered, and faded into sixth place, beaten six lengths. The explanation quickly became apparent. She was lame. It transpired she'd cracked her pelvis. Her racing days, though thankfully not her breeding days, were a thing of the past.

'I'm so sorry, Kirsten,' I overheard Sir Mark say to Miss Rausing as the filly was led away, 'we've got beat, and we've done her in.' Miss Rausing looked at him for a second, and then replied: 'Comment, I think, is superfluous.'

I'm afraid that observation is always forced to apply whenever a gamble comes unstuck.

17

'DON'T LET THE BASTARDS GRIND YOU DOWN'

I think there's a scene at the beginning of the classic television comedy series 'Porridge' where Ronnie Barker's character, the old lag Norman Stanley Fletcher, introduces his fresh-faced young cellmate Lenny Godber to the dos-and-don'ts of his first prison stretch with the advice 'Don't let the bastards grind you down!'

That sentiment kept crossing my mind throughout 1997, 1998 and 1999. Although I'd contemplated retirement briefly in 1994 when it seemed all the years of patience, application and sheer hard graft I'd expended to get in a position to ride quality horses had come to nought after I'd been jocked-off Unblest, I fought the urge to pack it all in and was rewarded by the arrival of the Last Seconds and the Pivotals. In 1997 I had to remind myself once more that G Duffield was no quitter.

My marriage had been on the rocks for a number of years. Gill and I were growing apart. I wasn't enjoying home life and there was a knock-on effect into my racing. I felt I was getting stale and that this was a reflection of my marriage. Gill had made such a success of training her point-to-pointers and Sheikh Hamdan's Arabs, and become so committed to that aspect of her life, that it took over her life and she forgot about me. The kids and I used to say the pecking order in our house was horses, dogs, kids – then me!

Whether she wants to believe it or not, I was just as keen as she was to see her make a go of it and her success gave me a big thrill. I backed her to the hilt, often accompanying her to meetings to help her saddle them up, but she rarely came racing with me or attended any functions. Unless it was an Arab Horse Society dinner or something I'd always appear alone at functions or parties because Gill preferred to stay at home reading or thinking about her horses. I wanted to be out and about. People grew to expect me to arrive alone and no one bothered to ask where Gill was.

When you're left pretty much a free agent for as long as I was you're going to get yourself into trouble. I had a couple of affairs towards the end, one up in the North and later one near Newmarket. Up till then I'd always been faithful. Gill had suspected something but chose to turn a blind eye. Nothing changed, we just carried on.

My problem was I never wanted to grow up. I was always younger than my years, always acting a bit silly, always up to mischief. I just couldn't grow up and, more importantly, I didn't want to grow up. My reasoning, however self-justifying it sounds, was simple enough. If I'd got to compete on the track with kids half my age or younger, I had to feel much younger than I actually was. I had to keep some kind of spark in my arse. I felt I was beginning to lose this vital spark. Gill was growing old gracefully and I wasn't. I still had to play the silly sod I was at 20 or 30. Then along came Ann Swinbank.

I first met Ann in 1993, 14 August it was, at Ripon. I'd just ridden the winner of the Seller at 2.45, Infantry Glen for Geoff Oldroyd (I actually got it in the stewards' room off one ridden by Lindsay

Charnock) and came out to put my saddle over the rack ready for the next race when John Lowe, who'd ridden a few of Ann's horses that season, introduced us. 'Pleased to meet you, Ann,' I said, shaking her hand. 'I'd be more than willing to ride for you any time.' Any hidden agenda of mine to make an impression on this attractive new addition to the training ranks obviously fell on stony ground because she had no idea who I was. 'I met George Duffield today,' she said on returning home, 'Who is he? Is he any good?'

Nevertheless, Ann Swinbank had certainly made an impression on me. Tall, leggy, long blonde hair – any red-blooded male couldn't help but sit up and take notice. In short: decidedly glamorous. 'I would leave home for her,' I told Nicky Connorton in the weighing room. Like Gill, she originated from Liverpool. A lifetime obsession with horses, which owed much to the present of a Shetland pony from her parents when she was four, had been put on hold when, at the age of 17, she bought her mother's nursing home as she had become too ill to continue running it.

In 1989 Ann sold the home and, eventually, after a few years buying, selling and training pointers and hunter-chasers, she chose to plough all her money into a new venture, training racehorses from Thorndale Farm, at Melsonby near Richmond. She was granted her licence in 1992 and had mainly National Hunt horses.

In 1993 Ann was 29 and had been married to Alan Swinbank for five years. He was a well-known face on the Northern racing circuit, standing as a part-time bookmaker. He was also a farmer, and dealt in second-hand farm machinery. Arnie, the valet, tried to warn me right from the start. Alan Swinbank spelt trouble. I never imagined in a million years just how much trouble.

I did get to ride one or two horses for Ann and gradually we became friendlier and friendlier, closer and closer. She would come to the weighing room for a chat, occasionally with her young son

A.J. and I'd give him a conducted tour. There was definitely an attraction on my side from the outset but even though Ann always made a point of coming to see me if we were at the same meeting, I was never conscious of anything on her part.

Things were to change at an alarming rate in the spring of 1997. The previous November I'd celebrated both my 50th birthday and 25th wedding anniversary. Whether I liked it or not, I could no longer avoid the twin realisations that as well as getting painfully close to hanging up my boots I was getting painfully close to the end of my marriage. I wanted more out of my private life. I was getting fed up with merely going through the motions. I'm sure Gill wasn't happy either. We had become more like brother and sister than man and wife.

One Sunday I decided I was going to phone Ann to see if I could arrange to go hunting with her, something we'd discussed several times during our chats in the weighing room. At that moment the phone rang. It was Ann. She said she had two horses to hunt with the Zetland and would I like a day out on one. I'd been hunting with the Puckeridge and Thurlow for years and jumped at the opportunity, though I must admit even if I'd never enjoyed a day's hunting in my life, I'd still have jumped at the opportunity.

This day's hunting proved to be the trigger. I soon discovered what I had long imagined and, in truth, had hoped to hear. Her marriage was shallow and unhappy. On the way back to Thorndale in the horsebox Ann poured out her heart to me concerning this thing and that thing which were wrong in her marriage. Something clearly was amiss and I told her what she needed was someone to look after her because what was missing in her life was a lot of love. The thought occurred to me that prior to this conversation I was a 50/1 shot, whereas now I felt like an even-money favourite. Later that evening, as I was about to drive back to Newmarket, I said: 'Look, if ever you want to ring me, I'm only at the end of a phone.'

I'd not got very far when Ann rang me on my mobile. Throughout the ensuing month we were constantly on the mobile to each other.

A deep affection was growing by the minute. Eventually, we arranged to meet in London. At this time Ann regularly visited London to be a studio guest on the Racing Channel. I excused myself by telling Gill I was going to meet Andy, an old friend of mine who owns a factory that retails catering equipment. See him I did, but it was just a ploy to meet up with Ann after she'd finished on the Racing Channel. Andy had booked us a room at the White House Hotel in Great Portland Street under an assumed name and we spent two or three hours together before dashing back to King's Cross to catch our respective trains. We spoke to each other on the way home – me on one train going to Cambridge and Ann on another going back to Darlington – until the batteries in our mobile phones were exhausted.

Guilt subsequently consumed me. Did I smell of Ann's perfume? Was there a tell-tale blonde hair on my jacket to give the game away? Would Gill spot Ann's number cropping up time and again on my mobile bill? Was the smell of another woman all over me? All manner of things fill your mind when you know you're a married man and you've been doing something you shouldn't. I just hoped I could bluff my way through each day without in some way spilling the beans.

My mind was in turmoil. I'd been married for over 25 years, I had two grown-up children and I'd met a woman I loved more than my wife. 'Is it possible to love two women?' I asked Ann. 'Even if it is, I love you more than I love my wife and it's tearing me apart. I don't know what to do and if you don't want me I don't know how I'll cope with it.' I eventually made up my mind that staying with Gill would only be living a lie if I knew I loved somebody more, and that even if Annie didn't want me I'd have to move out of Cedar Cottage. It wasn't fair to Gill for me to stay there, living a lie.

None of this was fair on Ann, either. I'd put her in a dilemma. She wanted to leave her husband, but she wasn't so sure I was the right man to leave her husband for. Jockeys have got a bad reputation when it comes to birds, booze and misbehaviour, and she had always made a point of not getting involved with them. She knew she liked me but not whether she loved me. It took me a while to convince Ann that I really did want her more than anything else. Eventually she started to believe me.

At the beginning of April I rode some work at Thorndale before the two of us drove up to Hamilton where I was to partner Sun Mark for her. I was to stay the night. At dinner, Ann, who was sat between me and Alan, started to play 'footsie' with me under the table. Although he didn't say anything, I sensed Alan knew something was going on because he leant back in his chair and looked under the table and my suspicions were confirmed when Ann left the room to fetch a tape of one of her horses for me to see. I tried to strike up a conversation with Alan and he was very frosty.

'He knows,' I told Annie as soon as I got the chance. 'You listen to me. He's seen you rubbing your foot on mine under the table. And I'm glad because I hate all this pretending. It's driving me mad!'

I went to bed and lay there with this awful gut-wrenching feeling. Alan had not said a word, not one, since dinner. It occurred to me he was the sort of fella who might just take it into his head to come into my room and give me a good hiding as I'm lying there in bed. Be prepared to smack him before he gets you, I told myself. So I lay there with my arms on top of the blankets just in case and merely cat-winked rather than went to sleep, ready to react if this fella decides to leap on me during the night. I heard a lot of shouting but nobody came into my room until Ann appeared with a cup of tea in the morning.

'You're right,' she said. 'He does know. He's been going round the house like a lunatic. He's threatened to embarrass me by telling the staff there's an affair going on between us.'

We agreed it would be foolish for me to ride out in the circumstances and I waited downstairs in the kitchen for the inevitable confrontation with Alan Swinbank. It came soon enough. He stormed in and began calling Ann a 'tart and a fucking cow', though he made no threat of physical menace toward me personally. He was blaming Annie for everything.

I tried my best to talk my way out of it. 'You misunderstood, Alan,' I said, 'You're being silly. She just moved her foot and accidently touched mine. You don't play footsie with your shoes on. You're imagining it.'

He replied: 'I would prefer it if you moved out of my house and never came back again.'

Ann came in and began to cry. She wasn't sure how I'd react now that we'd been found out. I put my arms round her. 'Look, I won't leave you. Whatever happens, I'll stick by you. It's a big relief to me now it's out in the open – a big burden lifted off my shoulders. Whatever you want to do, I'll stand right beside you.' At that, Annie seemed a different person.

It was still only 7.30 in the morning but Ann picked up the phone and made a call to Chris Williams, a barrister whose sons went to school with A.J. 'I need some advice,' she said to him. 'I need a good divorce lawyer, a very good one.' I left Ann and Alan to decide their future: divorce proceedings began in April 1997 on the grounds of his 'unreasonable behaviour.'

As for my own future, I decided not to say anything to Gill. Big mistake. A few months later I had to pay the price in full. At the end of July I'd got a suspension and Annie was due to go down to Ascot to cover the King George for the radio. I arranged for her to stay with Nigel and Cilla Day and told Gill I was going down to Royal

Birkdale to play golf with Nigel, which, of course, I wasn't.

Gill smelt a rat. 'There's something wrong, isn't there? Do you want to tell me about it? Is there someone else?'

'Yes, there is.'

'Is it Ann Swinbank?'

'It is, yes.'

'And do you love her?'

'I'm afraid I do.'

Gill walked out into the yard. I was ready to crawl into a hole. But I was determined to go through with the plan to see Ann at Ascot. I went after Gill to tell her I was about to leave and we met at the gate. I leant over and kissed her goodbye before getting in the car and driving away. I felt as guilty as hell. I'd betrayed her. I'd left her standing there in the yard so I could go off to meet another woman, a woman I loved more than her.

I'd not been in Ascot very long before the phone rang. It was Nicky. 'Dad, I think you should come home. Mum's in a real bad state.'

It turned out that young A.J. had been encourage to ring up to ask where his mother was. This lit Gill's fuse good and proper. I told Ann and the Days that I had to go home. I entered Cedar Cottage to find Gill in hysterics. She was sobbing her heart out, which made me feel even more of a traitor. She said she had to get away from the place and away from me. I could understand that. In response, I said that I wanted to sit down with the kids and try to explain to them what had happened and why it had happened. I spent the rest of the day sat outside on the step attempting to do just that, telling them to ask me whatever they wanted, even thump me if they wanted to. It must have been hard for them to take it all in, to understand why a man who has been married to their mother for 25 years should suddenly decide to leave her. I tried to put myself in their place. Maybe they thought I was in effect leaving them also, that they'd never see me again. You'll never get the exact same feelings as a child must when its father drops a bombshell like this on its head, I knew that, but I had to try. There were a lot of tears. Nathalie didn't handle it too well. Nicky was very brave and, although I think secretly he must have favoured his mother, he didn't take sides. I was proud of the way he dealt with the situation. All he'd say was how very disappointed in me he was. 'Nicky,' I said, 'Even though this happens to thousands of people every week and I'm just another statistic I'm disappointed in myself.'

Unfortunately my status as a sportsman, even one of exceedingly minor 'celebrity', ensured I was not just any other statistic. Most of the weighing room knew what was going on by now but although the racing press were very, very kind to me and Ann and left us alone once they got wind of the story, the tabloids didn't. For that we can thank Alan Swinbank. His story appeared in the *Daily Star*.

As Annie, me and young A.J. drove to Newcastle races on 6 August we were tipped off that reporters and photographers were already at the track and had been putting questions about us to all and sundry. I slipped in the weighing room by the back way and we kept our distance so the photographers could not get the shot they wanted of the two of us together. They thought their big chance was my first ride of the afternoon, which was a little two-year-old filly for Ann. She saddled the filly but foiled the photographers by avoiding the paddock and asking Linda Perratt to leg me up. Linda couldn't resist the opportunity of a joke at our expense. 'Ann says it's all right if I grope you on the way up,' she chuckled as she did the honours.

At every turn there were hacks from the tabloids. I couldn't walk to or from the paddock without one or more of them asking whether it was true I was leaving my wife to live with Ann Swinbank. They very nearly got the scoop they were sniffing around for after I'd won on a two-year-old of John Quinn's called Miss Main Street. As

I dismounted the crowd began clapping, causing the filly to rush forward and kick me on the way past. I went down like a sack of spuds. Ann heard the chorus of 'oohs and aahs' and was desperate to come and see me, but, thankfully, wise old Reg Hollinshead was on hand to hold her back because Ann cradling my head in her arms, for instance, would have provided precisely the photo opportunity these tabloid people were waiting for.

However, the damage had been done. The cat was well and truly out of the bag. I'd barely departed the track before Gill was on the mobile to say the house was being overrun with reporters. They were in the yard and trampling all over the garden. Some even knocked on the door and pretended to be prospective owners. All I could tell her was to call the police. I had been naïve enough to believe that someone as nondescript as me was not worth writing about. Now I was. I had no idea how low these journalists might stoop but remembering all the dirty tricks they'd pulled thus far, I decided to alert Sir Mark that something was in the offing, though as little ever passes him by I'm sure he knew exactly what was going on in any case. He was very supportive and concerned, but as long as the situation didn't affect my riding in any way he did not see my private life and all its turmoil being a problem.

Swinbank's 'sob-story' appeared in the *Daily Star* five days later. Under the banner headline 'Top Jock Gallops off With My Missus' he bleated 'It seemed everyone else knew about it … I was the last to know … I have been taken for a ride in every sense … our marriage was fine until Duffield came on the scene … I have been stitched up … I blame Duffield for wrecking everything I ever had … I want the pair of them painted black.'

We subsequently went through a bad time. Several of Ann's owners were contacted to be told their horses were unwell and not being cared for properly; horses' passports mysteriously disappeared from the office; trainers who rang Thorndale in an effort to locate me for a ride were being told I was sick or having a day off; and various people were informed that I was 'a bent jockey who had stopped horses in return for sexual favours from hookers.' More seriously, Ann's horses had cars deliberately driven at them on the way back from the gallops, necessitating a police escort on one occasion. One of her lads, Craig Wanless, was warned he faced being scarred for life; her head lad, Ricky Mills, quit under the strain. The list of incidents is endless and the police seemed powerless to stop them.

To begin with my divorce looked like being straightforward and reasonably civilised. Gill offered to feed and house me if I continued to ride work on her Arabs until the divorce was completed. I couldn't believe my ears. I was gobsmacked that Gill could be so understanding. After a week or two everything changed. By the time various individuals had been pouring poison down the phone, telling Gill I'd shagged virtually every woman in Newmarket, Gill wanted to hang, draw and quarter me. I came home from the races one night to be greeted with: 'That's another three you've shagged!' I could not believe Gill was buying all this crap. I'd never have gone racing if I'd been seeing to all the women I was alleged to have done. The bottom line, however, was that Gill was now ready to slaughter me and take every penny I'd got.

Things began to turn very nasty. Tempers would flare. Life became very difficult. All hopes of a routine divorce evaporated thanks to the input of a few meddling people – one woman in particular was keen to stab me in the back, no surprise since she'd had plentiful problems of her own. To give one example. In September I contracted measles, became quite ill and, with it being contagious, was confined to the house. One evening I asked Nathalie if she'd fetch me a takeaway but as she made to leave I heard Gill say to her: 'No, you're not getting food for him.' When I protested, Gill threw a cup of hot coffee at me which hit the wall behind me. That was the first – and only – time I felt like thumping her. Fortunately, I controlled my anger but it was the last straw. Although I felt like death warmed up, I packed a bag, jumped in the car and drove to Yorkshire. My marriage was effectively at an end. I'd finally abandoned the family home I'd helped to create plus the property I'd built up with every penny I'd earned. Annie and I rented a tiny one-bed-roomed cottage in Melsonby until, early in November, we moved into Hurgill Lodge in Richmond, after Bill Watts retired, renting the place from Lord Zetland.

Annie's divorce was dirtier than mine. I thought mine was bad but hers was worse. As Ann had made quite a bit of money from the sale of her nursing home, she was financially independent and was never after money from Alan Swinbank – who admitted to being 'a man of substantial means' – other than A.J.'s school fees and a contribution toward his maintenance. He had other ideas and his intimidatory tactics were no doubt designed to make her lose her nerve and back off. She didn't. However, her legal fees were escalating all the while. QCs were brought in toward the end which involved serious money and, after the dust had finally settled in February 1999 with the decree absolute, her final costs amounted to £110,000. She came out of the marriage with less than she went in. I was to be even more unlucky.

I was adamant Gill would not get Cedar Cottage off me. I'd worked too hard for it and was determined to give it up over my dead body. More to the point, a few years previously I had cashed in one of my own pensions in order to pay off the mortgage early. Even so, although my money had bought the property outright, I was more than happy to split everything 50-50. I took advice from Andrew Reid, a solicitor for whom I'd ridden when he had horses with Sir Mark Prescott – now a trainer in his own right – and Andrew's partner suggested a firm of solicitors, based in London.

I thought I was poorly represented from beginning to end. My case was passed from one solicitor to another – three in all – and at the hearing, in Cambridge in September 1998, Gill's firm took mine to the cleaners. Sour grapes? Yes and no. My team was too weak, Gill's was aggressive. Her Cambridge-based boys rode roughshod all over mine. My side hardly won a point throughout the case. And mine cost twice as much as hers because they were from London! At the hearing I continually passed notes to them, bringing particular points to their attention that demanded to be contested or raising questions that begged to be asked. And my man would just reply: 'That's just not my style, to be so aggressive. I'm a softly-softly man.'

As a result, they ran rings round us and I got shafted, big-time! Gill was awarded 80 per cent of our assets. That was bad enough, but my 20 per cent was deferred for eight years – my team had advised me the worse-case scenario would be seven – unless Gill remarried or sold the property (which fortunately she did in 2001). The judge's reasoning was that Mr Duffield could continue riding and earning until he reached 60 and Mr Duffield had private pensions, unlike Mrs Duffield. The judge failed to take into account two crucial facts. My ace card, or so I thought, was that a jockey like myself riding beyond the age of 50 was an exception not the rule. No way do jockeys ride till they're 60. Secondly, my pension was not worth much (£10,000 per year at the time) because I'd used one of them to pay off the mortgage on Cedar Cottage. I also had to pay both sets of costs which amounted to more than £40,000 – another kick in the bollocks.

So, Mrs Duffield gets to live in a £500,000 mortgage-free property from which she earned a very decent living training for one of the richest and most generous men in the world, and with no dependent children to worry about. Now, I'm not saying Gill was not entitled to a big share in what was, after all, her home as well as mine. She was my wife and the mother of my two children, and

I certainly did not wish her to suffer because of my choosing to make another life without her, but this outcome still seemed a bit unfair to put it mildly. There was no doubt about this result: Mr Duffield 20 Mrs Duffield 80.

Annie met me in the car outside the court. Not an awful lot was said. I don't think I was able to utter one single word until we reached Peterborough. She was gutted at the news, she felt entirely responsible for me losing virtually everything I had, and was ready to blame herself. She was also concerned that our relationship would suffer as a result. For a fleeting moment she had lost track of my priorities. I didn't care about money or my shattered ego. All I wanted was her.

After a while I leaned over as she drove, patted her on the leg and kissed her cheek. 'Annie,' I said, 'I still think I got you cheap.'

Our ordeal was not over by any stretch of the imagination. I was advised to appeal. Getting stuffed once was costly enough. Volunteering for the possibility of a second helping seemed a bold move. Nevertheless, we went for it. The appeal took six months to come to court, and again Gill's side were well prepared. They arrived with a new set of accounts showing how hard it would be for her to make a living if she had to give me more than my 20 per cent. The original judgement was allowed to stand – and once again I got lumbered with the costs.

Privately, I was reduced to tears of rage and frustration. Yes, I cried. But I didn't cry for long. And I wasn't about to allow anyone out there see me cry. Nor was I going to allow any of them to point at me behind my back and say: 'What a silly old bugger he is, throwing his career away for a woman. He should know better at his age.' My natural determination kicked in. I fully intended to turn this kick in the balls into something positive. I now had to be very focused and very positive. I had a job to do, and I needed to do it better than ever before to stop the vultures from circling overhead.

I was at the wrong end of my career to be starting all over again but I had no choice in the matter. I had lost virtually everything financially. It was time to get some back.

My single thought was: 'I'll show the bastards! G Duffield isn't finished. Far from it. You wait and see.'

18

THERE IS A GOD AFTER ALL

My single-minded determination to attack the remainder of my riding career – however short a period it turned out to be – with all the enthusiasm and vigour I could muster was rewarded with the kind of success I never could have imagined let alone hoped for. By my standards, I began winning Group 1 races as if they were going out of fashion. After 26 years of trying Sir Mark and I had broken our collaborative duck in the 1996 Nunthorpe and, like one long-awaited bus frequently being followed by plenty more, we immediately went on to add successive runnings of the Champion Stakes in 1998 and 1999 with Alborada. On top of that, young Irish genius Aidan O'Brien put me up on Aristotle and Giant's Causeway – probably the best horse I've ever ridden – to win the 1999 Racing Post Trophy and 2000 Eclipse Stakes respectively.

During the traumatic period of my divorce I had sought advice from Sir Mark Prescott on its likely impact on my riding career. 'Do you really want Ann Swinbank?' he asked. 'It's got to be 100 per cent from both sides, otherwise it'll be a total shambles and it'll mess your life up completely. You'll need to be 110 per cent dedicated to each other for this to succeed. I don't care about Mrs Duffield and I don't care about Ann Swinbank, but I have to care about you for the sake of my owners. You are stable jockey here and I owe it to my owners to ensure you are capable of doing the job.'

I knew then, without Sir Mark having to spell it out, what I had to prove and what I had to do in order to keep my job. I had to be on my mettle. I had to ride better than ever. I could not betray any weaknesses or reveal any evidence of declining powers. If anything went wrong, I was out with the washing. There were no ifs-and-buts about it. I couldn't afford to make mistakes. People were waiting to see how I handled the pressure I'd put myself under. Some of them would be waiting for the opportunity to kick me up the arse. It was as simple as that. Alborada was to be the first crucial test of both my resolve and my ability to continue delivering the goods.

The emergence of Kirsten Rausing's Alborada and her eventual confirmation as a genuine Group I performer was especially satisfying to both Sir Mark and myself because, like Cheveley Park's Pivotal had been, she was a home-bred animal. Sir Mark had inherited a Heath House full of home-breds from the studs of the Macdonald-Buchanans and the Fairhavens, for example, but, unfortunately for us, at a time when their fortunes were on the wane. These studs represented 'old money'. Pivotal and Alborada represented 'new money'. In Alborada's case, lots and lots of it.

Miss Kirsten Rausing is the only daughter of the Swedish billionaire Gad Rausing, the man who hit upon the wonderful idea of the milk carton. We are talking serious money here. On the death of her father in 2000, Miss Rausing's share of his empire (she has two brothers) was put at £1.5 billion, making her the eighth richest person in Britain. Easy enough, then, to believe the story that when some racecourse jobsworth was enticing her to enter one of her horses in a race by stressing the £125,000 prize money, Miss

Rausing's companion merely remarked: 'Don't be silly, she's got more than that in her purse!'

Thoroughbreds rather than cartons have been Miss Rausing's consuming passion. She had evented as a child but shifted into the bloodstock world to assume control of her grandfather's Simontorp Stud whilst graduating in business studies from Stockholm University. One of Miss Rausing's great mentors subsequently was Captain Tim Rogers of the Airlie Stud (his widow Sonia was her co-owner in Alleluia), whose knowledge and wisdom she began putting to good effect after purchasing Newmarket's Lanwades Stud in 1980, where she stood the Irish and French Leger winner Niniski. 'I was so exotic and outlandish, I was just a novelty,' she once admitted. 'I had none of the right credentials. I was a foreigner, I was a woman and I was young!' While Miss Rausing's imposing figure crowned by a teutonic mane of golden hair probably justifies the first part of her description, I suspect she did possess at least one of the 'right credentials' – whether Arab, Japanese or Swedish in origin, the racing world worships money like no other god!

Miss Rausing never spent 19,000 guineas better than the day she bought the two-year-old grey filly Alruccaba at the Newmarket December Sales of 1985. Michael Stoute had trained this filly from one of the Aga Khan's best families (her dam was closely related to Nishapour, the French Guineas winner of 1978) to win a small race at Brighton, but she easily outstripped this flimsy record at stud. She bred User Friendly's old adversary Arrikala, Last Second, of course, and Alouette (by the French Derby winner Darshaan), who won three races in Ireland. Alborada was Alouette's first foal. Enter Lady Luck. A fractured pedal bone in her near hind sustained as a foal caused Alborada (which means 'break of day' in Spanish) to forgo the sales ring in favour of being sent into training at Heath House instead.

Alborada's dam had won up to one and a half miles and although her sire, Alzao, had just the one Pattern-race success to his name (an Italian Group III over one and a half miles), he did represent the potent Northern Dancer sire line and had begun to do pretty well for himself after he was acquired by the Coolmore operation – particularly with his fillies, who included Last Second, of course, and the Irish Guineas winner Matiya. Alborada was much more robust than Last Second and far stronger mentally. Sir Mark always had to wrap Last Second in cotton wool because she was so delicate and was so easily drained. Alborada, on the other hand, was a wonderful 'doer' and had a marvellous constitution which meant she could take training, you could work her and she got to be better and better. In comparison, say, to Red Camellia, she may have lacked a bit of true brilliance – and she did possess a rather scuttly action – but she made up for any such deficiencies with a terrier-like determination and became very good by application.

The penny didn't drop straight away with Alborada: she lost her first two races at Nottingham and Goodwood before opening her account at Beverley over seven furlongs. We went a serious gallop that day but I won as I liked by six lengths in a good time. She showed us the ability we believed she possessed and was clearly going in the right direction. From then on, you knew where you were with Alborada because her work at home was always reflected on the track. Sir Mark concluded her juvenile campaign with a visit to the Curragh for the same Group III won by Last Second two years earlier, the CL Weld Park Stakes. Seb Sanders rode her because I was otherwise engaged winning the Cambridgeshire on Pasternak, and he drove her clear of another Alzao filly called Winona to win by two lengths. The following summer Winona landed the Irish Oaks.

There were to be no Classics for Alborada, however. Even though Heath House was struck by an outbreak of equine flu during April and did not have its first runner until 28 May, the Guineas mile would have been too short for Alborada, while the Oaks was going to be too far. She always struck us a one and a quarter-mile filly. So, the Curragh's Pretty Polly Stakes on 27 June was chosen as Alborada's seasonal debut. The ground was soft, very testing for a first run, and it was a bit of a struggle for her to win this Group II, even though she went two and a half lengths clear in the end. Guts, and guts alone, won this race for Alborada.

Alborada had to defy a 3lb penalty picked up at the Curragh if she was to win her next race, the Group II Nassau Stakes at Goodwood, on the first day of August. The favourite for this one and a quarter-mile event was Henry Cecil's Oaks third Midnight Line, but his second string, Digitalize, proved more influential as the race unfolded. The pace we thought would materialise, didn't materialise. Darryll Holland finally decided to take the bull by the horns on Digitalize at no more than a steady gallop, and I immediately grabbed a position in his slipstream. If there was going to be a rush on in the final few furlongs, I wanted to be on the front of it not the back. Fillies like Midnight Line were one and a half milers, and if they were behind me when the sprint began our chances of winning had to be improved. True to form, Darryll went for his filly passing the three pole and, to begin with, I wasn't so sure we'd catch him. The *Racing Post* headlined the outcome as 'Duffield dynamic on Alborada', but she had plenty to do with it herself. Alborada demonstrated what a great athlete and enthusiast she was to get up and edge out Digitalize by a neck.

Alborada had now won four races on the trot, the last three of them in Group company. The streak was to be broken when she was elevated to Group I class and took on the colts for the first time in the Irish Champion Stakes. She finished second but, for me, this was her best race of the lot. The horse that beat her was Swain, the top 10 to 12-furlong horse in Europe, fresh from a second consecutive victory in the King George. Nor did Swain have everything his own way – he only beat her a length. Full marks to Miss Rausing for having the balls – if she'll excuse the expression – to take him on in a Group I rather than play safe by opting for another Group II confined to her own sex, such as the Sun Chariot Stakes.

With Swain being reserved for the Breeders' Cup Classic, Godolphin's representative in the Champion Stakes was Daylami, the only horse on the book with form surpassing Alborada's. As a three-year-old, the grey had won a French Guineas for the Aga Khan, and since changing hands he'd won further Group Is like the Eclipse and, most recently, the Man o'War Stakes at Belmont Park. But there were rumours around to the effect that his trip to New York had taken a bit out of him. If he were removed from the shake-up, for instance, Alborada had as good a chance as any of the remaining eight runners.

We didn't fear any lack of pace on this occasion because Godolphin, as is their wont, were running a pacemaker for Daylami. However, Happy Valentine only set a moderate gallop, so I once more occupied the 'box seat' – close up behind him – in readiness for the inevitable sprint in the closing stages. We passed him three furlongs from home, which was plenty long enough to be left in the lead, and all the way to the line I could make out Olivier Peslier and Insatiable creeping up the rail closer and closer. We got there first by a neck. Alborada had proved her run against Swain was no fluke. The massive first prize of £228,200 – our biggest ever payday – was going back to Heath House, and the home-town crowd gave us – all three of us, Alborada, me and Sir Mark, I like to think – a fantastic reception as we came back in to unsaddle. 'You spend a lifetime watching races like this and wishing you had a runner that good,' an elated, yet drained, Sir Mark told Channel 4, 'and when you do it kills you!'

The trainer was not alone. His jockey had a lot riding on this race. I knew I had to get it right on Alborada. Luckily, I did, and she gave me the boost I needed at the end of a tough year, what with my divorce and everything. A great weight had been lifted from my shoulders and, mentally, this win granted me enormous peace of mind. I sat quietly in the corner of the Newmarket weighing room, reflecting 'There is a God after all!' Miss Rausing, too, had been as nervous as a kitten beforehand, a total bag of nerves. She recovered her poise soon enough, and organised a special lunch in the Jockey Club Rooms for everyone involved with Alborada. Little did we suspect we'd be enjoying another one the following year.

For most of 1999 there seemed not a cat-in-hell's chance of Alborada becoming just the 11th horse – and the only filly besides Triptych – in the race's 122-year history to achieve the Champion Stakes double. It was a catalogue of woe from the outset. During the winter she was turned out at Lanwades. As befitted the Stud's superstar, everything was done to ensure her comfort and safety. Her paddock was painstakingly searched for any dangerous objects, for instance. So what happens? Alborada steps on a flint and drives it into her hoof with the result that her leg blows up like a balloon. Only rapid intervention from Miss Rausing's vet prevented permanent impairment. Consequently, she came back to Heath House a month later than intended. She eventually began cantering toward the end of April with the aim of contesting the Eclipse on 3 July.

Alborada didn't make that date owing to a mucky throat – thankfully, from my selfish point of view, as I was suffering with that self-inflicted broken finger thanks to poking Tomoe Gozen in a fit of temper. Then every little thing imaginable seemed to go wrong. She banged a splint bone, cutting herself in the process, which again put her back. An added complication was that every time Sir Mark had to stop working her she'd get 'setfast' – a muscular problem like a cramp caused by the sudden release of lactic acid into the muscle – which meant putting her on a reduced diet and having to start her training programme all over again. Sir

Mark finally got her to the track for the Nassau which was run on very firm ground and, coming round the top turn, Alborada took a bump and lost her legs on turf made greasy by watering. She ran a blinder in the circumstances to finish fifth, less than two lengths behind Zahrat Dubai. But, in all honesty, this was not the Alborada of old.

The ensuing weeks afforded Sir Mark Prescott ample opportunity of living up to his credo 'It takes nerves of steel not to run a good horse.' He was helped immeasurably by having the right owner, one who was prepared to wait. And, boy, was Miss Rausing made to wait! The Irish Champion came and went – Alborada had a corn which held her back for nearly a month. Twice she worked so moderately, by her standards, on the Al Bahathri, that Sir Mark ('She couldn't even beat me!') was on the verge of advising Miss Rausing to retire her. Desperate for any sign of encouragement, Sir Mark began working her in front rather than from behind. The filly responded. Slowly, she began to show some of the old sparkle – so many fillies do seem to prosper in the autumn. Then, eight days before the Champion Stakes, we received concrete proof that she was back to her old self.

At exactly the same point in her build-up to the previous season's Champion, Sir Mark had galloped Alborada a mile on the gallops known as Across the Flat on Racecourse Side, with old Farmost, whom he rates the best workhorse in the country. Farmost will go a fierce gallop but, more importantly, he will keep going when the good horse in the gallop duly comes by him – most workhorses will stop once they're passed. If the good horse is not on song and does not pull away, Farmost will go past it again. Consequently, he is an absolutely reliable yardstick. Before that 1998 Champion, Alborada gave Farmost 35lb and beat him a length. Now, eight days before the 1999 Champion, we were set to give Farmost the same 35lb. The result? We beat him by a length. Same piece of work, same location, same galloping companion, same outcome. The previous year's gallop had been reproduced to the pound. We were over the moon. Alborada was back. Sir Mark went into the office and rang Miss Rausing. 'I don't know whether Alborada will win the Champion,' he said, 'but Farmost says that she will.'

We now knew Alborada was back to the form that had won last year's Champion, but would that be good enough to win this year's race? To my reading of the formbook, yes. The favourite was Henry Cecil's filly Shiva, a Group I winner in the spring but not seen out since Royal Ascot and probably a gallop or two short of peak fitness. The 1998 Derby winner, High-Rise, was in the field, but he'd shown next to nothing as a four-year-old; the rest were not much more than Group II or III horses.

The race, which this October was on the July Course as the Rowley Mile grandstand was being rebuilt, turned out to be totally problem-free and resulted in a more comfortable victory that the first one. John Reid made the pace on Kabool, and I followed him – nudging Olivier Peslier on High-Rise out of the way in order to do so. I drove Alborada into the lead coming out of the Dip and she stuck to her guns really well up the hill to hold Shiva at bay by one and a quarter lengths. 'The people's champions scoop the big one again,' blazed the following day's headlines.

This had to go down as a truly great training performance from Sir Mark Prescott because Alborada must have been a complete headache to train in 1999, a fact he owned up to when later admitting, in uncharacteristic – though perfectly permissible – fashion, that this second success was 'one of our better efforts – it had to be one of the most enjoyable days of my life.' I shared Sir Mark's satisfaction at a job well done ('I felt like I was playing a video game and was in charge of all the controls,' he added) for it was a tremendous achievement to win back-to-back Champion Stakes. Coincidentally, the last to do so, in 1986-87, was the only other filly, Triptych, and one of her successes was also on the July Course.

Since Alborada had obviously now come to herself and had had only two races, it was planned to run her again before she commenced her career in the paddocks with a visit to the crack American stallion Danzig in the spring. The Premio Roma was mooted but ultimately rejected, bypassed in favour of an ambitious tilt at the Japan Cup. Alborada had never gone one and a half miles and they always go some gallop in the Japan Cup. Whether or not she would have stayed or been effective at the distance became entirely academic when she was found to have injured her off-hind heel two days before the race. Alborada was retired forthwith. Timeform rated her at only 122 – the equal of Wizard King and below Missed Flight (123), Pivotal (124) and Noalcoholic, Environment Friend and User Friendly (all on 128) among the top horses I rode on a regular basis (Giant's Causeway, whom I partnered just the once, was awarded 132 in 2000). I can't agree with Timeform's assessment. I accept that Alborada means a lot to me because she arrived as a bonus when the curtain could so easily have been brought down on my career after my divorce, yet to me, at least, she was a superstar. She was as good as User Friendly and was blessed with more speed.

Alborada brought further benefits. Shortly after that second Champion Stakes, Sir Mark took a telephone call from Aidan O'Brien, the Irish 'wunderkind' who had taken the racing world by storm and the son-in-law of his good friend, Joe Crowley of Spindrifter fame. In a matter of a few years, Aidan had won Champion Hurdles with Istabraq and was collecting Classics at home and abroad as if there was no tomorrow. There's little to no point writing more about Aidan O'Brien at this stage of his career because he is still in his early thirties, and it seems as inevitable as night following day that he will have rewritten the record books by the time he finally chooses to pack in training. However, one thing already crystal clear about Aidan's approach to Group I races was that he was not averse to attacking them 'mob-handed' with two or three runners, and sometimes even more. This raised the possibility now and again of a choice 'spare' ride for some lucky jock.

Aidan got straight to the point. 'Sir Mark, is George Duffield as strong in a finish as I've heard?' Once given an answer in the affirmative, and gaining my release from one of Sir Mark's down at Newbury, he contacted my agent Keith Bradley to offer me the mount on one of his three entries in the following Saturday's Group I Racing Post Trophy at Doncaster. 'That's a bit of a shock to the system – great!' was my reaction to the news. I didn't care which of the three I was to ride.

My mount turned out to be Aristotle, a white-socked bay by Sadler's Wells, who had won his only race at Galway in mid-summer. Apparently, he required plenty of stoking up, and my performance on Alborada had alerted Aidan to the fact that I might be just the man to fill such a job description. Aristotle was presumed to be Aidan's third string, with stable jockey Mick Kinane on the Dewhurst third Zentsov Street (11/2) and Paul Scallan aboard Lermontov, on whom he'd won a Group race at the Curragh. The 2/1 favourite was Scarteen Fox from David Elsworth's, the winner of the Group III Somerville Tattersall Stakes at Newmarket on his last start. The going was soft, which always tends to suit the progeny of Sadler's Wells and, as Zentsov Street drifted in the betting toward the off, Aristotle joined Lermontov on 10s.

I had never met Aidan before, but I knew he was – like Sir Mark Prescott – a great one for tactics and race plans, a trainer of considerable intelligence. I was not disappointed. He got his three jockeys together. 'Paul will make the running on Lermontov,' he said very, very softly, before turning toward me. 'George, you be on his tail and keep punching – this horse is lazy. Michael will ride his own race.' All his thoughts were concentrated on those three horses of his. Nothing else was allowed to intrude. Even after he'd legged me up, he followed me around the paddock, saying 'Don't forget, George, he's tough, this horse.'

Aidan's instructions were carried out to the letter. Lermontov led into the straight with us close up, until Ekraar slipped up the inside rail to take him on, travelling all over like a winner. The resultant increase in pace instantly had Aristotle in trouble, and we were under pressure and off the bridle straight away, seemingly going nowhere in a great hurry. The two leaders must have gone four or five lengths clear of us by the two pole. But recalling Aidan's final rejoinder, I kept shoving and shoving at Aristotle. He kept plugging on for me and, running to the furlong marker, I sensed Lermontov and Ekraar were beginning to tire and at this rate I was going to pick them both up. We caught them 50 yards out and won, rather comfortably, going away by one and a quarter lengths. Zentsov Street ran as disappointingly as the market suggested, finishing a well-beaten fifth.

The papers had a field day. 'By George! Old boy Duffield is simply amazing,' wrote Tim Richards in the *Raceform Update;* 'Group I George proves a wise choice – Duffield booking a stroke of pure genius,' declared the *Racing Post*. Explaining the choice of G Duffield for Aristotle, Aidan said: 'We though George would suit Aristotle because he is strong, fit and wise. You could work this fellow against a donkey at home and Aristotle would only beat it a neck. All he does is eat and sleep. He's so lazy we knew we had to have someone like George on him.'

'Group One George' was one nickname I could grow to cope with quite easily. Two on consecutive Saturdays was a habit worth having! Alborada had got me the ride on Aristotle and Aristotle was to get me the ride on probably the best horse I've ridden – Giant's Causeway. That's how a snowball builds when it's rolling in your favour. I'd just ridden Ciro, one of Aidan's four in the race, to finish third in the Irish Derby of 2000 when I got the call to stand by for the mount on Giant's Causeway in the following Saturday's Eclipse in case Mick Kinane failed to recover from a tweaked muscle in his back. Sadly for Mick, his back made insufficient progress by declaration time and the mount was confirmed as mine.

I was chuffed to bits. I'd already been offered the ride on Border Arrow in the race by Ian Balding – which in any other circumstances would have been a decent enough each-way ride – but I had no qualms turning him down when there was the slightest possibility of getting on Giant's Causeway who had a chance of winning. This big, striking chestnut, sporting two white stockings, had finished second in both the English and Irish 2000 Guineas prior to winning the Group I St James's Palace Stakes at Royal Ascot. No three-year-old had gone on to add the Eclipse in the same season since Rhodes Scholar in 1936, and plenty of 'experts' expressed reservations about Giant's Causeway's ability to last the extra quarter of a mile. 'If Aidan O'Brien thinks he'll stay that's good enough for me,' I told Channel 4 viewers before the race. 'He won't bring him here half-cocked.'

The opposition was headed by the Derby runner-up, Sakhee (at 7/4), supported by Sir Michael Stoute's Kalanisi (7/2) and Godolphin's Fantastic Light (5/1). When you consider that trio went on to win an Arc, a Juddmonte International, an Irish Champion, a Hong Kong Cup and a brace of Breeders' Cup Turfs, to name only the major Group races they accumulated, you realise how good Giant's Causeway (an 8/1 shot) must have been this day at Sandown in order to beat them.

Aidan's orders were to 'have him handy, get a lead and make the best of your way home once you've turned for home. And remember, George, he'll only do what you ask him.' The Godolphin pacemaker Sun Charm was slow leaving the stalls and it took him a while to get to the front. As he passed me, I pushed Sakhee and Richard Hills in behind him so that I could get first run on them in the straight. I kept Sakhee safely pocketed until the pacemaker had been dropped passing the three pole, but then he quickly stole a length off me. The challenge was all Giant's Causeway needed because, given something to fight against, he buckled down to the task, got stuck into Sakhee and battled his way into the lead.

Everything seemed to be going like clockwork. Then, just as Aidan had warned, Giant's Causeway thought he'd done enough and began to idle. All of a sudden, Kalanisi and Pat Eddery appeared on my outside with all guns blazing. They must have gone a head up. My horse was actually waiting for him, it seemed to me. Now I had to earn my riding fee and justify the faith Aidan had placed in me. I changed my hands, picked Giant's Causeway up again and pulled my stick through into my right hand. Crack! Crack! Crack! All told, I hit Giant's Causeway 15 times. But he responded like the tough and courageous animal he was to regain the lead in the dying strides to win by a head. Pat is a tough man to beat when he gets upsides you, but I can honestly say Giant's Causeway wanted to win more than I did, which is saying something. Winning these top races is like an athlete winning an Olympic gold medal, and to be selected at my age by someone like Aidan who is spoilt for choice and could have picked anyone he wanted was a huge compliment. Then, to go and achieve the victory through the exact attributes I'd been chosen for made it all exceptionally special. Later, Sir Mark received another phone call: 'Sir Mark,' said a cheery Aidan, 'make sure you breed from him before you let him go!'

I awoke the next day to headlines like 'Age came before beauty' and 'Old-Timers set up a stunner', plus another 'By George!' headline on the front page of the *Racing Post*. Inside there was fulsome praise from Alastair Down in a piece entitled 'Older, wiser and with an irrepressible desire to win – Duffield eclipses them all with a vintage display of skill and strength.' The article went on to say: 'Ludicrously fit for a man in his fifties, this is a man who grafts like the most ambitious of youngsters...I know 53 is not 93, but it is still a hell of an age at which to be competing at the very top level in a multi-million pound sport, often against people in their twenties.' Those sort of comments made welcome reading, particularly given my personal circumstances of late.

Less welcome, were the column inches devoted to the repercussions of my efforts to win one of the most prestigious all-aged races in the calendar. 'Duffield and Eddery are referred for whip abuse.' I held my hands up to the charge of 'excessive frequency', no bother. I broke the Rules and knew full well what I was doing. And I would do it again. What I was doing, was doing my utmost to win a race on a horse who was responding and who otherwise would not have won. What I was not doing was abusing the horse. Did this 'thrashing' do Giant's Causeway any harm? Considering he went from strength to strength by adding the Sussex Stakes, Juddmonte International and Irish Champion Stakes to his Group I tally, even the disciplinary panel at Portman Square would have to concede that it did not. Giant's Causeway wasn't dubbed the 'Iron Horse' for nothing. However, I'd broken the rule and was perfectly prepared to abide by the punishment. Pat and me each received ten days. 'How does a disciplinary steward pass wind?' queried Alastair Down. 'Through his ears as usual! We have lost our backbone and replaced it with a broad yellow stripe,' he concluded. I can't help agreeing with him.

The press subsequently referred to Pat and me as the 'Whipping Boys'. In the main, rather than vilify two senior, experienced professionals trying to do their best for the owner and trainer who'd employed them and the punters who'd supported them, virtually every writer chose to highlight the iniquity of the Jockey Club's cock-eyed two-tier system of justice. In essence, a jockey was automatically referred to Portman Square, and thus the likelihood of a heftier ban, for breaking the Rules in major races like the

Eclipse because he had brought racing into 'disrepute' on one of its high-profile days, whereas if he committed the same offence in a Redcar seller he would be dealt with at the track and escape with a lighter punishment. Whoever made up this rule wants his bumps feeling. It was a stupid rule.

My twelfth Group I victory had come at some cost, but after what I had been through in the previous few years, any punishment meted out by the Jockey Club was strictly small potatoes by comparison. G Duffield had finally emerged from the darkest tunnel imaginable – and the sunshine greeting me seemed absolutely bloody gorgeous.

EPILOGUE

METHUSELAH OF THE
WEIGHING ROOM

In 2002 I began my 36th full season in the saddle with as much optimism as ever before.

The day I find that buzz has gone will be the day I call it quits. At the end of each year I always ask myself the same question: 'Do you want to do this again?' And the answer continues to be 'Yes, I do!' I take far less interest in racing during the winter these days, which freshens me up nicely for the coming season. I want to feel 'Great! Here we go again' not 'Bloody hell! Here we go again!' There's plenty to look forward to at Heath House in 2002, what with Danehurst (on whom I won the Group III Cornwallis Stakes in 2000) going for the top sprints, and Alborada's full sister Albanova due to start her three-year-old career after winning her only start at two. How many more seasons after that? Who knows. I can't see myself riding until I'm knocking 60 like Lester, let alone until I'm 65 like Frank Buckle, the first great jockey on the British Turf, whose Classic-winning record Lester eventually surpassed.

There was also much to look back on as the 2002 season approached. My 61st domestic winner of 2001 saw me pass Eph Smith in the British all-time list with a total of 2,313 (up to 2,372 by the end of the year) which gets me into the top ten. I can't tell you how proud I am to have scaled such heights, someone who has never been champion jockey or ridden more than 116 winners in a single season. The company I'm keeping takes my breath away. Just take a look at the nine names above me: Sir Gordon Richards, Pat Eddery, Lester Piggott, Willie Carson, Doug Smith, Joe Mercer, Fred Archer, Eddie Hide, George Fordham...and then me, George Duffield! Probably more satisfying still, is the class of jockey I've edged out of the top ten besides Eph Smith: legends like Scobie Breasley and Billy Nevett. Have I come a long way since Syllable at Yarmouth!

My fellow jockeys also voted me a third 'special recognition award' at the annual 'Lesters', our version of the Oscars, following those of 1998 and 1999. Recognition from your peers always means a hell of a lot. Not that I'm spared in the weighing room, mind you, where 'dad', 'old boy', 'grandad' and even Methusaleh are some of the politer things I'm called. It's only piss-taking, really. I don't mind, and I try to give as good as I get. I know I'm the oldest but I don't let it bother me. To be competing against these kids – who are younger than my own – and regularly beating them gives me a great thrill, and I think the fact that I'm 55 and still so bloody hard to beat tends to earn their respect. Some of them do ask me for advice, just like I used to ask people like Eric Eldin and Frank Durr

all those years ago, but they don't take any liberties in a race. We've not reached the stage like when, back in the 60s, you'd hear

Lester shouting across at Scobie 'Move over, grandad! I'm coming through!' They are all well aware that anyone trying to get up G Duffield's inside in a race is making a big, big mistake. No matter who you are, you don't poke up there. If you do, you're going to be flattened!

Although my temper can still flash, the fuse is considerably longer nowadays. I don't think I'm fooling myself when I say that my whole outlook on life has taken a turn for the better. I'm no longer the firebrand of old. I'm more at ease with myself. For that I can thank Annie.

Annie and me were married on 18 December 1999 at Leyburn registry office, and the following January we moved into Sun Hill Farm, a 40-acre property at Constable Burton, between Bedale and Leyburn, in Wensleydale. Annie's training operation is up and running, incorporating a six-furlong uphill all-weather gallop and three new barns containing 40 boxes. We've also done a lot to the 18th century house, and any visitor to Sun Hill is quite likely to come across a slight figure in overalls, wellingtons and flat cap happily busying himself around the garden. Nothing gives me greater pleasure than gardening, you may be surprised to hear, especially landscaping: putting in rockeries, ornamental streams and ponds. It may not be Castle Howard but Duffield Towers is coming on!

Who knows, perhaps at long last I truly have become 'Gentleman George'.

APPENDIX 1: BRITISH CAREER TOTALS

1966...**0**	1979...**76**	1992..**108**
1967...**10**	1980...**78**	1993..**116**
1968...**39**	1981...**94**	1994...**65**
1969...**35**	1982...**92**	1995...**60**
1970...**51**	1983...**98**	1996...**74**
1971...**16**	1984...**86**	1997...**79**
1972...**33**	1985...**61**	1998...**74**
1973...**30**	1986...**94**	1999...**80**
1974...**49**	1987...**64**	2000...**68**
1975...**26**	1988...**77**	2001...**95**
1976...**50**	1989...**87**	TOTAL: 2,372
1977...**60**	1990...**84**	= 10th in All-Time
1978...**75**	1991...**88**	List

APPENDIX 2: PRINCIPAL RACES WON

1968 Cecil Frail Handicap, Haydock: CHARLIE'S PAL (Ryan Jarvis)

1970 Duke of York Stakes, York: FLUKE (John Oxley)
Jersey Stakes, Royal Ascot: FLUKE (John Oxley)
Royal Hunt Cup, Royal Ascot: CALPURNIUS (Bill Watts)

1971 Great Metroplitan Handicap, Epsom: TARTAR PRINCE (Tom Waugh)

1972 Autumn Cup, Newbury: DANTON (John Winter)

1974 **OAKS, CALCUTTA: GOLDFINDER (CAPTAIN FOWNES)**

1976 Prix Gladiateur d'Ostende: BUSTIFFA (Sir Mark Prescott)

1979 Andy Capp Handicap, Redcar: SIDE TRACK (GAVIN PRITCHARD-GORDON)
Criterium de Vitesse de la Mer du Nord, Ostende: MARCHING ON (SMP)
Happy Valley Handicap, Sandown: MARCHING ON (SMP)
Bovis Stakes, Ascot: MARCHING ON (SMP)

1980 Zetland Gold Cup, Redcar: SIDE TRACK (GP-G)
Child Stakes (Group III), Newmarket: STUMPED (Bruce Hobbs)

1981 Ascot Stakes, Royal Ascot: ATLANTIC TRAVELLER (Bill Watts)
November Handicap, Doncaster: LAFONTAINE (Clive Brittain)

1982 Lanson Champagne Stakes, Goodwood: ALL SYSTEMS GO (GP-G)
Seaton Delaval Stakes (Group III), Newcastle: ALL SYSTEMS GO (GP-G)
Van Geest Stakes, Newmarket: NOALCOHOLIC (GP-G)

Prix Messidor (Group III), Maisons-Laffitte: NOALCOHOLIC (GP-G)
Bovis Handicap, Ascot: BRI-EDEN (Jack Berry)
Challenge Stakes (Group II), Newmarket: NOALCOHOLIC (GP-G)
November Handicap, Doncaster: DOUBLE SHUFFLE (GP-G)

1983 Lockinge Stakes (Group II), Newbury: NOALCOHOLIC (GP-G)
SUSSEX STAKES (GROUP I), GOODWOOD: NOALCOHOLIC (GP-G)

1984 Holsten Pils Trophy Stakes, Leicester: HARLOW (Sir Mark Prescott)
Blue Riband Trial Stakes (Group III), Epsom: LONG POND (Paul
    Kelleway)
Prix du Palais-Royal (Goup III), Longchamp): HARLOW (SMP)

1986 Rapid Lad Handicap, Beverley: FORWARD RALLY (SMP)
Zetland Gold Cup, Redcar: FORWARD RALLY (SMP)

1988 Cambridgeshire, Newmarket: QUINLAN TERRY (SMP)

1990 Ostermann-Pokal (Group III), Cologne: MAXIMILIAN (John Gosden)
Solario Stakes (Group III), Sandown: RADWELL (James Fanshawe)
Atalanta Stakes, Sandown: ARPERO (JF)
Ben Marshall Stakes, Newmarket: TWO LEFT FEET (SMP)

1991 Dante Stakes (Group II), York: ENVIRONMENT FRIEND (JF)
Porcelanosa Sprint Stakes, Sandown: CASE LAW (SMP)
**ECLIPSE STAKES (GROUP I), SANDOWN: ENVIRONMENT
    FRIEND (JF)**
Gordon Stakes (Group III), Goodwood: STYLISH SENOR (JF)
Solario Stakes (Group III), Sandown: CHICMOND (SMP)
October Stakes, Ascot: CHIPAYA (JF)

1992 Oaks Trial, Lingfield: USER FRIENDLY (Clive Brittain)
OAKS (GROUP I), EPSOM: USER FRIENDLY (CB)
Northumberland Plate, Newcastle: WITNESS BOX (John Gosden)
IRISH OAKS (GROUP I), CURRAGH: USER FRIENDLY (CB)
YORKSHIRE OAKS (GROUP I), YORK: USER FRIENDLY (CB)
ST LEGER (GROUP I), DONCASTER: USER FRIENDLY (CB)
Stubbs Rated Stakes, Newmarket: SPECIFICITY (John Gosden)
Autumn Handicap, Newmarket: CAMBRIAN (Julie Cecil)
**CLICO STEWARDS CUP (GROUP I), SANTA ROSA: SWEET TASSA
    (COLT DURRANT)**

1993 Sandy Lane Handicap, Haydock: LOOK WHO'S HERE (Bryan McMahon)
GRAND PRIX DE SAINT-CLOUD (GROUP I): USER FRIENDLY (CB)
Batleys Cash & Carry Handicap, York: HASTEN TO ADD (SMP)
Laurent-Perrier Champagne Stakes (Group II), Doncaster: UNBLEST (JF)

1994 Field Marshal Stakes, Haydock: GREAT DEEDS (Mike Channon)
Spring Handicap, Newbury: MISSED FLIGHT (Chris Wall)
Ebor Handicap, York: HASTEN TO ADD (SMP)

Tote Festival Handicap, Ascot: WIZARD KING (SMP)
Prix du Rond-Point (Group II), Longchamp: MISSED FLIGHT (CW)

1995 Sandown Mile (Group II): MISSED FLIGHT (CW)
Sandy Lane Handicap, Haydock: STAR TULIP (John Dunlop)
Prix de Meautry (Group III), Deauville: MISSED FLIGHT (CW)
CL Weld Park Stakes (Group III), Curragh: LAST SECOND (SMP)

1996 Kingís Stand Stakes (Group II), Royal Ascot: PIVOTAL (SMP)
Nassau Stakes (Group II), Goodwood: LAST SECOND (SMP)
NUNTHORPE STAKES (GROUP I), YORK: PIVOTAL (SMP)
Solario Stakes (Group III), Sandown: BRAVE ACT (SMP)
Prestige Stakes (Group III), Goodwood: RED CAMELLIA (SMP)
Sun Chariot Stakes (Group II), Newmarket: LAST SECOND (SMP)
Concorde Stakes (Group III), Tipperary: WIZARD KING (SMP)
Knockaire Stakes, Leopardstown: WIZARD KING (SMP)

1997 Leicestershire Stakes, Leicester: WIZARD KING (SMP)
Ballycorus Stakes (Group III), Leopardstown: WIZARD KING (SMP)
John Smithís Magnet Cup, York: PASTERNAK (SMP)
Concorde Stakes (Group III), Tipperary: WIZARD KING (SMP)
Cambridgeshire, Newmarket: PASTERNAK (SMP)
Two-Year-Old Trophy, Redcar: GRAZIA (SMP)
Wulfrun Stakes, Wolverhampton: FARMOST (SMP)

1998 Pretty Polly Stakes (Group II), Curragh: ALBORADA (SMP)
Nassau Stakes (Group II), Goodwood: ALBORADA (SMP)
Ballycullen Stakes, Leopardstown: ON CALL (SMP)
CHAMPION STAKES (GROUP I), NEWMARKET: ALBORADA (SMP)

1999 Stardom Stakes, Goodwood: SARAFAN (SMP)
CHAMPION STAKES (GROUP I), NEWMARKET: ALBORADA (SMP)
**RACING POST TROPHY (GROUP I), DONCASTER: ARISTOTLE
(AIDAN O'BRIEN)**

2000 **ECLIPSE STAKES (GROUP I), SANDOWN: GIANT'S CAUSEWAY
(AOB)**
Empress Stakes, Newmarket: IN THE WOODS (David Cosgrove)
Cornwallis Stakes (Group III), Newbury: DANEHURST (SMP)
Matron Stakes (Group III), Curragh: IFTIRAAS (John Dunlop)
Prix des Reservoirs (Group III), Deauville: PERFECT PLUM (SMP)
Prix Saint-Roman (Group III), Saint-Cloud: PERFECT PLUM (SMP)

2001 Bonusprint Handicap, Newmarket: ALPHAEUS (SMP)
John Smith's Cup, York: FOREIGN AFFAIRS (SMP)
Wentworth Stakes, Doncaster: DANEHURST (SMP)

INDEX